The Document Foundation

LibreOffice 4.2 Impress Guide

Presentations in LibreOffice

Copyright

Contributors

Peter Schofield	Michele Zarri	Jean Hollis Weber
T. Elliot Turner	Chad D. Lines	Muhammad Sufyan Zainalabidin
Low Song Chuan	Jaimon Jacob	Hazel Russman

Feedback

Please direct any comments or suggestions about this document to the Documentation Team's mailing list: documentation@global.libreoffice.org

Note: Everything you send to a mailing list, including your email address and any other personal information that is written in the message, is publicly archived and cannot be deleted.

Acknowledgments

This book is adapted and updated from the *OpenOffice.org 3.3 Impress Guide*. The contributors to that book are listed on page 11.

Publisher

Friends of OpenDocument, Inc.
544/60 Beck Drive North
Condon, QLD 4815, Australia
http://friendsofopendocument.com/
ISBN 978-1-921320-41-5

Publication date and software version

Published 26 August 2014. Based on LibreOffice 4.2.

Documentation for LibreOffice is available at http://www.libreoffice.org/get-help/documentation

Contents

Preface

Who is this book for?

Anyone who wants to get up to speed quickly with LibreOffice Impress will find this book valuable. You may be new to presentation software, or you may be familiar with another program such as Microsoft PowerPoint.

What's in this book?

This book covers the main features of Impress, the presentations (slide show) component of LibreOffice. Using Impress, you can create slides that contain text, bulleted and numbered lists, tables, charts, clip art, and other objects.

Impress comes with prepackaged text styles, slide backgrounds, and Help. It can open and save to Microsoft PowerPoint formats and can export to PDF, HTML, Adobe Flash, and numerous graphic formats.

Where to get more help

This book, the other LibreOffice user guides, the built-in Help system, and user support systems assume that you are familiar with your computer and basic functions such as starting a program, opening and saving files.

Help system

LibreOffice comes with an extensive Help system. This is your first line of support for using LibreOffice.

To display the full Help system, press *F1* or select **LibreOffice Help** from the Help menu. In addition, you can choose whether to activate Tips, Extended tips, and the Help Agent (using **Tools > Options > LibreOffice > General**).

If Tips are enabled, place the mouse pointer over any of the icons to see a small box ("tooltip") with a brief explanation of the icon's function. For a more detailed explanation, select **Help > What's This?** and hold the pointer over the icon.

Free online support

The LibreOffice community not only develops software, but provides free, volunteer-based support. See Table 1 and this web page: http://www.libreoffice.org/get-help/

You can get comprehensive online support from the community through mailing lists and the Ask LibreOffice website, http://ask.libreoffice.org/en/questions/. Other websites run by users also offer free tips and tutorials.

This forum provides community support for LibreOffice: http://en.libreofficeforum.org/

This site provides support for LibreOffice, among other programs: http://forum.openoffice.org/en/forum/.

Paid support and training

Alternatively, you can pay for support services. Service contracts can be purchased from a vendor or consulting firm specializing in LibreOffice.

Table 1: Free support for LibreOffice users

Free LibreOffice support	
Ask LibreOffice	Questions and answers from the LibreOffice community http://ask.libreoffice.org/en/questions/
Documentation	User guides, how-tos, and other documentation. http://www.libreoffice.org/get-help/documentation/ https://wiki.documentfoundation.org/Documentation/Publications
FAQs	Answers to frequently asked questions http://wiki.documentfoundation.org/Faq
Mailing lists	Free community support is provided by a network of experienced users http://www.libreoffice.org/get-help/mailing-lists/
International support	The LibreOffice website in your language. http://www.libreoffice.org/international-sites/ International mailing lists http://wiki.documentfoundation.org/Local_Mailing_Lists
Accessibility options	Information about available accessibility options. http://www.libreoffice.org/get-help/accessibility/

What you see may be different

Illustrations

LibreOffice runs on Windows, Linux, and Mac OS X operating systems, each of which has several versions and can be customized by users (fonts, colors, themes, window managers). The illustrations in this guide were taken from a variety of computers and operating systems. Therefore, some illustrations will not look exactly like what you see on your computer display.

Also, some of the dialogs may be differ because of the settings selected in LibreOffice. You can either use dialogs from your computer system (default) or dialogs provided by LibreOffice. To change to using LibreOffice dialogs:

1) On Linux and Windows operating systems, go to **Tools > Options > LibreOffice > General** on the main menu bar to open the dialog for general options.

2) On a Mac operating system, go to **LibreOffice > Preferences > General** on the main menu bar to open the dialog for general options.

3) Select *Use LibreOffice dialogs* in *Open/Save dialogs* and, in Linux and Mac OS X operating systems only, *Print dialogs* to display the LibreOffice dialogs on your computer display.

4) Click **OK** to save your settings and close the dialog.

Icons

The icons used to illustrate some of the many tools available in LibreOffice may differ from the ones used in this guide. The icons in this guide have been taken from a LibreOffice installation that has been set to display the Galaxy set of icons.

If you wish, you can change your LibreOffice software package to display Galaxy icons as follows:

1) On Linux and Windows operating systems, go to **Tools > Options > LibreOffice > View** on the main menu bar to open the dialog for view options.

2) On a Mac operating system, go to **LibreOffice > Preferences > View** on the main menu bar to open the dialog for view options.

3) In *User interface > Icon size and style* select *Galaxy* from the options available in the drop-down list.

4) Click **OK** to save your settings and close the dialog.

Note	Some Linux operating systems, for example Ubuntu, include LibreOffice as part of the installation and may not include the Galaxy set of icons. You should be able to download the Galaxy icon set from the software repository for your Linux operating system.

Using LibreOffice on a Mac

Some keystrokes and menu items are different on a Mac from those used in Windows and Linux. The table below gives some common substitutions for the instructions in this chapter. For a more detailed list, see the application Help.

Windows or Linux	Mac equivalent	Effect
Tools > Options menu selection	**LibreOffice > Preferences**	Access setup options
Right-click	*Control+click* and/or *right-click* depending on computer setup	Open a context menu
Ctrl (Control)	⌘ *(Command)*	Used with other keys
F5	*Shift+⌘+F5*	Open the Navigator
F11	*⌘+T*	Open the Styles and Formatting window

What are all these things called?

The terms used in LibreOffice for most parts of the *user interface* (the parts of the program you see and use, in contrast to the behind-the-scenes code that actually makes it work) are the same as for most other programs.

A *dialog* is a special type of window. Its purpose is to inform you of something, or request input from you, or both. It provides controls for you to use to specify how to carry out an action. The technical names for common controls are shown in Figure 1. In most cases we do not use the technical terms in this book, but it is useful to know them because the Help and other sources of information often use them.

1) Tabbed page (not strictly speaking a control).

2) Radio buttons (only one can be selected at a time).

3) Checkbox (more than one can be selected at a time).

4) Spin box (click the up and down arrows to change the number shown in the text box next to it, or type in the text box).

5) Thumbnail or preview.

6) Drop-down list from which to select an item.

7) Push buttons.

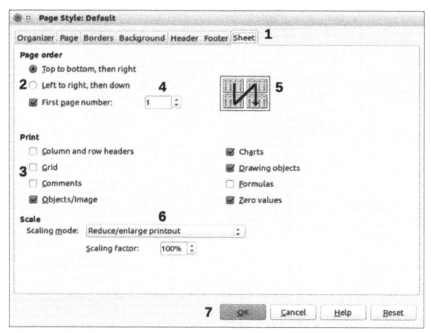

Figure 1: Dialog showing common controls

In most cases, you can interact only with the dialog (not the document itself) as long as the dialog remains open. When you close the dialog after use (usually, clicking **OK** or another button saves your changes and closes the dialog), then you can again work with your document.

Some dialogs can be left open as you work, so you can switch back and forth between the dialog and your document. An example of this type is the Find & Replace dialog.

Who wrote this book?

This book was written by volunteers from the LibreOffice community. Profits from sales of the printed edition will be used to benefit the community.

Acknowledgements

This book is adapted and updated from *OpenOffice.org 3.3 Impress Guide*. The contributors to that book are:

Michele Zarri	Jean Hollis Weber	Dan Lewis
Agnes Belzunce	Peter Hillier-Brook	Gary Schnabl
Claire Wood	Rachel Kartch	Hazel Russman
Jared Kobos	Martin J Fox	Paul Miller
Nicole Cairns	Rachel Kartch	

Frequently asked questions

How is LibreOffice licensed?

LibreOffice 4.2 is distributed under the Open Source Initiative (OSI) approved Mozilla Public License (MPL). The MPL license is available from http://www.mozilla.org/MPL/2.0/.

May I distribute LibreOffice to anyone?

Yes.

How many computers may I install it on?

As many as you like.

May I sell it?

Yes.

May I use LibreOffice in my business?

Yes.

May I distribute the PDF of this book, or print and sell copies?

Yes, as long as you meet the requirements of one of the licenses in the copyright statement at the beginning of this book. You do not have to request special permission. In addition, we request that you share with the project some of the profits you make from sales of books, in consideration of all the work we have put into producing them.

How can I contribute to LibreOffice?

You can help with the development and user support of LibreOffice in many ways, and you do not need to be a programmer. For example, you can help with producing and maintaining written user documentation, producing video tutorials, and other user support services. To start, check out this webpage: http://www.documentfoundation.org/contribution/

What's new in LibreOffice 4.2?

The LibreOffice 4.2 Release Notes (changes from version 4.1) are here: https://wiki.documentfoundation.org/ReleaseNotes/4.2.

You may also want to read the LibreOffice 4.1 Release Notes (changes from version 4.0) here: https://wiki.documentfoundation.org/ReleaseNotes/4.1.

Chapter 1
Introducing Impress

What is Impress?

Impress is the presentation (slide show) program included in LibreOffice. You can create slides that contain many different elements, including text, bulleted and numbered lists, tables, charts, and a wide range of graphic objects such as clipart, drawings and photographs. Impress also includes a spelling checker, a thesaurus, text styles, and background styles.

This chapter introduces the Impress user interface and describes how to create a simple slide show using the Presentation Wizard. The other chapters in this guide explain all the features available in Impress that can be used to create more sophisticated slide shows.

To use Impress for more than very simple slide shows requires some knowledge of the elements which the slides contain. Slides containing text use styles to determine the appearance of that text. Creating drawings in Impress is similar to using the Draw program included in LibreOffice. See the *Draw Guide* for more details on how to use the drawing tools.

Starting Impress

You can start Impress in several ways:

- From the LibreOffice Start Center, if no component is open: click on the Impress Presentation icon to create a new presentation, or click on the Open File icon and navigate to the folder where there is an existing presentation.
- From the system menu, the standard menu from which most applications are started. On Windows, it is called the Start menu. On Linux with a Gnome desktop, it is called the Applications menu; on a KDE desktop, it is identified by the KDE logo. On Mac OS X, it is the Applications menu. Details vary with your operating system; see the *Getting Started Guide Chapter 1 Introducing LibreOffice.*
- On Windows, use the Presentation selection in the LibreOffice Quickstarter. Similar functions exist for Mac OS X and Linux; see the *Getting Started Guide Chapter 1 Introducing LibreOffice.*
- From any open component of LibreOffice. Click the triangle to the right of the **New** icon on the main menu bar and select *Presentation* from the drop-down menu or choose **File > New > Presentation** on the main menu bar.

Note	When LibreOffice was installed on your computer, in most cases a menu entry for each component was added to your system menu. The exact name and location of these menu entries depend on the operating system and graphical user interface.

When you start Impress for the first time, the Presentation Wizard is shown by default. Here you can choose from the following options:

- **Empty presentation**, which gives you a blank document
- **From template,** which is a presentation designed with a template of your choice
- **Open existing presentation**
- Click **Create** to open the main Impress window.

For detailed instructions about how to use the Presentation Wizard, see "Creating a new presentation" on page 23.

If you prefer not to use the Presentation Wizard, select the **Do not show this wizard again** option before clicking **Create**. You can enable the wizard again later under **Tools > Options > LibreOffice Impress > General > New document** on the main menu bar and select the **Start with wizard** option.

Main Impress window

The main Impress window (Figure 2) has three parts: the *Slides pane*, *Workspace*, and *Sidebar*. Additionally, several toolbars can be displayed or hidden during the creation of a presentation.

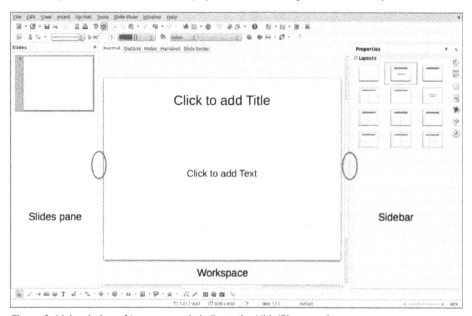

Figure 2: Main window of Impress; ovals indicate the Hide/Show markers

Tip	You can close the *Slides pane* or the *Sidebar* by clicking the *X* in the upper right corner of each pane or go to **View > Slide Pane** or **View > Sidebar** on the main menu bar to deselect the pane. To reopen a pane, go to **View** on the main menu bar and select **Slide Pane** or **Sidebar** again.
	You can also maximize the Workspace area by clicking on the Hide/Show marker in the middle of the vertical separator line (indicated by ovals in Figure 2). Using the Hide/Show marker hides, but does not close, the Slides pane or Sidebar. To restore the pane, click again on its Hide/Show marker.

Slides pane

The Slides pane contains thumbnail pictures of the slides in your presentation, in the order the slides will be shown, unless you change the slide show order that is described in *Chapter 9 Slide Shows*. Clicking a slide in this pane selects it and places it in the Workspace. When a slide is in the Workspace, you can make any changes you like.

Several additional operations can be performed on one or more slides simultaneously in the Slides pane:

- Add new slides to the presentation.
- Mark a slide as hidden so that it will not be shown as part of the presentation.
- Delete a slide from the presentation if it is no longer needed.

- Rename a slide.
- Duplicate a slide (copy and paste) or move it to a different position in the presentation (cut and paste).

It is also possible to perform the following operations, although there are more efficient methods than using the Slides pane, as you will see later in this chapter:

- Change the slide transition following the selected slide or after each slide in a group of slides.
- Change the sequence of slides in the presentation.
- Change the slide design.
- Change slide layout for a group of slides simultaneously.

Sidebar

The *Sidebar* has seven sections. To expand a section you want to use, click on its icon or click on the small triangle at the top of the icons and select a section from the drop down list. Only one section at a time can be open.

Properties

Shows the layouts included within Impress. You can choose the one you want and use it as it is, or modify it to meet your own requirements. However, it is not possible to save customized layouts.

Master Pages

Here you define the page (slide) style for your presentation. Impress includes several designs of Master Pages (slide masters). One of them – Default – is blank, and the rest have background and styled text.

Custom Animation

A variety of animations can be used to emphasize or enhance different elements of each slide. The Custom Animation section provides an easy way to add, change, or remove animations.

Slide Transition

Provides a number of slide transition options. The default is set to *No Transition*, in which the following slide simply replaces the existing one. However, many additional transitions are available. You can also specify the transition speed (slow, medium, fast), choose between an automatic or manual transition, and choose how long the selected slide should be shown (automatic transition only).

Styles and Formatting

Here you can edit and apply graphics styles, but you can only edit presentation styles. When you edit a style, the changes are automatically applied to all of the elements formatted with this style in your presentation. If you want to ensure that the styles on a specific slide are not updated, create a new master page for the slide.

Tip	Go to **Format > Styles and Formatting** on the main menu bar or press the *F11* key to open the Styles and Formatting dialog, where you can modify the styles used in any master page to suit your purpose. This can be done at any time.

Gallery

Opens the Impress gallery where you can insert an object into your presentation either as a copy or as a link. A copy of an object is independent of the original object. Changes to the original object have no effect on the copy. A link remains dependent on the original object. Changes to the original object are also reflected in the link.

Navigator

Opens the Impress navigator, in which you can quickly move to another slide or select an object on a slide. It is recommended to give slides and objects in your presentation meaningful names so that you can easily identify them when using the navigator.

Workspace

The Workspace (normally in the center) has five tabs: **Normal**, **Outline**, **Notes**, **Handout**, and **Slide Sorter** (Figure 3). These five tabs are called View buttons. The Workspace below the View buttons changes depending on the chosen view. The workspace views are described in detail "Workspace views" on page 19.

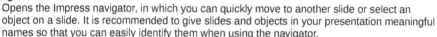

Figure 3: Workspace tabs

Toolbars

Many toolbars can be used during slide creation; they can be displayed or hidden by going to **View > Toolbars** on the main menu bar and selecting from the context menu.

You can also select the icons that you wish to appear on each toolbar. For more information, refer to *Chapter 11 Setting Up and Customizing Impress*.

Many of the toolbars in Impress are similar to the toolbars in Draw. Refer to the *Draw Guide* for details on the functions available and how to use them.

Status bar

The *Status* bar (Figure 4), located at the bottom of the Impress window, contains information that you may find useful when working on a presentation. You can hide the Status Bar by going to **View** on the main menu bar and deselecting **Status Bar** in the context menu.

Note	The sizes are given in the current measurement unit (not to be confused with the ruler units). This measurement unit is defined in **Tools > Options > LibreOffice Impress > General**.

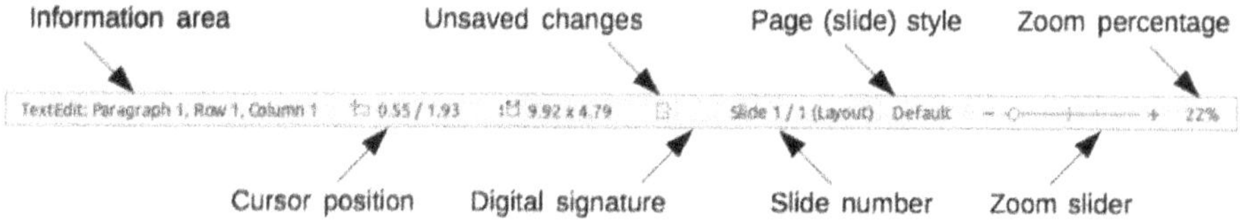

Information area   Unsaved changes   Page (slide) style   Zoom percentage

TextEdit: Paragraph 1, Row 1, Column 1   0.55 / 1.93   9.92 x 4.79   Slide 1 / 1 (Layout) Default   22%

Cursor position   Digital signature   Slide number   Zoom slider

Figure 4: Status bar

From left to right, you will find:

- **Information area** – changes depending on the selection. For example:

Example selection	Examples of information shown
Text area	Text Edit: Paragraph x, Row y, Column z
Charts, spreadsheets	Embedded object (OLE) "ObjectName" selected
Graphics	Bitmap with transparency selected

- **Cursor position** – the position of the cursor or of the top left corner of the selection measured from the top left corner of the slide, followed by the width and height of the selection or text box where the cursor is located.
- **Unsaved changes** – a flag indicating that the file needs saving. Double-clicking on this flag opens the file save dialog.
- **Digital signature** – a flag indicating whether the document is digitally signed. After the file has been saved, double-clicking on this flag opens the digital signatures dialog.
- **Slide number** – the slide number currently displayed in the Workspace and the total number of slides in the presentation.
- **Page (slide) style** – the style associated with the slide, handout, or notes page currently in the Workspace. Double-clicking on the style name opens the slide design dialog.
- **Zoom slider** – adjusts the zoom percentage of the Workspace displayed.
- **Zoom percentage** – indicates the zoom percentage of the Workspace displayed. Double-clicking on zoom percentage opens the zoom and layout dialog.

Navigator

The Navigator displays all objects contained in a presentation. It provides another convenient way to move around a presentation and find items in it. To open the Navigator dialog (Figure 5), click the **Navigator** icon ⊘ on the Standard toolbar, or go to **View > Navigator** on the main menu bar, or use the keyboard shortcut *Ctrl+Shift+F5*. Alternatively, click on the *Sidebar Navigator* icon ⊘ to open a page that is similar to the Navigator dialog.

Figure 5: Navigator dialog

The Navigator is more useful if you give your slides and objects (pictures, spreadsheets, and so on) meaningful names, instead of leaving them with default names, such as "Slide 1" and "Shape 1" and so on.

Workspace views

Each of the Workspace views is designed to ease the completion of certain tasks; it is therefore useful to familiarize yourself with them to quickly accomplish those tasks.

Note	Each Workspace view displays a different set of toolbars when selected. These toolbar sets can be customized by going to **View > Toolbars**, then check or uncheck the toolbar you want to add or remove.

Normal view

Normal view is the main view for creating individual slides. Use this view to format and design slides and to add text, graphics, and animation effects.

To place a slide in the slide design area of the Normal view (Figure 2 on page 15), either click the slide thumbnail in the Slides pane or double-click it in the Navigator.

Outline view

Outline view (Figure 6) contains all of the slides of the presentation in their numbered sequence. It shows topic titles, bulleted lists, and numbered lists for each slide in outline format. Only the text contained in the default text boxes in each slide is shown. If you have added text boxes or graphic objects to the slides, then these objects are not displayed. Slide names are not included.

Figure 6: Outline view

Figure 7: Outline level and movement arrows in Text Formatting toolbar

Use Outline view for:
1) Making changes in the text of a slide:
   a) Add or delete text in a slide just as in the Normal view.
   b) Move the paragraphs of text in the selected slide up or down by using the up and down arrow buttons (Move Up or Move Down) on the Text Formatting toolbar (highlighted in Figure 7).
   c) Change the outline level for any of the paragraphs in a slide using the left and right arrow buttons (Promote or Demote) on the Text Formatting toolbar.
   d) Simultaneously move a paragraph and change its outline level using a combination of these four arrow buttons.
2) Comparing the slides with your outline (if you have prepared one in advance). If you notice from your outline that another slide is needed, you can create it directly in the Outline view, or you can return to the Normal view to create it.

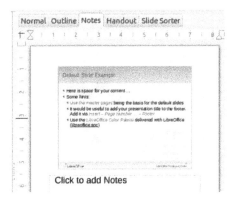

Figure 8: Notes view

Notes view

Use the Notes view (Figure 8) to add notes to a slide. These notes are not seen when the presentation is shown to an audience on an extra display monitor connected to your computer.

1) Click the **Notes** tab in the Workspace.
2) Select the slide to which you want to add notes.
3) Click the slide in the Slide pane, or double-click the slide name in the Navigator.
4) In the text box below the slide, click on the words *Click to add notes* and begin typing.

You can resize the Notes text box using the resizing handles which appear when you click on the edge of the box. You can also move the box by placing the pointer on the border, then clicking and dragging. To make changes in the text style, press the *F11* key to open the Styles and Formatting dialog or click on the Styles and Formatting icon ![icon] on the Sidebar.

Handout view

Handout view is for setting up the layout of your slide for a printed handout. Click the *Handout* tab in the workspace and the **Layouts** section opens on the Sidebar (Figure 9) where you can then choose to print 1, 2, 3, 4, 6, or 9 slides per page. If the Layouts section does not open, then click on the Properties icon ![icon] at the side of the Sidebar.

You can also use this view to customize the information printed on the handout. Refer to *Chapter 8 Adding and Formatting Slides, Notes, and Handouts* for more information.

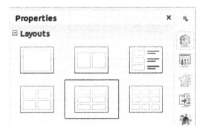

Figure 9: Handout layouts

Select from the main menu **Insert > Page Number** or **Insert > Date and Time** and the **Header and Footer** dialog opens. Click on the *Notes and Handouts* tab (Figure 10) and use this dialog to select the elements you want to appear on each handout page and their contents.

Figure 10: Header and Footer dialog – Notes and Handouts page

Slide Sorter view

The Slide Sorter view (Figure 11) contains all of the slide thumbnails. Use this view to work with a group of slides or with only one slide.

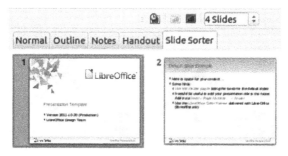

Figure 11: Slide Sorter view

Customizing Slide Sorter view

To change the number of slides per row:

1) Check **View > Toolbars > Slide Sorter** and **Slide View** to show or hide the slide sorter and view toolbars (Figure 12).

2) Adjust the number of slides (up to a maximum of 15).

Figure 12: Slide Sorter and Slide View toolbars

Moving a slide using Slide Sorter

To move a slide in a presentation using the Slide Sorter:

1) Click the slide to highlight it (Figure 11).
2) Drag and drop it to the location you want.

Selecting and moving groups of slides

To select a group of slides, use one of these methods:

- Using the *Ctrl* key – click on the first slide and, while pressing the *Ctrl* key, select the other desired slides.
- Using the *Shift* key – click on the first slide, and while pressing the *Shift* key, select the final slide in the group. This selects all of the other slides between the first and the last slide selected.
- Using the mouse – click slightly to one side (left or right) of the first slide to be selected. Hold down the left mouse button and drag the cursor until all of the slides you want selected are highlighted.

To move a group of slides:

1) Select a group of slides.
2) Drag and drop the group to their new location.

Working in Slide Sorter view

You can work with slides in the Slide Sorter view just as you can in the Slide pane. To make changes, right-click a slide and choose any of the following from the context menu:

- **New Slide** – adds a new slide after the selected slide.
- **Duplicate Slide** – creates a duplicate of the selected slide and places the new slide immediately after the selected slide (see "Duplicate slide" on page 26).
- **Delete Slide** – deletes the selected slide.
- **Rename Slide** – allows you to rename the selected slide.
- **Slide Layout** – allows you to change the layout of the selected slide.
- **Slide Transition** – allows you to change the transition of the selected slide.
    - For one slide, select a slide and add the desired transition.
    - For more than one slide, select a group of slides and add the desired transition.
- **Hide Slide** – any slides that are hidden are not shown in the slide show.
- **Cut** – removes the selected slide and saves it to the clipboard.
- **Copy** – copies the selected slide to the clipboard without removing it.
- **Paste** – inserts a slide from the clipboard after the selected slide.

Creating a new presentation

This section shows you how to create a new presentation using the Presentation Wizard.

Tip	The first thing to do is decide on the purpose of the presentation and plan the presentation. Although you can make changes as you go, having an idea of who the audience will be, the structure, the content, and how the presentation will be delivered, will save you a lot of time from the start.

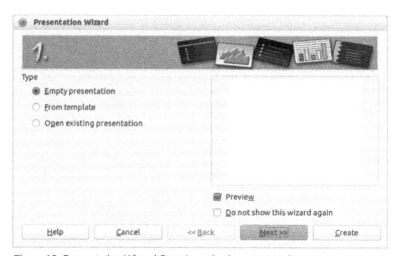

Figure 13: Presentation Wizard Step 1 – selecting presentation type

When you start Impress, the Presentation Wizard Step 1 (Figure 13) appears.

1) Under **Type**, choose one of the options:

   - *Empty presentation* creates a blank presentation.

   - *From template* uses a template design already created as the basis for a new presentation. The wizard changes to show a list of available templates. Choose the template you want. More details can be found in *Chapter 2, Using Slide Masters, Styles, and Templates.*

   - *Open existing presentation* continues work on a previously created presentation. The wizard changes to show a list of existing presentations. Choose the one you want.

2) Click **Next** and the Presentation Wizard Step 2 opens. It appears as shown in Figure 14 if you selected *Empty presentation* at step 1. If you selected *From template*, an example slide is shown in the Preview box.

3) Choose a design under **Select a slide design**. The slide design section gives *Presentation Backgrounds* with a list of choices for slide designs. If you want to use one of these other than <Original>, click it to select it.

   The types of Presentation Backgrounds are shown in Figure 14. When you select a presentation background, you will see a preview of the slide design in the Preview window.

   <Original> is for a blank presentation slide design.

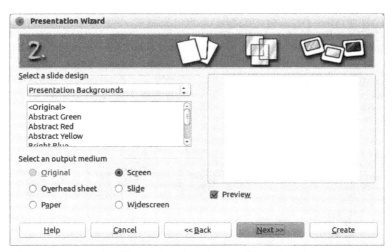

Figure 14: Presentation Wizard Step 2 – selecting slide design & output medium

4) Select how the presentation will be used under **Select an output medium**. Most often, presentations are created for computer screen display, so you would select **Screen**. You can change the page format at any time.

Note	The default Screen page is for a 4:3 display (28cm x 21cm) which is not suitable for modern wide-screen displays. You can change the slide size at any time by switching to Normal view and selecting **Format > Page**.

5) Click **Next** and the Presentation Wizard Step 3 (Figure 15) opens.

   a) Select the desired slide transition from the *Effect* drop-down menu.

   b) Select the desired speed for the transition between the different slides in the presentation from the **Speed** drop-down menu. *Medium* is a good choice for now.

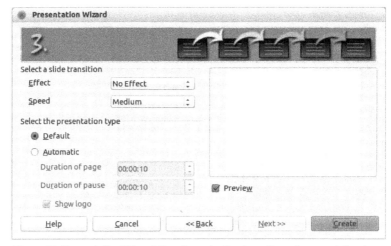

Figure 15: Presentation Wizard Step 3 – selecting transitions & presentation type

6) Select the presentation type – *Default* or *Automatic*.

- Choosing *Default* displays the presentation as a full screen presentation with the specified speed you selected from the Speed drop down list.
- Choosing *Automatic* allows you to set the duration the slide is displayed and the duration of the pause between the end and restart of the presentation.

7) If you did not select *From template* in Step 1 of the Presentation Wizard, click **Create** and your new presentation is created.

Tip	You can accept the default values for both *Effect* and *Speed* unless you are skilled at creating presentations. Both of these values can be changed later while working with **Slide transitions** and **animations**. These two features are explained in more detail in *Chapter 9 Slide Shows*.

Note	If you selected *From template* in Step 1 of the Presentation Wizard, then the **Next** button is active and, when clicked, Steps 4 and 5 become available. These extra steps when using a template are described below.

8) Click **Next** and Step 4 of the Presentation Wizard (Figure 16) appears. Here you can enter the name of your company, your presentation topic, and the basic ideas you want to cover in the presentation you are creating.

9) Click **Next** and step 5 of the Presentation Wizard (Figure 17) appears showing a preview of what each slide in your presentation will look like. If the preview does not appear, select *Preview*.

10) If you want to create a summary of your presentation, select *Create summary*. This creates a new slide that contains a bulleted list from the titles of the slides that follow the selected slide. The summary slide is inserted behind the last slide of your presentation.

11) Click **Create** and your new presentation is created.

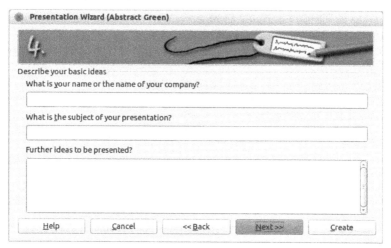

Figure 16: Presentation Wizard Step 4 – presentation information

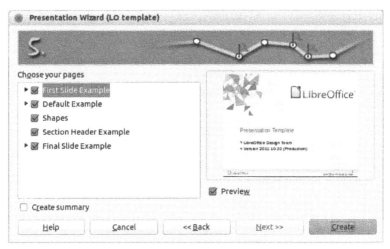

Figure 17: Presentation Wizard Step 5 – presentation preview

Formatting a presentation

A new presentation only contains one empty slide. In this section we will start adding new slides and preparing them for the intended contents.

Inserting slides

New slide

A new slide can be inserted into a presentation as follows:

1) Go to **Insert** on the main menu bar and select **Slide**.

   Or, right-click on a slide in the Workspace, Slides Pane, or Slide Sorter view and select **Slide > New Slide** from the context menu.

   Or, click the **Slide** icon ⊞ in the Presentation toolbar. If the Presentation toolbar is not visible, go to **View > Toolbars** on the main menu bar and select **Presentation** from the list.

2) A new slide is inserted after the selected slide in the presentation.

Duplicate slide

Sometimes, rather than starting from a new slide you may want to duplicate a slide already included in your presentation. To duplicate a slide:

1) Select the slide you want to duplicate from the Slides Pane.

2) Right-click on the slide in the Slides Pane or Workspace and select **Duplicate Slide** from the context menu.

   Or, go to Slide Sorter view, right-click on a slide and select **Duplicate Slide** from the context menu.

   Or, go to **Insert** on the main menu bar and select **Duplicate Slide**.

Or, click on the triangle to the right of the **Slide** icon in the Presentation toolbar and select **Duplicate Slide** from the context menu. If the Presentation toolbar is not visible, go to **View > Toolbars** on the main menu bar and select **Presentation** from the list.

3) A duplicate slide is inserted after the selected slide in the presentation.

Selecting a slide layout

Click on the Properties icon at the side of the Sidebar to open **Layouts** section and display the available layouts (Figure 18). The layouts included in Impress range from a blank slide to a slide with six contents boxes and a title.

The first slide in a presentation is normally a title slide. The *Title Slide* (which also contains a section for a subtitle) or *Title Only* are suitable layouts for the first slide, while for most of the remaining slides you will probably use the *Title, Contents* layout.

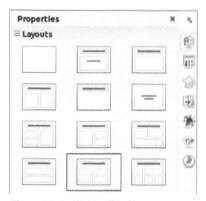

Figure 18: Available slide layouts

Selecting layout

Assuming that the *Blank Slide* layout was not selected:

1) Click on *Click to add title* and then type the title text. To adjust the formatting of the title, modify the *Title* presentation style; see *Chapter 2 Using Slide Masters, Styles, and Templates* for instructions.

2) If you are using the *Title Slide* layout, click on *Click to add text* to add a subtitle. To adjust the formatting of the subtitle, modify the *Subtitle* presentation style; see *Chapter 2 Using Slide Masters, Styles, and Templates* for instructions.

Note	Text and graphic elements can be readjusted at any time during the preparation of the presentation, but changing the layout of a slide that already contains some contents can have a dramatic effect. It is therefore recommended that you pay particular attention to the layout you select. If you do need to change the layout after contents have been added, the contents are not lost though they may need to be reformatted.

Tip	To view the names for the included layouts, use the Tooltip feature: position the cursor on an icon in the Layout section (or on any toolbar icon) and its name will be displayed in a small rectangle.

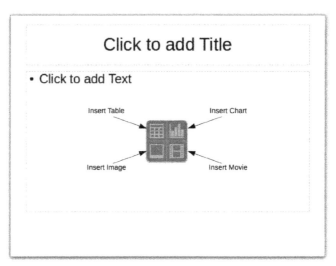

Figure 19: Selecting contents type

Changing layout

To select or change the layout:

1) Place the slide in the work area and select the desired layout from the layout section in Sidebar Properties. Several layouts contain one or more content boxes. Each of these boxes can be configured to contain one of the following elements: Text, Movie, Image, Chart or Table.

2) Select the type of contents by clicking on the icon that is displayed in the middle of the contents box as shown in Figure 19.

3) If instead you intend to use the contents box for text, just click on the *Click to add text* and type your text.

Note	If you have selected a layout with one or more contents boxes, this is a good time to decide what type of contents you want to insert.

Modifying slide elements

A slide contains elements that were included in the slide master, as well those elements included in the selected slide layout. However, it is unlikely that the predefined layouts will suit all your needs for your presentation. You may want to remove elements that are not required or insert objects such as text and graphics.

Although Impress does not have the functionality to create new layouts, it allows you to resize and move the layout elements. It is also possible to add slide elements without being limited to the size and position of the layout boxes.

To resize a contents box, click on the outer frame so that the 8 resizing handles are displayed. To move it place the mouse cursor on the frame so that the cursor changes shape. You can now click the left mouse button and drag the contents box to its new position on the slide.

To remove any unwanted elements, click the element to highlight it and the resizing handles show it is highlighted. Press the *Delete* key to remove it.

Adding text

To add text to a slide that contains a text frame, click on *Click to add text* in the text frame and then type your text. The Outline styles are automatically applied to the text as you insert it. You can change the outline level of each paragraph as well as its position within the text by using the arrow buttons on the *Text Formatting* toolbar (see Figure 7 and "Outline view" on page 19). For more information on text, see *Chapter 3 Adding and Formatting Text*.

Adding objects

To add any pictures or objects to a slide, for example a picture, clipart, drawing, photograph, or spreadsheet, click on **Insert** then select from the drop down menu what type of insert you require. For more information, see the following chapters:

- For pictures, see *Chapter 4 Adding and Formatting Images*.
- For graphic objects, see *Chapter 5 Managing Graphic Objects* and *Chapter 6 Formatting Graphic Objects*.
- For OLE and other objects, see *Chapter 7 Including Spreadsheets, Charts, and Other Objects*.

Modifying slide appearance

To change the background and other characteristics of all slides in the presentation, you need to modify the master page or choose a different master page.

A *Slide Master* is a slide with a specified set of characteristics that acts as a template and is used as the starting point for creating other slides. These characteristics include the background, objects in the background, formatting of any text used, and any background graphics.

Impress has included a range of slide masters, found in the **Master Pages** section of the Sidebar. You can also create and save additional slide masters or add more from other sources. See *Chapter 2 Using Slide Masters, Styles, and Templates* for information on creating and modifying slide masters.

If all you need to do is to change the background, you can use a shortcut:

1) Select **Format > Page** and go to the *Background* tab on the **Page Setup** dialog that opens.
2) Select the desired background between solid color, gradient, hatching and bitmap.
3) Click **OK** to apply it. A dialog box opens, asking if the background should be applied to all the slides. If you click **Yes**, Impress automatically modifies the master page for you.

Modifying a slide show

By default the slide show will display all the slides in the same order as they appear in the slide sorter, using any transition between slides specified in the Presentation Wizard, and you need some keyboard or mouse interaction to move from one slide to the next.

Now is a good time to review the entire presentation and answer some questions. Run the slide show at least once (see "Running a slide show" on page 31) before answering them. You might want to add some questions of your own.

- Are the slides in the correct order? If not, some of them will need to be moved.
- Is the information well spaced and visible to members of an audience at the back of a large room? They may not be able to see information at the bottom of a slide, so you may need to design your presentation to fit the top three-quarters of the screen.
- Would an additional slide make a particular point clearer? If so, another slide needs to be created.
- Do some of the slides seem unnecessary? Hide or delete them.
- Would custom animations help some of the slides? (Advanced technique.)
- Should some of the slides have a different slide transition than others? The transition of those slides should be changed.

Tip	If one or more slides seem to be unnecessary, hide the slide or slides, and view the slide show a few more times to make sure they are not needed. To hide a slide, right-click the slide in the Slides pane and select **Hide Slide** from the context menu. Do not delete a slide until you have done this; otherwise you may have to create that slide again.

Once you have answered these and your own questions, make the necessary changes. This is done most easily in the Slide Sorter view (see "Slide Sorter view" page 21). Use the Slide Show menu to change the order of the slides, choose which ones are shown, automate moving from one slide to the next, and other settings. To change the slide transition, animate slides, and make other enhancements, use the various selections in the Task pane.

Custom animations

If you wish to add a custom animation to a slide, do it now. Custom animations are found in the **Custom Animation** section of the Sidebar. This is an advanced technique and is explained in *Chapter 9 Slide Shows*.

Slide transitions

Your first slide show will probably have the same slide transition for all slides. Setting *Advance slide* to **On mouse click** is the default. If you want each slide to be shown for a specific amount of time, click **Automatically after** and enter the number of seconds. Click **Apply to all slides**.

Transition choices are found under **Slide Transition** on the Sidebar. For more information about slide transitions see *Chapter 9 Slide Shows*.

Tip	The Slide Transition section has a very useful option: *Automatic preview*. With this option selected, when you make any changes in a slide transition, the new slide is previewed in the Slide Design area, including its transition effect.

Running a slide show

1) To run the slide show, do one of the following:

   • Click **Slide Show > Slide Show** on the main menu bar.

   • Click the **Slide Show** icon 📊 on the Presentation toolbar or the Slide Sorter toolbar.

   • Press *F5* or *F9*. (*F9* does not work on a Mac.)

2) If the slide transition is *Automatically after x seconds*, let the slide show run by itself.

3) If the slide transition is *On mouse click*, do one of the following to move from one slide to the next.

   • Click the mouse button to advance to the next slide.

   • Use the arrow keys on the keyboard to go to the next slide or back to the previous one.

   • Press the *Spacebar* on the keyboard to advance to the next slide.

4) Right-click anywhere on the screen to open a menu from which you can navigate the slides and set other options.

5) When you advance past the last slide, the message *Click to exit presentation...* appears. Click the mouse or press any key to exit the presentation.

6) To exit the slide show at any time including at the end, press the *Esc* key.

Presenter Console

LibreOffice Impress has a Presenter Console function that can be used when an extra display for presentation has been connected your computer. The Presenter Console (Figure 20) provides extra control over slide shows by using different views on your computer display and on the display that the audience sees. The view you see on your computer display includes the current slide, the upcoming slide, any slide notes, and a presentation timer.

For more information and details about using the Presenter Console, see *Chapter 9 Slide Shows*.

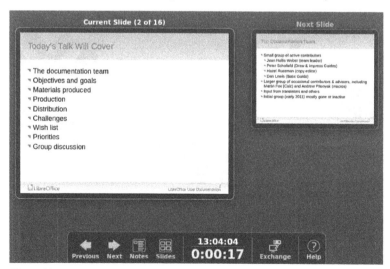

Figure 20: Impress Presenter Console

Chapter 2
Using Slide Masters,
Styles, and Templates

Designing a presentation

In addition to careful planning of the content, as discussed in *Chapter 1 Introducing Impress*, you need to plan the appearance of the presentation. It is best to do this after you have developed an outline, because the outline will determine some of the requirements for the appearance of the slides. For example:

- What color combinations (background and text) will look good and also be easy for your audience to read?
- Would a picture help your audience understand the contents better?
- Do you want particular text and a picture to appear on all the slides? For example a company name and logo.
- Would the audience benefit from having the slides numbered so that they can quickly refer to one of them?
- Do you want a background graphic or gradient? If so, you need to pick something that does not interfere or clash with content such as the colors used in charts.
- Will you need one slide master or more than one? Will one slide design suit all of the content?

You can change the appearance of slides as you develop the presentation, but planning ahead will save you time in the long run.

What are slide masters?

A *slide master* is a slide that is used as the starting point for other slides. It is similar to a page style in Writer: it controls the basic formatting of all slides based on it. A slide presentation can have more than one slide master.

Note	LibreOffice uses three terms for one concept: *slide master*, *master slide*, and *master page*. All refer to a slide which is used to create other slides. This book uses the term *slide master*, except when describing the user interface.

A slide master has a defined set of characteristics, including the background color, graphic, or gradient; objects (such as logos, decorative lines, and other graphics) in the background; headers and footers; placement and size of text frames; and the formatting of text.

All of the characteristics of slide masters are controlled by *styles*. The styles of any new slide you create are inherited from the slide master from which it was created. In other words, the styles of the slide master are available and applied to all slides created from that slide master. Changing a style in a slide master results in changes to all the slides based on that slide master. It is, however, possible to modify each individual slide without affecting the slide master.

Note	Although it is highly recommended to use the slide masters whenever possible, there are occasions where manual changes are needed for a particular slide, for example to enlarge the chart area when the text and chart layout is used.

Slide masters have two types of styles associated with them: *presentation styles* and *image styles*. The prepackaged presentation styles can be modified, but new presentation styles cannot be created. For image styles, you can modify the prepackaged styles and also create new styles.

Presentation styles are discussed in detail in *Chapter 3 Adding & Formatting Text*. The use of image styles is covered in *Chapter 6 Formatting Graphic Objects*. See also "Working with styles in Impress" on page 47.

Working with slide masters

Impress comes with a collection of slide masters. These slide masters are shown in the Master Pages section of the Sidebar (Figure 21). This section has three subsections: *Used in This Presentation*, *Recently Used*, and *Available for Use*. Click the expand marker next to the name of a subsection to expand it and show thumbnails of the slides, or click the collapse marker to collapse the subsection to hide the thumbnails.

Each of the slide masters shown in the *Available for Use* list is from a template of the same name. If you have created your own templates, or added templates from other sources, slide masters from those templates will also appear in this list. See "Working with templates" on page 47 for more information about templates.

Figure 21: Sidebar Master Pages section

Creating slide masters

You can create a new slide master which is similar to modifying the default slide master.

1) Enable editing of slide masters by selecting **View > Master > Slide Master** on the main menu bar and the **Master View** toolbar opens (Figure 22). If the Master View toolbar does not appear, go to **View > Toolbars** and select **Master View**.

2) Alternatively, right-click on a slide master you want to use in the Master Pages section of the Sidebar that and select **Edit Master** from the context menu to open the Master View toolbar.

3) On the Master View toolbar, click the **New Master** icon.

4) A new slide master appears in the Slides pane. Modify this slide master to suit your requirements.

Figure 22: Master View toolbar

5) It is recommended that you rename this new slide master. Right-click on the slide in the Slides pane and select **Rename master** from the context menu.

6) When finished creating a slide master, click **Close Master View** on the Master View toolbar and return to normal slide editing mode.

Applying a slide master

To apply a slide master to all the slides in your presentation:

1) In the Sidebar, click on the **Master Pages** icon to open the Master Pages section (Figure 21).

2) To apply one of the slide masters to *all slides* in your presentation, right-click on the slide master you want to use and select **Apply to All Slides** on the context menu.

To apply a different slide master to one or more selected slides:

1) In the Sidebar, click on the **Master Pages** icon to open the Master Pages section (Figure 21).

2) In the Slide Pane, select the slide or slides where you want to use a new slide master.

3) In the Sidebar, right-click on the slide master you want to apply to the selected slides and select **Apply to Selected Slides** on the context menu.

Loading additional slide masters

Sometimes, in the same set of slides, you may need to mix multiple slide masters that may belong to different templates (the use of templates is explained in "Working with templates" on page 47). For example, you may need a completely different layout for the first slide of the presentation, or you may want to add a slide from a different presentation to your current presentation.

1) Go to **Format > Slide Design** on the main menu bar or right-click on a slide in the Slides Pane and select **Slide Design** from the context menu to open the Slide Design dialog (Figure 23). This dialog shows the slide masters already available for use.

2) To add more slide masters, click **Load** to open the Load Slide Design dialog (Figure 24).

3) Select in the Load Slide Design dialog the template from which to load the slide master and click **OK.**

4) Click **OK** again to close the Slide Design dialog.

5) The slide masters in the template you selected are now shown in the *Available for use* subsection of Master Pages.

Note	The slide masters you have loaded will also be available the next time you load the presentation. If you want to delete the unused slide masters, click the corresponding checkbox in the Slide Design dialog. If the slide master was not used in the presentation, it is removed from the list of available slide masters.

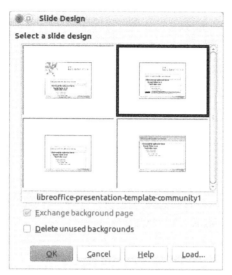

Figure 23: Slide Design dialog

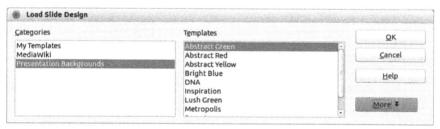

Figure 24: Load Slide Design dialog

Tip	To limit the size of the presentation file, you may want to minimize the number of slide masters used.

Modifying slide masters

The following items can be changed on a slide master:

- Background (color, gradient, hatching, or bitmap)
- Background objects (for example, adding a logo or decorative graphics)
- Text attributes for the main text area and notes
- Size, placement, and contents of header and footer elements to appear on every slide
- Size and placement of default frames for slide titles and content

To select the slide master for modification:

1) Select **View > Master > Slide Master** from the main menu bar. This opens the master view and unlocks the properties of a slide master.
2) Select a slide master you want to modify in the Slide Pane

---

Figure 25: Example master view

3) Right-click in the Workspace on your selected slide master that you want to modify so you can edit the slide master (Figure 25).

4) Select an object on the slide master, then right-click on the object and make any necessary changes using the options available in the context menu that opens. Selecting one of the options in the context menu may open a dialog where you can make the necessary changes to your selected object.

5) Click **Close Master View** on the Master View toolbar or go to **View > Normal** on the main menu bar to exit from editing slide masters.

6) Save your presentation file before continuing.

Note	Any changes made to one slide when in Master View mode will appear on all slides using this slide master. Always make sure you close Master View and return to Normal view before working on any of the presentation slides.

The changes made to one of the slides in Normal view (for example, changes to the bullet point style, the color of the title area, and so on) will not be overridden by subsequent changes to the slide master. There are cases, however, where it is desirable to revert a manually modified object of the slide to the style defined in the slide master: to do that, select that object and choose **Format > Default Formatting** from the main menu bar, or right-click on an object and select **Default** from the context menu.

Sometimes, depending on the contents of the slide, you may want to apply a different layout. The title and text boxes will inherit the properties of the slide master, but if you have changed the position of these text boxes in the slide master, the layout may appear corrupted and you may need to re-position some of the layout elements manually.

Selecting and applying backgrounds

Backgrounds can be applied to a number of elements in Impress: a slide, a default text area, an image and so on. The procedures to apply a background are always the same and the following procedure is used to apply a background to the slide.

1) Select **Format > Page** on the main menu bar, or right-click on the slide and select **Slide >Page Setup** from the context menu to open the Page Setup dialog.

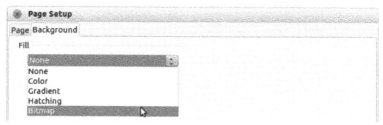

Figure 26: Background types in Page Setup dialog

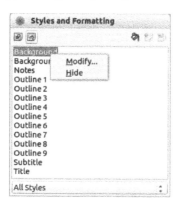

Figure 27: Presentation Styles

2) Select the *Background* tab and then type of *Fill* from the drop down list (Figure 28). The options available for backgrounds will depend on the fill type selected.

3) Alternatively, select **Format > Styles and Formatting** from the main menu bar, or press *F11*, or click the **Styles and Formatting** icon on the Line and Filling toolbar to open the Styles and Formatting dialog (Figure 27). Alternatively, click on the Styles and Formatting icon on the Sidebar to open the Styles and Formatting section.

4) Select the Presentation Styles icon and right-click *Background* style and select **Modify** from the context menu. This opens the Background dialog, which has one tab (*Area*) and offers the same options as the *Background* tab in the Page Setup dialog.

5) Select the type of fill you want for your background from the five options in the drop-down menu: *None, Color, Gradient, Hatching*, or *Bitmap*. A list of options for the selected fill type then appears. Figure 28 shows the options available if you select a bitmap for your background.

6) Select one of the options on the Fill list and click **OK**. The option you have selected is added to the slide master, replacing any previously selected fill.

Tip	You can make custom additions to each type of background, with the obvious exception of *None*. After you create new fills, they are listed in the Background dialog along with the fills provided with LibreOffice, see *Chapter 6 Formatting Graphic Objects* for more information.

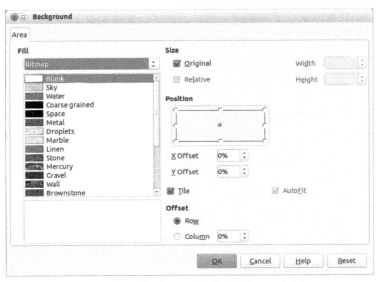

Figure 28: Selecting a bitmap background in the Background dialog

Adding image objects

When you want the same image to appear on every slide of your presentation, the easiest and quickest solution is to use the slide master. It saves time while creating the presentation and when you want to modify or reposition the image on all the slides. If the same image is added to each slide manually, these operations have to be performed on each individual slide in the presentation. LibreOffice supports a large number of image formats.

For example, one of the most common actions in preparing a presentation is to add an image to the slide master. To insert an image already available on the computer, follow these steps:

1) Select **View > Master > Slide Master** on the main menu bar to open the master view.
2) Select the slide master where you want to add an image.
3) Select **Insert > Image > From File** on the main menu bar to open the file browser.
4) Navigate to the directory where your image is located and select it. If you want to see a preview, select the *Preview* checkbox in the file browser dialog.
5) Click **Open** and the image is placed into your slide.

Once the image is inserted onto your slide, you have to move it to the background so that any information you add to the slide when creating a presentation appears over the background image.

1) With the image selected, right-click on the image and select **Arrange > Send to Back** from the context menu.
2) If necessary, reposition the image and modify its size. See *Chapter 4 Adding and Formatting Images* for more information.

In addition to images you can add a number of other objects in the background, for example decorative lines, text, and shapes.

Note	LibreOffice offers the option to insert an image as a link to the file rather than embedding it in your presentation. This can be useful when a presentation is **not** intended for distribution onto other computers, but where it will remain in the same computer and directory structure. For example, it could be created on a notebook computer, which is to be used to give the presentation to a group of clients. However, if the presentation file is to be distributed onto other computers, the image must be embedded to avoid the "missing image" syndrome when the presentation is given using a different computer.

Tip	If you want the image to blend with the background, you can set the background color of the image as transparent. Select the image, then go to **Tools > Color Replacer** on the main menu bar. Select the first checkbox, move the mouse cursor onto the picture and click on the color you want to make transparent. This color appears next to the checkbox. Make sure that *Replace with...* is set to **Transparent** and click **Replace**.

Tip	An easy way to make the image lighter so that the text stands out better against its background, is to increase the transparency of the image or change the gamma luminance of the image. Both these adjustments can be quickly made from the Picture toolbar.

Slide master styles

Within the slide master you can define a complete set of styles for the default appearance of text and images inserted in slides based on that background. If for example your slide master has a dark background, you may want to set the font color of the title and text areas to be light. Rather than manually changing the font color for every new slide you create, a time-consuming operation prone to errors and omissions, simply modify the style in the slide master. Changes made to styles in the slide master only apply to the slides based on that particular slide master.

Styles in Impress are sub-divided into two main categories: *presentation styles* and *image styles*.

Figure 29: Image styles

To work on the slide master styles, press *F11*, or select **Format > Styles and Formatting** from the main menu, or click the **Styles and Formatting** icon on the Line and Filling toolbar to open the Styles and Formatting dialog (Figure 27 on page 39 for Presentation styles and Figure 29 for

Image styles). Alternatively, click on the Styles and Formatting icon 🔀 on the Sidebar to open the Styles and Formatting section.

Presentation styles

Presentation styles (Figure 27) affect three elements of a slide master: the background, background objects (such as icons, decorative lines, and text frames), and the text placed on the slide. Text styles are further divided into *Notes*, *Outline 1* through *Outline 9*, *Subtitle*, and *Title*. The outline styles are used for the different levels of the outline to which they belong. For example, Outline 2 is used for the sub-points of Outline 1, and Outline 3 is used for the sub-points of Outline 2.

The presentation styles can be modified, but new presentation styles cannot be created.

Image styles

Image styles (Figure 29) apply to lines, shapes and text boxes created using the Impress drawing tools and define the formatting of such objects. You can create additional styles or modify the included styles.

Note	The presence of text and title styles both in the Presentation and Image styles may seem confusing. This apparent duplication is because Impress uses special text boxes when adding structured text to slides where Presentation styles apply (AutoLayout boxes). The title and other text styles in Image styles continue to apply to other text boxes you may want to add, or to text associated with shapes or lines.

Tip	At the bottom of the Styles and Formatting dialog is a drop-down list where you can choose to show either *Hierarchical*, *All Styles*, *Hidden Styles*, *Applied Styles* or *Custom Styles*.

Modifying default text areas

When a slide master is opened for editing, it contains five areas, as shown in Figure 25 on page 38.

- Title area for AutoLayouts
- Object area for AutoLayouts
- Date area
- Footer area
- Slide number area

Position and size

Click with the left mouse button on any of these areas to display the selection handles around the rectangle. Use these handles to modify the size and position of the area.

- To change the position, move the mouse towards one of the edges, not on a selection handle, and click the left mouse button. The cursor changes shape which is dependent on your computer setup (normally a clenched hand).
- To modify the shape and size of one of the rectangular areas, use one of the selection handles. The corner handles modify the height and width of the rectangle simultaneously while the side handles modify only one dimension at a time. The shape of the mouse cursor

usually changes shape when over a handle, giving a clear visual indication of how it will affect the shape of the rectangular area.

Tip	To keep the shape of the rectangular area constant, move the mouse to one of the four corner handles and keep the *Shift* key pressed while dragging the handle with the mouse. The rectangle maintains the ratio between the width and height dimensions of the rectangle.

To accurately control the shape and size as well as the position of the default text area, it is better to use the Position and Size dialog than the mouse.

1) Select the rectangular area by clicking on the border.

2) Press *F4*, or go to **Format > Position and Size** on the main menu bar, or right-click on the border and select **Position and Size** from the context menu to open the Position and Size dialog (Figure 30).

3) Alternatively, click on the **Properties** icon on the Sidebar and open the *Position and Size* subsection.

Note	Clicking on the **More Options** icon on the *Position and Size* subsection on the Sidebar will open the Position and Size dialog.

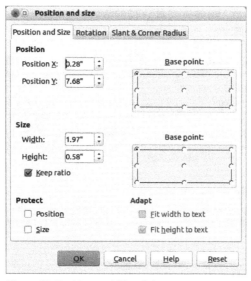

Figure 30: Position and Size dialog

The functions of the Position and Size dialog are explained in the *Draw Guide*, so only short descriptions of the most important fields are provided in this chapter.

- Use the *Position* section to specify the X (horizontal) and Y (vertical) position of the rectangular area. The values represent the distance of the selected base point and the default position is the top left corner of the slide.

- Use the *Size* section to specify the width and height of the rectangular area. In the *Base point* section, select a point on the rectangular area that you do not want to move while resizing. The default setting of top left corner means that the position of the top left corner of the area will not change after resizing.

- Use the *Rotation* page of the dialog to rotate the default text area. For example, you can place the footer area on the side by rotating each text area by 90 degrees and obtain a more modern-looking layout. In general it is preferable to use only right angles for ease of editing, although the program does not impose restrictions on the values that can be used.

Background, border, arrangement and alignment

Besides the shape, size and position, it is also possible to modify other aspects of the editable areas on the slide master, such as the background, border, alignment relative to the slide, and position relative to other objects.

- To edit the background of an object, go to **Format > Area** on the main menu bar, or right-click on the object and select **Area** from the context menu. This opens the Area dialog where you can change the type of fill used for object backgrounds. Alternatively, click on the **Properties** icon on the Sidebar and open the *Area* subsection. See *Chapter 6 Formatting Graphic Objects* for more information.

- To edit the borders of an object, go to **Format > Line** on the main menu bar, or right-click on the object and select **Line** from the context menu. This opens the Line dialog where you can change the type and color of the line used for object borders. Alternatively, click on the **Properties** icon on the Sidebar and open the *Line* subsection. See *Chapter 6 Formatting Graphic Objects* for more information.

- To change the alignment of an object on a slide or the alignment between two or more objects, right-click on the object and select **Alignment** then the type of alignment from the context menu, or click on the small triangle to the right of the **Alignment** icon on the Line and Filling toolbar and select the type of alignment from the options available. See *Chapter 5 Managing Graphic Objects* for more information.

- To arrange the position of an object on a slide in relation to other objects on a slide, right-click on the object and select **Arrange** then the object position from the context menu, or click on the small triangle to the right of the **Arrange** icon on the Line and Filling toolbar and select the object position from the options available. See *Chapter 5 Managing Graphic Objects* for more information.

Adding text and fields to all slides

Adding text and fields to a master slide allows you to place information that you want to appear on all the slides in your presentation, for example presentation title, company, date and slide number.

Text

Text objects can be placed anywhere on the master page so that it appears on every slide in your presentation. Text objects can also be placed in the footer if you do not want to use the footer default fields in your presentation.

1) Select **View > Master > Slide Master** from the main menu bar to open Master View.

2) To add text to the main area of the slide, select the **Text** icon on the Drawing toolbar, or press the *F2* key.

3) Click once in the master page and drag to draw a text object, then type or paste your text into the text object.

4) To add text to the slide footer, click in one of the footer areas of the slide and highlight the text field, then type of paste your text into the footer area.

5) To format the text after placing it on your master page, see *Chapter 3 Adding and Formatting Text* for more information.

6) Click **Close Master View** on the Master View toolbar or go to **View > Normal** on the main menu bar when you are finished.

Footer default fields

By default, the footer used in an Impress slide consists of three sections with each section containing a default field as follows:

- Left section – date and time. The field name is <date>.

- Center section – footer text, for example this could be the presentation title, file name and so on. The field name is <text>.

- Right section – slide (page) number. The field name is <number>.

Figure 31: Date and Time dialog

The default footer fields are set up as follows:

1) Select **View > Master > Slide Master** from the main menu bar to open Master View.

2) Go to **Insert > Page Number** or **Date and Time** to open the Date and Time dialog (Figure 31) and make sure the **Slides** tab is selected.

3) For a fixed **Date and time** in the left section of the footer, select *Fixed* and enter the date you want to use in the text box.

4) For a variable **Date and time** in the left section of the footer, select *Variable*, then select the *Format* and *Language* from the drop down lists that you want to use. Using a variable date and time means that each time the file is opened, the date and time are updated.

5) To place text in the center section of the footer, select **Footer** and then type or paste your text into the *Footer text* box.

6) To place the slide number in the right section section of the footer, select **Slide number**.

7) If you do not want the footer to appear on the first slide of your presentation, then select **Do not show on the first slide**. The first slide is normally the title slide of your presentation.

8) Click **Apply to All** to close the dialog.

9) To format the text used for the default fields, see *Chapter 3 Adding and Formatting Text* for more information.

10) Click **Close Master View** on the Master View toolbar or go to **View > Normal** on the main menu bar when you are finished.

Note	The default fields in the footer can be replaced with text or manual fields. For more information, see "Text" on page 44 and "Manual fields" on page 46. These default sections in a footer can also be formatted, resized and repositioned. See "Modifying default text areas" on page 42 for more information.

Manual fields

Manual fields, for example date or page number (slide number), can be added as text objects on a slide master or replace one of the default footer fields. The fields you can use in Impress are:

- Date (fixed)
- Date (variable): updates automatically when you reload the file
- Time (fixed)
- Time (variable): updates automatically when you reload the file
- Author: first and last names listed in the LibreOffice user data
- Page number (slide number)
- File name

To place a field on your slide master:

1) Select **View > Master > Slide Master** from the main menu bar to open Master View.

2) Click anywhere on the slide master.

3) Go to **Insert > Fields** on the main menu bar and select the required field from the submenu.

4) By default the field is placed in the center of the slide master. Reposition the field text box to the desired position on your slide master.

5) To format the text used in a field, see *Chapter 3 Adding and Formatting Text* for more information.

6) Click **Close Master View** on the Master View toolbar or go to **View > Normal** on the main menu bar when you are finished.

To replace a default field in the footer on your slide master:

1) Select **View > Master > Slide Master** from the main menu bar to open Master View.

2) Highlight all of the characters used in the default field you want to replace in the footer.

3) Go to **Insert > Fields** on the main menu bar and select the required field from the submenu.

4) To format the text used in a field, see *Chapter 3 Adding and Formatting Text* for more information.

5) Click **Close Master View** on the Master View toolbar or go to **View > Normal** on the main menu bar when you are finished.

Tip	To change the number format (1,2,3 or a,b,c or i,ii,iii, etc.) for the slide number, go to **Format > Page** on the main menu bar and select a format from the list in the **Layout Settings** area.
	To change the author information, go to **Tools > Options > LibreOffice > User Data** on the main menu bar.

Working with styles in Impress

If you are familiar with styles in Writer, you will find both similarities and differences in Impress. The presentation styles are comparable to paragraph styles in Writer and are used in a similar fashion. You cannot create new presentation styles but you can fully configure the existing ones. Note that, as with the Heading styles in Writer, the Outline styles are hierarchically linked, so that a change in the Outline 1 will cascade through all the other Outline levels.

In Impress you will also find the image styles very useful. They define the characteristics of graphic objects (including text objects). For example, if you need to create an organization chart diagram in one of the slides of your presentation, you will probably want all of the objects to have a consistent appearance, such as line style, font type, shadow, and so on. The easiest way to achieve this result with the minimum effort is to create an image style for the objects and apply it to each object. The major benefit is that if you decide to change, say, the background color of objects, all you need to do is modify the style rather than each individual object.

Presentation styles are discussed in more detail in *Chapter 3 Adding and Formatting Text* and image styles are discussed in detail in *Chapter 6 Formatting Graphic Objects*. More information on styles can also be found in the *Getting Started Guide Chapter 3 Using Styles and Templates*.

Working with templates

A *template* is a special type of document that you use as a basis to create other documents from. For example, you can create a template for business presentations so that any new presentations has your company logo and name on the first slide and the remaining slides in your presentation only show the company name.

Templates can contain anything that regular documents can contain, such as text, graphics, a set of styles, and user-specific setup information such as measurement units, language, the default printer, and toolbar and menu customization.

All documents created using LibreOffice are based on templates. You can create a specific template for any document type (text, spreadsheet, drawing, presentation). If you do not specify a template when you start a new document, then the document is based on the default template for that type of document. If you have not specified a default template, LibreOffice uses the blank template for that type of document that is installed with LibreOffice. This default template can be changed, see "Setting default template" on page 49 for more information.

However, Impress is a little different from other LibreOffice components, in that it starts with the Presentation Wizard, unless you have decided to turn off this wizard. When you choose **File > New > Presentation** from the menu bar and, if the wizard is active, it opens offering several choices for a new presentation, one of which is *From template*.

If you have turned off the Presentation Wizard, when you start a new presentation by choosing **File > New > Presentation** from the menu bar, LibreOffice uses the default presentation template. If you have not defined your own default template, LibreOffice uses the blank template supplied with Impress.

Any slide masters created from a template created by yourself or created from imported templates will appear in *Available for Use* in the Master Pages section of the Sidebar.

For more information on templates, see the *Getting Started Guide Chapter 3 Using Styles and Templates*.

Templates supplied with LibreOffice

Impress comes with a set of predefined templates and these are located in the *Presentation backgrounds* folder. These templates only contain backgrounds and background objects providing you with a starting point to create your own templates. Any templates that you create from this default set will be located in the *My Templates* folder after you have saved your presentation as a template. Create a new presentation from a presentation template as follows:

1) Click on **Templates** in LibreOffice start up window or go to **File > New > Templates** on the main menu bar to open the Template Manager dialog (Figure 32).

2) Click on the **Presentations** tab to open the page containing all the templates for use in Impress.

3) Navigate to the folder that contains the selection of presentation templates you want to use.

4) Select the template you want to use.

5) Click on the **Open** icon 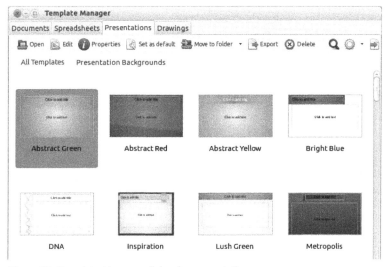 on the Template Manager toolbar or double-click on the template and a new presentation will be created using the selected template.

Figure 32: Template Manager dialog for presentations

Templates from other sources

You can download templates for LibreOffice from many sources, including the official template repository at http://templates.libreoffice.org/, and install them on your computer. On other websites you may find collections of templates that have been created using open document format (.OTP file extension) that Impress uses as its default format. These templates from other sources are installed using the Extension Manager, as described in "Importing template collections" on page 53.

Some of these templates are free of charge; others are available for a fee. Check the descriptions to see what licenses and fees apply to the ones that interest you. To import individual templates, see "Importing templates" on page 52 for more information and to import a template collection, see "Importing template collections" on page 53 for more information.

Creating your own templates

To create a template from a presentation and save it to *My Templates* folder or a folder of your own choosing:

1) Open the presentation that you want to use for a template, or open a template that you want to use as a basis for your template.

2) Add any extra content and styles to your presentation.

3) Go to **File > Templates > Save As Template** on the main menu bar to open the Template Manager dialog (Figure 33).

4) Open the *My Templates* or your own template folder as your destination folder to activate

the **Save** icon 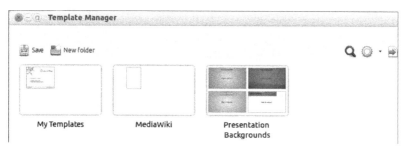, then click the **Save** icon.

5) Type a name for the new template in the *Enter template name* text box.

6) Click **OK** to save the new template in the destination folder.

7) Close the Template Manager dialog.

8) To use the template for a new presentation, follow the procedure in "Templates supplied with LibreOffice" on page 48 and select your newly created template.

Figure 33: Saving a new template in the Template Manager dialog

Setting default template

If you create a presentation by using **File > New > Presentation** on the main menu bar and do not select a template, LibreOffice creates the presentation from the default Impress template, which is normally a blank template. However, you can set any presentation template to be the default template, even a template that you have created, so long as it is located in a folder displayed in the Template Manager dialog. You can always reset to the default template back to the blank template later if you choose.

Setting a custom template as default

To set a template that you have created or imported as default instead of using the Impress default template:

1) Click on **Templates** in LibreOffice start up window or go to **File > New > Templates** to open the Template Manager dialog and select the **Presentations** tab (Figure 32 on page 48).

2) Double-click on the *My Templates* folder or the folder that contains the template you want to use to open the folder.

3) Select the template you want to use as the default template.

4) Click the **Set as default** icon and your selected template becomes the default template. The next time that you create a new presentation using Impress, the presentation will be created from the default Impress template.

Note	By default, the Presentation Wizard will have *From template* selected if the default template has been changed. If you select *Empty presentation* in the Presentation Wizard and then click **Create**, an empty presentation will be created and the default template will not be used.

Resetting default template

To reset the default template for a new presentation to use the Impress default template:

1) Click on **Templates** in LibreOffice start up window or go to **File > New > Templates** to open the Template Manager dialog.

2) Select the **Action Menu** icon and choose **Reset Default Template** from the drop-down menu (Figure 34). This command does not appear unless the default template has been previously changed to a template of your choosing.

3) Select **Presentation** from the drop down list to reset the default template. If other modules in LibreOffice have had their default template changed, then these modules will also appear in this drop down list.

4) The next time that you create a new presentation using Impress, the presentation will be created from the default Impress template.

Figure 34: Resetting the default template

Editing a template

You can edit template styles and content, and then, if you wish, you can reapply the template styles to presentations that were created from that template.

Note	You can only reapply styles. You cannot reapply content.

Editing

1) Click on **Templates** in LibreOffice start up window or go to **File > New > Templates** to open the Template Manager dialog (Figure 32 on page 48).

2) Navigate to the folder where the template you want to edit is located and click once on it to activate the file handling controls.

3) Select the **Edit** icon ![icon] and the template opens in Impress. Edit the template just as you would any other presentation.

4) To save your changes, go to **File > Save** on the main menu bar.

Updating a document from a changed template

The next time that you open a presentation that was created from the changed template, the following message appears (Figure 35).

Click **Update Styles** to update any styles in the template that have been changed in the document. Click **Keep Old Styles** if you do not want to update any styles in the template that have been changed in the document. Whichever option you choose, the message box closes and the presentation opens in Impress.

Figure 35. Update styles message

Note	If you select **Keep Old Styles** in the message box shown in Figure 35, then this message will not appear again the next time you open the document after changing the template it is based on. You will not get another chance to update the styles from the template.

Organizing templates

LibreOffice can only use templates that are in LibreOffice template folders. You can create new LibreOffice template folders and use them to organize your templates. For example, separate template folders for different projects or clients. You can also import and export templates.

Tip	The location of LibreOffice template folders varies with your computer operating system. To learn where the template folders are stored on your computer, go to **Tools > Options > LibreOffice > Paths**.

Creating template folders

To create a template folder:

1) Go to **File > New > Templates** on the main menu bar to open the Template Management dialog.

2) Select the **Presentations** tab to open the dialog page for presentations (Figure 32 on page 48).

3) Click the **New Folder** icon ![icon] and enter a name for the new folder in the *Enter folder name* box, then click **OK**.

4) Alternatively, click on the template you want to move to a new folder and the file handling controls are displayed.

5) Click the **Move to folder** icon and select **New folder** from the drop list that appears.

6) Type a name for the new folder in the *Enter folder name* box, then click **OK**. The selected template is then moved to the new folder you have just created.

Deleting template folders

You cannot delete the template folders supplied with LibreOffice or installed using the Extension Manager. You can only delete folders that you have created.

To delete a template folder that you have created:

1) Go to **File > New > Templates** on the main menu bar to open the Template Management dialog.

2) Select the **Presentations** tab to open the dialog page for presentations (Figure 32 on page 48).

3) In the Template Management dialog select the folder that you want to delete.

4) Select the **Delete** icon and a message box appears and asks you to confirm the deletion. Click **Yes**.

Moving templates

To move a template from one template folder to another template folder:

1) Go to **File > New > Templates** on the main menu bar to open the Template Management dialog.

2) Select the **Presentations** tab to open the dialog page for presentations (Figure 32 on page 48).

3) Navigate to the template that you want to move and then select it.

4) Click the **Move to folder** icon and select the folder from the drop down list to move your selected template.

Deleting templates

You cannot delete the templates supplied with LibreOffice or installed using the Extension Manager. You can only delete templates that you have created or imported.

To delete a template:

1) Go to **File > New > Templates** on the main menu bar to open the Template Management dialog.

2) Select the **Presentations** tab to open the dialog page for presentations (Figure 32 on page 48).

3) Navigate to the template that you want to delete and then select it.

4) Click the **Delete** icon and a message box appears and asks you to confirm the deletion. Click **Yes**.

Importing templates

If the template that you want to use is in a different location, you must import it into an LibreOffice template folder.

To import a template into a template folder:

1) In the Template Manager dialog, select the folder into which you want to import the template.

2) Click the **Import** icon 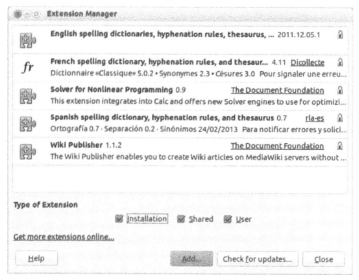 and a standard file browser dialog opens.

3) Navigate to the template on your computer that you want to import, select it and click **Open.** The file browser window closes and the template appears in the selected folder.

4) Alternatively, click the **Get more templates from LibreOffice** icon on the right of the Template Manager toolbar to open your web browser at the LibreOffice template page.

5) Locate the template you want to import and select it.

6) Download the template to your computer, then repeat Steps 1 to 3 above to import the template into LibreOffice.

Importing template collections

The Extension Manager provides an easy way to install collections of templates that have been packaged as extensions. For more about the Extension Manager, see the *Getting Started Guide Chapter 14 Customizing LibreOffice*.

1) Download the extension package (.OXT file) and save it anywhere on your computer. You can find several templates at http://templates.libreoffice.org/template-center that have been developed for use with LibreOffice.

2) Go to **Tools > Extension Manager** on the main menu bar to open the Extension Manager dialog (Figure 36).

3) Click **Add** to open a file browser window.

4) Find and select the template package you want to install and click **Open**. The package begins installing. You may be asked to accept a license agreement.

5) When the package installation is complete, the templates are available for use through **File > New > Templates** and the extension is listed in the Extension Manager.

Figure 36: Extension Manager

Exporting templates

To export a template from a template folder to another location:

1) Go to **File > New > Templates** on the main menu bar to open the Template Management dialog.

2) Select the **Presentations** tab to open the dialog page for presentations (Figure 32 on page 48).

3) Navigate to the template that you want to export and then select it.

4) Click the **Export** icon and a standard file browser dialog opens.

5) Navigate to the folder into which you want to export the template and click **OK**.

Chapter 3
Adding and Formatting Text

Introduction

Any text used in slides is contained in text boxes. This chapter describes how to create, modify, use, and delete text boxes. It also discusses the various types of text that can be inserted and explains how to format the text. Finally, it provides information on how to insert special forms of text such as numbered or bulleted lists, tables, fields, and hyperlinks.

Working with text boxes

There are two ways of adding text boxes to slides:

- Choose a predefined layout from the *Layouts* section of the Tasks pane containing text elements as described in *Chapter 1 Introducing Impress*. These text boxes are called **AutoLayout** text boxes.

- Create a text box using the Horizontal text tool T or Vertical text tool in the Drawing toolbar (Figure 37) or the Text toolbar (Figure 38).

Figure 37: Drawing Toolbar

Figure 38: Text toolbar

Note	In addition to the normal text boxes where text is horizontally aligned, it is possible to insert text boxes where the text is aligned vertically. Click on the Vertical Text icon in the Drawing or Text toolbars (Figure 37 and Figure 38) to create a vertical text box. The Vertical Text tool is available only when *Asian* languages and *Complex text layout (CTL)* are enabled in **Tools > Options > Language Settings > Languages** on the main menu bar.

Entering text into AutoLayout text boxes

To enter text into an AutoLayout text box:

1) Make sure Normal view is selected.
2) Click in the text box that reads *Click to add text*.
3) Type or paste your text into the AutoLayout text box.

For more information on AutoLayout text boxes, see "Creating bulleted and numbered lists" on page 74 for more information.

Entering text into text boxes

To enter text into a text box created using the text tool:

1) Make sure Normal View is selected.

Figure 39: Entering text in a text box

2) Click on the **Text** icon ⊤ on the Drawing toolbar (Figure 37) or the Text toolbar (Figure 38). The default position of the drawing toolbar is towards the bottom of the screen. If the Drawing or Text toolbars with the text icon are not visible, got **View > Toolbars > Drawing** or **Text** on the main menu bar.

3) Click in the slide and drag to draw a text box setting the width. Do not worry about the height because the text box will expand as you type.

4) To reposition the text box to a different part of the slide, see "Moving text boxes" on page 57; to change the width, see "Resizing text boxes" on page 58.

5) Release the mouse button when finished. The cursor appears in the text box, which is now in edit mode with the border highlighted (Figure 39).

6) Type or paste your text in the text box.

7) Click outside the text box to deselect it.

Moving text boxes

In Normal view, the cursor changes from an arrow to an I-beam (depending on your computer setup) as you move it over the text in a text box.

1) Click when the pointer becomes an I-beam. The text box is now in edit mode. In this mode the border is visible around the text box edges (Figure 39).

2) Move the cursor over the highlighted border and it changes shape, becoming the usual "move" symbol for your operating system (for example, a hand).

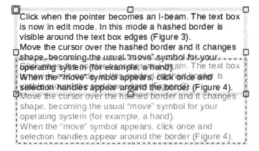

Figure 40: Moving text boxes

3) When the "move" symbol appears, click once and selection handles appear around the border (Figure 40).

4) Click anywhere on the border and drag to move the text box. A semi-transparent copy of the text box shows where your text box will be placed. Do not click on a selection handle as this will not move the text box, but resize the text box.

5) Release the mouse button when the text box is in the desired position. To return to edit mode, click outside the text box area.

Resizing text boxes

In Normal view, the cursor changes from an arrow to an I-beam (depending on your computer setup) as you move it over the text in a text box.

1) Click when the pointer becomes an I-beam. The text box is now in edit mode. In this mode the border is visible around the text box edges (Figure 39).

2) Move the cursor over the border and it changes shape, becoming the usual "move" symbol for your operating system (for example, a hand).

3) When the "move" symbol appears, click once and selection handles appear around the border (Figure 41).

4) Move the pointer over any handle. The cursor changes shape, indicating in which direction the text box will be resized. The corner handles change the two dimensions of the text box simultaneously, while the four handles at the center of each side modify only one dimension.

5) When the two-headed arrow is displayed, click and drag to resize the text box. As you resize the text box, a dashed outline appears indicating the new size of the text box.

6) Release the mouse button when the text box is at the desired size. To return to edit mode, click outside the text box area.

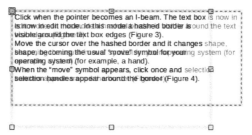

Figure 41: Resizing text boxes

Tip	To maintain the proportions of a text box while resizing, press and hold the *Shift* key, then click and drag. Make sure to release the mouse button **before** releasing the *Shift* key.

Using Position and Size dialog

For more accurate control over the size and position of a text box, use the Position and Size dialog instead of using the mouse.

1) Select the text box, then click on the text box border to display the selection handles.

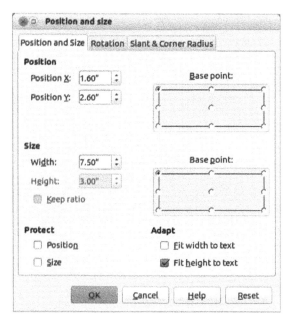

Figure 42: Position and Size dialog

2) Press *F4,* or select **Format > Position and Size** from the main menu bar, or right-click and select **Position and Size** from the context menu to open the Position and Size dialog (Figure 42).

3) Alternatively, click on the **Properties** icon on the Sidebar, then open the *Position and Size* subsection where you can change position, size, and rotation angle of the text box. To open the Position and Size dialog, click on the **More Options** icon at the top right of the *Position and Size* title bar.

4) Use the **Position** to specify the X (horizontal) and Y (vertical) position of the text box. The values represent the distance of the base point relative to the top left corner of the slide.

5) Use the **Size** section to specify the width and height of the text box. The values represent the distance of the base point relative to the top left corner of the slide. To maintain the ratio of width to height, select the *Keep ratio* option.

6) Select one of nine base points that correspond to the selection handles on the text box and the center of the text box. The default selection is the top left corner of a text box.

7) To prevent accidental modification of the position or size of the text box, select the *Position* and/or *Size* options in the **Protect** section of the dialog.

8) To allow the text box to adjust its height and/or width as you enter text, select *Fit width to text* and/or *Fit height to text* in the **Adapt** section of the dialog.

9) Click **OK** and the text box is moved or re-positioned on your slide.

Note	The unit of measurement for this dialog and other dialogs used in Impress is set in **Tools > Options > LibreOffice Impress > General** on the main menu bar.

Deleting text boxes

1) Click the text once to display the text box border.
2) Move the cursor to the border and click to display the selection handles, then press *Delete*.

Tip	Sometimes it is faster to to delete a text box by dragging a selection rectangle around the text box and then hitting the *Delete* key. Take care to avoid selecting and accidentally deleting other text boxes or shapes.

Inserting text

Pasting text

Text may be inserted into the text box by copying it from another document and pasting it into Impress. However, the pasted text will probably not match the formatting of the surrounding text or that of the other slides in the presentation. This may be what you want on some occasions; however, in most cases you may want to make sure that the presentation style is consistent. There are several ways to ensure consistency and these methods are explained below.

Pasting text unformatted

It is good practice to paste text without formatting and apply the formatting later. After highlighting and copying the text, use one of these methods to paste the text into your slide without formatting:

- Use the keyboard shortcut *Control+Shift+V* and select **Unformatted text** from the dialog that opens.

- Click on the small triangle to the right of the **Paste** icon on the Standard toolbar and select **Unformatted text** from the context menu that opens.

- Select **Edit > Paste Special** on the main menu bar and select **Unformatted text** from the dialog that opens.

The text will be pasted at the cursor position and formatted with the outline style in an AutoLayout text box or with the default graphic style in a normal text box.

Pasting text formatted

To paste text straight into an **AutoLayout** text box on your slide with its formatting retained, use one of these methods:

- Use the keyboard shortcut *Control+V*.

- Click on the **Paste** icon on the Standard toolbar.

- Select **Edit > Paste** on the main menu bar.

The text will be pasted into your slide at the cursor position. To give the pasted text the same appearance as the rest of your presentation, apply the appropriate outline style to the text:

1) Select the text you have just pasted (see "Selecting text" on page 63 for more information).
2) Select **Format > Default formatting** on the menu bar. This operation assigns one of the nine Presentation styles to the text. The style depends on where the text was pasted into your slide.

Figure 43: Text Formatting toolbar

3) Use the four positioning arrows ⇐ ⇒ ⇧ ⇩ on the Text Formatting toolbar (Figure 43) to move the text to the appropriate position and give it the appropriate outline level. The left arrow promotes the list entry by one level (for example from Outline 3 to Outline 2), the right arrow demotes the list entry by one level, the up and down arrows move the list entry.

4) Apply necessary manual formatting to the text changing font attributes, tabs, and so on.

If you are pasting text into a normal text box, you can still use styles to quickly format the text. Note that only one graphic style can be applied to the copied text.

1) Paste the text in the desired position.

2) Select the text you have just pasted (see "Selecting text" on page 63 for more information).

3) Select the desired graphic style.

4) Apply necessary manual formatting to the text changing font attributes, tabs, and so on.

Tip	Presentation styles are very different from Writer styles and are applied differently. Refer to "Using styles to format text" on page 64 for details.

Inserting special characters

To insert special characters, such as copyright, math, geometric, or monetary symbols, or characters from another language.

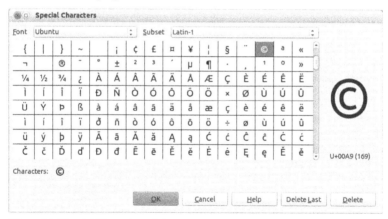

Figure 44: Special Characters dialog

1) Click at the position where you want to insert the special character into the text.

2) Select **Insert > Special Character** on the main menu bar to open the Special Characters dialog (Figure 44). Alternatively, and if the Text Formatting toolbar has been customized, click the **Special Character** icon 🎛 to open the Special Characters dialog.

Tip	To show toolbar tools that are not visible on a toolbar, right-click in a blank area on the toolbar and select **Visible Buttons** from the context menu that opens. Click on the icon you wish to add to the toolbar.

3) Choose the font and character subset from the *Font* and *Subset* drop-down menus.

4) Select the special character you want to insert. You may have to scroll to find the one you want.

5) Click **OK** to close the dialog and insert the special character at the cursor position in the text.

6) Alternatively, double-click on the special character you want to insert. This closes the dialog and inserts the special character at the cursor position in the text.

Characters you selected will be inserted in the order they were selected, even if you accidentally click on the wrong character. Clicking on another character will only add it to the ones being inserted. Use one of the following methods to delete any unwanted characters:

- Click **Delete Last** to delete the last special character that you selected and then click on the correct character.

- Click **Delete** to delete all the characters selected and then click on the correct characters.

- Alternatively, you can insert all the selected characters and then delete any unwanted characters from the slide because special characters behave like any other character.

Inserting formatting marks

Formatting marks are a type of special character that you can insert into your text to correct the formatting. For example, it may not be desirable for words that are separated by a space or a hyphen to span over two lines, you can insert a non-breaking space or non-breaking hyphen. To access formatting marks, select **Insert > Formatting marks** on the main menu bar to open a context menu that lists the formatting marks that Impress supports, which are as follows:

- **Non-breaking space** – inserts a space that will keep bordering characters together on line breaks (keyboard shortcut *Control+Shift+Space*).

- **Non-breaking hyphen** – inserts a hyphen that will keep bordering characters together on line breaks.

- **Optional hyphen** – inserts an invisible hyphen within a word that will appear and create a line break once it becomes the last character in a line.

- **No-width optional break** – inserts an invisible space within a word that will insert a line break once it becomes the last character in a line. Only available when complex text layout (CTL) is enabled (keyboard shortcut *Control+Slash*).

- **No-width no break** – inserts an invisible space within a word that will keep the word together at the end of a line. Only available when complex text layout (CTL) is enabled.

- **Left-to-right mark** – inserts a text direction mark that affects the text direction of any text following the mark. Only available when complex text layout (CTL) is enabled.

- **Right-to-left mark** – inserts a text direction mark that affects the text direction of any text following the mark. Only available when complex text layout (CTL) is enabled.

Formatting text

Introduction

The appropriate use of text formatting can give a presentation a consistent look and a dynamic feel and it can even enhance the understanding of an audience by preventing any distracting elements in your message.

When you enter text, either in an AutoLayout text box or in a normal text box, it is formatted with a set of predefined attributes known as a style. The style used depends on the outline level of the point where the text was entered into a text box. For example, if you paste text at a level 2 position, Impress will format it either according to the Outline 2 presentation style for AutoLayout text boxes or the Default Graphic style for text boxes.

| Tip | Sometimes, as seen in the "Pasting text" section on page 60, it is very useful to re-apply the baseline style to a selection of text eliminating any manual formatting applied to it, especially if you made a mistake and you do not know how to undo it. To use the baseline style, select the formatted text and then select **Format > Default formatting** on the main menu bar. |

Formatting text may require some intervention in three areas:

- Character attributes (for example font color)
- Paragraph attributes (for example alignment)
- List attributes (for example type of bullet)

Sometimes it is quicker and more efficient to apply manual formatting. However, in situations where you need to perform the same modifications to many different parts of the presentation, the use of styles is recommended. Both these techniques are described here.

| Note | Unlike LibreOffice Writer, where it is recommended to use styles whenever possible, in Impress manual formatting has to be used more often. This is because presentation styles are fixed in Impress. Therefore, it is not possible, for example, to have two different level 1s or different types of bullet points for the same outline level. Also, the lack of support for character styles forces the use of manual formatting to modify sections of the text. |

Selecting text

Text must be selected before it can be formatted. Any formatting changes will apply only to the selected text.

- To format *all* the text in a text box, click once on the text, then click once on the border of the text box to display the selection handles. Now any formatting changes will apply to all the text in the text box.
- To format only *part* of the text and after clicking once on the text, you can select text using one of the following methods:
    - Click and drag the cursor over the text to highlight the text.
    - Double-click to select a complete word or triple click to select a whole paragraph.
    - Press and hold the *Shift* key and then use the keyboard arrow keys to extend your selection.

| Tip | To select text word by word, instead of character by character, press the *Ctrl* key and *Shift* key together. To speed up the selection even further, you can combine the *Shift* key with the *Home* key or the *End* key to extend the selection up to the start or end of the line in which the cursor is positioned, respectively. |

Using styles to format text

Impress has two categories of styles: presentation styles and graphics styles. Presentation styles are used on text inserted into an AutoLayout text box, slide master backgrounds, and background objects. However, for text inserted in a text box or a graphic object, you need to apply a graphic style.

In this chapter we focus on Presentation styles. For information on graphic styles, see *Chapter 6 Formatting Graphic Objects*.

Modifying presentation styles

To modify a presentation style, follow these steps:

1) Open the Styles and Formatting dialog (Figure 45) by pressing *F11* or selecting **Format > Styles and Formatting** on the menu bar.

2) Make sure the **Presentation Styles** icon  is selected.

3) Right-click on the style to be modified and select **Modify** from the context menu. The tabbed pages available in this dialog for modifying a presentation style are shown in Figure 46.

Figure 45: Presentation Styles and Formatting dialog

Figure 46: Dialog for modifying a presentation style

This modifying dialog consists of fifteen tabbed pages, which can be divided in two groups: pages that determine formatting of the text, and pages that determine the properties of slide master background and background objects.

There is no difference between attributes that determine a style and attributes used manually on portions of text. In fact the pages that open when manually applying formatting are the same that you use when configuring styles in the Styles and Formatting dialog. Therefore, once you master the formatting of text, you will know how to create and modify a style.

- For the *Font* and *Font Effects* style pages, refer to "Formatting characters" on page 65.

- For the *Indents and Spacing*, *Alignment*, and *Tabs* style pages, refer to "Formatting paragraphs" on page 68.

- For the *Bullet and numbering type*, *Graphics*, *Customize* style pages, refer to "Creating bulleted and numbered lists" on page 74.

The pages that relate to formatting background and background objects are described in detail in *Chapter 6 Formatting Graphic Objects*.

Updating a style from a selection

To update a style from a portion of text that you have just modified or would like to use:

1) Select an item in a text box that has the format you want to adopt as a style.

2) In the Styles and Formatting dialog (Figure 45), select the style you want to update and then click the **Update Style** icon .

Applying a presentation style

To apply a presentation style, move the paragraph to the appropriate outline level as described in "Creating bulleted and numbered lists" on page 74.This is different from Writer, where you select the desired style from the Styles and Formatting window.

Formatting characters

Character dialog

To view the character formatting options, select **Format** > **Character** on the main menu bar or click the **Character** icon on the Text Formatting toolbar (Figure 51 on page 69) and the Character dialog opens (Figure 47). If Text Formatting toolbar is not visible, choose **View** > **Toolbars** > **Text Formatting.** Note that character styles do not exist in Impress.

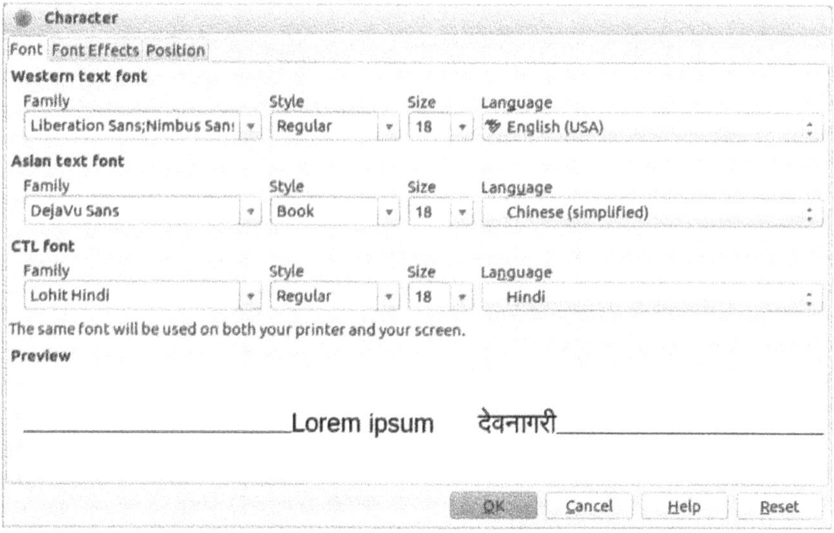

Figure 47: Font page in Character dialog with Asian and CTL fonts enabled

Font page

Use the *Font* page (Figure 47) to select the desired font type, its base attributes (*Italic*, **Bold**, etc.) as well as the size. A sample of the font is displayed in the lower part of the dialog. You can also specify the language of this style. This font page is also available when creating or modifying a presentation style or a graphics style.

Tip	When writing a presentation in multiple languages, you can use the language setting to create two styles that only differ in the language but are otherwise the same. This allows you to check the spelling of all of the contents without affecting appearance.

If support for Asian language and Complex Text Layout (CTL) font has been enabled (**Tools > Options > Language Settings > Languages**), then Asian text font and CTL text font are available in the Character dialog. Each part of the Character dialog has the same functionality, so you can specify the Asian and CTL text fonts and their attributes as well as Western text fonts.

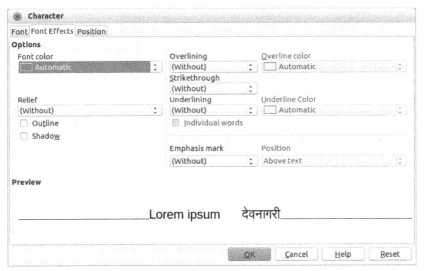

Figure 48: Font Effects page in Character dialog

Font Effects page

Use the *Font Effects* page (Figure 48) to apply special effects to the text, such as over lining and underlining, color, shadow, and so on. As for the *Font* page, a sample of the text is displayed in the lower part of the dialog, providing a quick visual check of the effects applied. This page is also available when creating or modifying a presentation style or a graphics style.

Position page

The *Position* page (Figure 49) has advanced options to customize text. Use this page to set the text position relative to the baseline when you need to insert subscripts or superscripts. This page is not available when creating or modifying a presentation style or a graphics style.

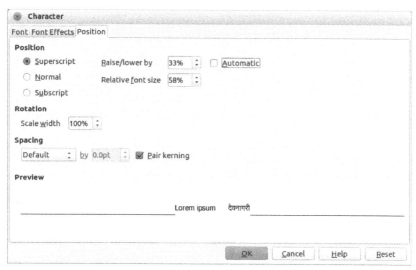

Figure 49: Position page in Character dialog

In **Position**, create a superscript or a subscript as follows:

1) Select *Superscript* or *Subscript* as applicable.
2) Specify the amount as a percentage by which the text should be raised (superscripts) or lowered (subscripts). If *Automatic* is selected, this option is not available.
3) Specify the percentage of the character to be used relative to the baseline character size.

The other attributes that can be set on this page are as follows:

- *Scale width* in **Rotation** – specifies the percentage of the font width by which to horizontally stretch or compress the individual characters of the selected text.
- **Spacing** – specifies the spacing between the characters of the selected text. For expanded or condensed spacing, enter the amount that you want to expand or condense the text in the **by** box using the options from the drop-down list.
    - *Default* – uses the character spacing specified in the font type
    - *Expanded* – increases the character spacing
    - *Condensed* – decreases the character spacing
    - *Pair kerning* – automatically adjust the character spacing for specific letter combinations. Kerning is only available for certain font types and requires that your printer support this option.

Sidebar Character subsection

An alternative method of formatting characters is to use the *Character* subsection (Figure 50) on the Sidebar. Click on the **Properties** icon on the Sidebar, then open the *Character* subsection. If you require more character formatting, click on the **More Options** icon at the top right of the *Character* title bar to open the Character dialog.

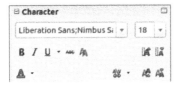

Figure 50: Sidebar Character Subsection

The character formatting options available in the *Character* subsection on the Sidebar are as follows:

- **Font Name** and **Font Size** – select the font name and size that you want to use from the drop-down lists. These options are also available on the Text Formatting toolbar.

- **Bold**; *Italic*; Underline – these options are also available on the Text Formatting toolbar. Click on the small triangle to the right of Underline and select the type of underlining you want to use from the drop-down list. Click **More Options** at the bottom of this drop-down list to open the Character dialog.

- ~~Strikethrough~~ – draws a line through the selected text.

- Shadow – adds a shadow to the selected text.

- **Increase Font** and **Reduce Font** – each click increases or reduces the size of the selected characters by the same amount. Actual size depends on your computer setup.

- **Font Color** and **Highlighting** – click on the small triangle to the right of these icons and select the color you want to use. These options are also available on the Text Formatting toolbar.

- **Character Spacing** – click on the small triangle to the right Character Spacing and select the type of spacing between characters that you require. Spacing between characters is also know as kerning.

- **Superscript** – reduces the font size of the selected text and raises the text above the baseline.

- **Subscript** – reduces the font size of the selected text and lowers the text below the baseline.

Formatting paragraphs

Paragraph dialog

To view the paragraph formatting options, select **Format > Paragraph** on the main menu bar or click the **Paragraph** icon on the Text Formatting toolbar (Figure 58 on page 78) and the Paragraph dialog opens (Figure 51). If the Text Formatting toolbar is not visible, select **View > Toolbars > Text Formatting** on the main menu bar.

Normally the paragraph formatting dialog contains three pages: *Indents and Spacing*; *Alignment* and *Tabs*. However, if Asian language support has been enabled in **Tools> Options > Language Settings > Languages**, a page called *Asian Typography* is also becomes available.

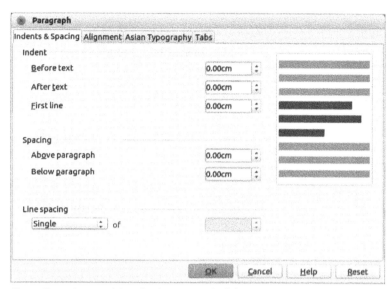

Figure 51: Indents and Spacing in Paragraph dialog

Indents and Spacing page

The *Indents and Spacing* page (Figure 51) has four sections and is also available in Presentation Styles dialog and Graphics Styles dialog.

- **Indent** – specifies the amount of space to leave between the left and the right page margins and the paragraph.

  - *Before text* – enter the amount of space that you want to indent the paragraph from the page margin. If you want the paragraph to extend into the page margin, enter a negative number. In Left-to-Right languages, the left edge of the paragraph is indented with respect to the left page margin. In Right-to-Left languages, the right edge of the paragraph is indented with respect to the right page margin.

  - *After text* – enter the amount of space that you want to indent the paragraph from the page margin. If you want the paragraph to extend into the page margin, enter a negative number. In Left-to-Right languages, the right edge of the paragraph is indented with respect to the right page margin. In Right-to-Left languages, the left edge of the paragraph is indented with respect to the left page margin.

  - *First line* – indents the first line of a paragraph by the amount that you enter. To create a hanging indent enter a positive value for *Before text* and a negative value for *First line*.

- **Spacing** – specifies the amount of space to leave between selected paragraphs.

  - *Above paragraph* – enter the amount of space that you want to leave above the selected paragraph(s).

  - *Below paragraph* – enter the amount of space that you want to leave below the selected paragraph(s).

Note	If spacing is specified for both before and after a paragraph and *Do not add space between paragraphs of the same style* is selected, only the spacing below a paragraph is applied when the preceding and following paragraphs are of the same paragraph style.

- **Line spacing** – specifies the amount of space to leave between lines of text in a paragraph. The options available from the drop-down list are as follows:
    - *Single* – applies single line spacing to the current paragraph. This is the default setting.
    - *1.5 lines* – sets the line spacing to 1.5 lines.
    - *Double* – sets the line spacing to two lines.
    - *Proportional* – select this option and then enter a percentage value in the box, where 100% corresponds to single line spacing.
    - *At Least* – sets the minimum line spacing to the value that you enter in the box. If you use different font sizes within a paragraph, the line spacing is automatically adjusted to the largest font size. If you prefer to have identical spacing for all lines, specify a value in *At Least* that corresponds to the largest font size.
    - *Leading* – sets the height of the vertical space that is inserted between two lines.
    - *Fixed* – enter a fixed value to be used for line spacing.

Tip	Setting the line spacing to less than 100% is a good method to place a lot of text into a text box when space is limited. However, care must be taken as too small a value will make the text hard to read.

Tip	You can change the default unit of measurement, for example from inches to centimeters, in **Tools > Options > LibreOffice Impress > General** on the main menu bar.

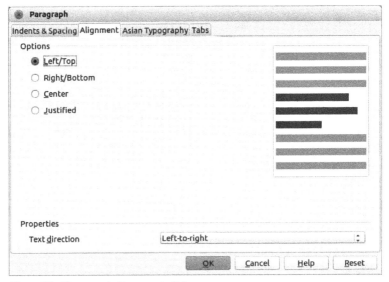

Figure 52: Alignment in Paragraph dialog

Alignment page

Use the *Alignment* page (Figure 52) to determine the paragraph alignment as follows. This page is also available in Presentation Styles dialog and Graphics Styles dialog.

- *Left* – aligns the paragraph to the left page margin. If Asian language support is enabled, this option is named *Left/Top*.
- *Right* – aligns the paragraph to the right page margin. If Asian language support is enabled, this option is named *Right/Bottom*.
- *Centered* – centers the contents of the paragraph on the page.
- *Justify* – aligns the paragraph to the left and to the right page margins.
- *Text direction* – specifies the text direction for a paragraph that uses complex text layout (CTL) and is only available if complex text layout support is enabled.

The paragraph alignment options can also be accessed using the paragraph alignment icons ▤ ▤ ▤ ▤ on the Text Formatting toolbar (Figure 58 on page 78) or the *Paragraph* subsection (Figure 55) on the Sidebar.

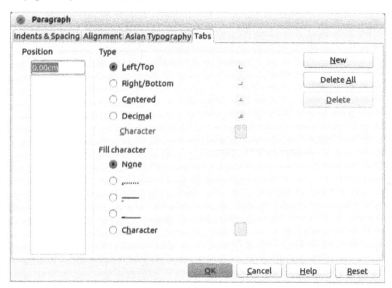

Figure 53: Tabs in Paragraph dialog

Tabs page

Use the *Tabs* page (Figure 53) to determine the tab stops. This page is also available in Presentation Styles dialog and Graphics Styles dialog.

You can create tabs within a paragraph as follows:

1) Set the size of the tab stop in the **Position** text box.
2) Select the type of tab in **Type**. If you set the type to *Decimal*, specify the character to be used as the decimal point In *Character* box.
   - Left – aligns the left edge of the text to the tab stop and extends the text to the right. The name of this tab stop is *Left/Top* if Asian language support is enabled.

- *Right* – aligns the right edge of the text to the tab stop and extends the text to the left of the tab stop. This name of this tab stop is *Right/Bottom* if Asian language support is enabled.
- *Center* – aligns the center of the text to the tab stop.
- *Decimal* – aligns the decimal point of a number to the center of the tab stop and text to the left of the tab.
- *Character* – enter a character that you want the decimal tab to use as a decimal separator.

3) Select a **Fill character** which will be drawn from the tab insertion point up to the tab stop.
- *None* – inserts no fill characters and removes any existing fill characters to the left of the tab stop.
- .... – fills the empty space to the left of the tab stop with dots.
- ------ – fills the empty space to the left of the tab stop with dashes.
- _____ – draws a line to fill the empty space to the left of the tab stop.
- *Character* – specify a character to fill the empty space to the left of the tab stop.

4) Click the **New** button to apply the new tab stop to the current paragraph.
5) Click **OK** to save your changes and close the dialog.

You can edit tabs within paragraphs as follows:
1) Select the tab you want to edit in the **Position** box.
2) Select the **Type** and **Fill character** you want to use.
3) Click **OK** to save your changes and close the dialog.

Note	To change the tab position, you have to delete the tab first, then create a new tab with the changes you require.

You can delete tabs within paragraphs as follows:
1) Select the tab in the **Position** box.
2) Click **Delete** to delete the selected tab.
3) Click **Delete All** to delete all of the tab stops that are set for the current paragraph.
4) Click **OK** to save your changes and close the dialog.

Asian Typography page

Use the *Asian Typography* page (Figure 54) to set the following properties relative to line changes. This page is also available in Presentation Styles dialog and Graphics Styles dialog.

- *Apply list of forbidden characters to the beginning and end of lines* – prevents the characters in the list from starting or ending a line. The characters are relocated to either the previous line or the next line. To edit the list of restricted characters that start or end a line, go to **LibreOffice > Language Settings > Asian Layout**.

- *Allow hanging punctuation* – prevents commas and periods from breaking the line. Instead, these characters are added to the end of the line, even in the page margin.

- *Apply spacing between Asian, Latin and Complex text* – inserts a space between Asian, Latin and complex characters.

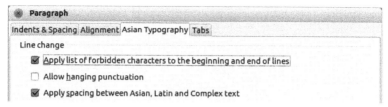

Figure 54: Asian Typography in Paragraph dialog

Sidebar Paragraph subsection

An alternative method of formatting paragraphs is to use the *Paragraph* subsection (Figure 55) on the Sidebar. Click on the **Properties** icon 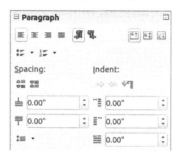 on the Sidebar, then open the *Paragraph* subsection. If you require more paragraph formatting, click on the **More Options** icon at the top right of the *Paragraph* title bar to open the Paragraph dialog.

Figure 55: Sidebar Paragraph Subsection

The character formatting options available in the *Paragraph* subsection on the Sidebar are as follows:

- **Align Left**; **Align Center**, **Alight Right**, **Align Justified** – determines how a paragraph is aligned to the page margins. These icons are also available on the Text Formatting toolbar.

- **Left-To-Right**, **Right-To-Left** – only available when *Asian* and *Complex text layout (CTL)* options have been selected in **Tools > Options > Language Settings > Languages**.

- **Align Top**, **Align Center Vertically**, **Align Bottom** – aligns the selected paragraph to the top, center or bottom of the text box. This is similar to vertical alignment of data within a table cell.

- **Bullets**, **Numbering** – creates a bulleted or numbered list from selected paragraphs. Click on the small triangle to the right of the icon to select a bullet or numbering formatting option from a drop-down list. Click **More Options** at the bottom of these drop-down lists to open the Bullets and Numbering dialog.

- **Increase Spacing**, **Decrease Spacing** – increases or decreases the spacing above and below the selected paragraphs.

- **Above Paragraph Spacing**, **Below Paragraph Spacing** – increases or decreases the spacing either above or below the selected paragraph. Enter the amount of spacing you want to use in the text box.

- **Line Spacing** – adjust the spacing between the lines of a selected paragraph. Click on the small triangle to the right of the icon and select the type of line spacing you want to use from the drop-down list.

- **Increase Indent** – this tool is only active when a list item is selected. Each click demotes the outline level of the selected list paragraph. Works in the same way as the **Demote** icon on the Text Formatting toolbar.

- **Decrease Indent** – this tool is only active when a list item is selected. Each click promotes the outline level of the selected list paragraph. Works in the same way as the **Promote** icon on the Text Formatting toolbar.

- **Switch to Hanging Indent** – this tool is only active when a standard paragraph is selected and does not work on list items. Each click switches the hanging indent of the first line of a selected paragraph from a positive value to a negative value or from a negative value to a positive value.

- **Left Indent**, **Right Indent**, **Hanging Indent** – enter the value for each type of indent in the text boxes.

Creating bulleted and numbered lists

The procedure to create a bulleted or numbered list varies depending on the type of text box used, although the tools to manage the list and customize the appearance are the same. In AutoLayout text boxes created automatically by Impress, the outline styles available are, by default, bulleted lists. For normal text boxes an additional step is required to create a bulleted list.

Creating lists in AutoLayout text boxes

Every text box included in the available layouts is already formatted as a bulleted list, therefore to create a bulleted list the only necessary steps are as follows:

1) From the Layout pane, choose a slide design that contains a text box. Those are easily recognizable from the thumbnail.

2) Click on the text •**Click to add text** in the text box and start typing your first item.

3) Press *Enter* to start a new bulleted line.

4) Press *Shift+Enter* to start a new line without creating a new bullet or number. The new line will have the same indentation as the previous line.

5) Press *Tab,* or the **Demote** icon ⇨ on the Text Formatting toolbar (Figure 43 on page 61), or use the keyboard shortcut *Alt+Shift+Right* to demote or move your item down to the next outline level.

6) Press *Shift+Tab,* or the **Promote** icon ⇦ on the Text Formatting toolbar, or use the keyboard shortcut *Alt+Shift+Left* to promote or move your item up to the next outline level.

7) Click the **Bullets On/Off** icon ≔ on the Text Formatting toolbar or **Bullets** in the Sidebar *Paragraph* subsection to create a list without bullet points or an item without a bullet point.

By default, the list created is a bulleted list. To customize the list appearance or to change from bulleted to numbered or numbered to bulleted, refer to "Changing list appearance" below.

In AutoLayout text boxes, promoting or demoting an item in the list corresponds to applying a different outline style. This means that the second outline level corresponds to Outline 2 style, the third to Outline 3 style, and so on. As a consequence, a change in the level also produces other changes (for example font size, bullet type, and so on).

Note	Do not try to change the outline level by selecting the text and then clicking the desired outline style as you would in Writer. Due to the way that presentation styles work in Impress it is not possible to apply outline levels in this way.

Creating lists in other text boxes

To create a list in a text box, follow these steps:

1) Place the cursor in the text box.
2) Click the **Bullets On/Off** icon ☷ in the Text Formatting toolbar, or **Bullets** or **Numbering** in the Sidebar *Paragraph* subsection.
3) Type the text and press *Enter* to start a new bulleted line.
4) Press *Shift+Enter* to start a new line without creating a new bullet or number. The new line will have the same indentation as the previous line.
5) Press *Tab* to increase the indent level of your item.
6) Press *Shift+Tab* to decrease the indent level of your item.

To customize the list appearance or to change from bulleted to numbered or numbered to bulleted, refer to "Changing list appearance" below.

Changing list appearance

You can customize the appearance of a list, change the bullet type or numbering for the entire list or for a single entry. All changes can be made using the Bullets and Numbering dialog (Figure 56), or the **Bullets** or **Numbering** tools in the Sidebar *Paragraph* subsection.

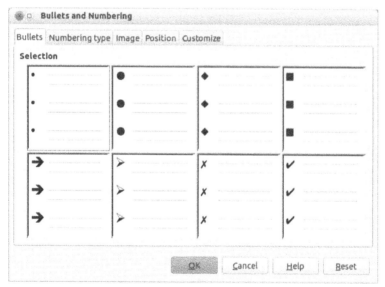

Figure 56: Bullets and Numbering dialog – Bullets page

Changing list type

1) To change the type of list for all the items in an entire list, select the entire list by highlighting all the text in the text box or click on the border of the text box so that the selection handles are displayed.

2) To change the appearance of a single item in a list, click anywhere in the list item to place the cursor in the line.

3) Select **Format > Bullets and Numbering** on the main menu bar or click on the **Bullets and Numbering** icon ⯐ on the Text Formatting toolbar to open the Bullets and Numbering dialog (Figure 56). This dialog contains five pages: *Bullets*, *Numbering type*, *Image*, *Position*, and *Customize*. Alternatively, click on **Bullets** or **Numbering** in the Sidebar *Paragraph* subsection.

4) If a bulleted list is required, select the bullet style from the default styles available on the *Bullets* page of the Bullets and Numbering dialog. Alternatively, click on the small triangle to the right of the **Bullets** tool in the Sidebar *Paragraph* subsection and select a bullet type from the drop-down list.

5) If a numbered list is needed, select a numbering style from the default numbering styles on the *Numbering type* page of the Bullets and Numbering dialog. Alternatively, click on the small triangle to the right of the **Numbering** tool in the Sidebar *Paragraph* subsection and select a numbering type from the drop-down list.

6) If you want to use a graphics style, select a graphic style from the default styles available on the *Image* page of the Bullets and Numbering dialog.

7) If you want to adjust the indentation and spacing of your list, see "Position page" below for more information.

8) If you want to use a customized list, select *Customize* in the Bullets and Numbering dialog and use the available options to customize your list. See "Customize page" below for more information.

9) If using the Bullets and Numbering dialog, click **OK** to save your changes and close the dialog. When using the **Bullets** or **Numbering** tool in the Sidebar *Paragraph* subsection, any changes to a list are immediate.

Note	To open the Bullets and Numbering dialog when using the **Bullets** or **Numbering** tool in the Sidebar *Paragraph* subsection, click on **More Options** at the bottom of the drop-down list that appears when click the small triangle to the right of the tool.

Note	If the list was created in an AutoLayout text box, then an alternative way to change the entire list is to modify the Outline styles. Changes made to the outline style will apply to all the slides using them, so be careful before using this command.

Position page

Use the *Position* page (Figure 57) to adjust the indentation and spacing of the bullet point and its text. This page is particularly effective when used in combination with the *Customize* page.

Set up an outline level as follows:

1) Select the level from the list on the left hand side of the page. Select level *1 – 10* to modify all levels simultaneously.

2) Set the *Indent* value to create spacing between the bullet or number and the text. If level *1 – 10* is selected, *Indent* is not available.

3) Select the *Relative* option to measure the indent value relative to the previous level and not from the margin.

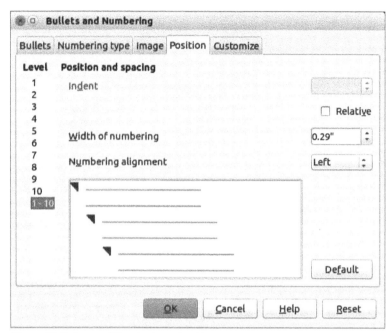

Figure 57: Bullets and Numbering – Position page

4) Set *Width of numbering* to make sure there is enough room in a numbered list for numbers when they consist of two or more digits.

5) Set *Numbering alignment* to specify the alignment of numbers when creating a numbered list. For example, you may want to align numbers to the right when your numbered list includes numbers with two or more digits.

6) Click **Default** to set indent and spacing values to the Impress default values.

7) Click **OK** to save your changes and close the dialog.

Note	The *Position* page is not available if you are modifying a presentation style or graphics style. However, the same effects can be obtained using the *Indents and Spacing* page of the Paragraph dialog (Figure 51 on page 69) for creating or modifying a slide.

Customize page

Use the *Customize* page (Figure 58) to alter the style of outline levels. The options available on this page depend on the type of marker selected for the list. Using the *Customize* page, you can create complex structured layouts, for example a nested list with numbering followed by bullets.

1) To modify each level independently, select each level you want to modify on the left hand side of the box. The right hand side of the screen shows a preview of the modifications made.

2) To modify all levels at once, select **1 – 10** as the level. With these levels being arranged in a hierarchical structure, changing, for example, the font attribute of one of the levels ripples through all the lower levels.

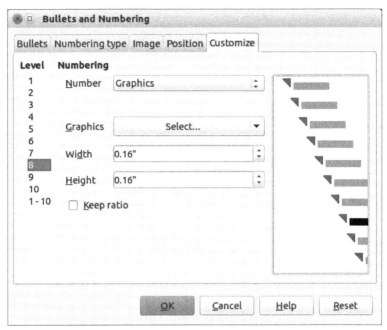

Figure 58: Bullets and Numbering – Customize page

3) Select the options you want to use when customizing your list. The options available are described below.

4) To revert to the default values used in Impress, click **Reset**.

5) When you have finished customizing the list, click **OK** to save your changes and close the dialog.

Depending on the bullet or numbering style selected, some of the following options may not be available on the *Customize* page:

- *Numbering* – select the type of numbering you want to use in your list from the drop-down list.

- *Before* – enter any text or characters to appear before the number (for example, *Step*).

- *After* – enter any text or characters to appear after the number (for example, a punctuation mark).

- *Color* – select the color for the list marker (number or bullet character) from the drop-down list.

- *Relative size* – specify the size of the number relative to the size of the characters used in the paragraph for each item.

- *Start at* – enter the first value of the list (for example, you might want the list to start at 4 instead of 1).

- *Character button* – select a special character for the bullet.

- *Graphics* – select a graphic from the gallery of available graphics or a file on to be used as a marker.

- *Width* – specifies the width of the graphic used as a marker.

- *Height* – specifies the height of the graphic used as a marker.

- *Keep ratio* – if selected, the ratio between the width and the height of the graphic marker is maintained.

Using tables

Tables are a powerful mechanism to convey structured information quickly, so they represent an important tool when creating a presentation. You can create tables directly in Impress eliminating the need to embed a Calc spreadsheet or a Writer text table in your presentation. However, in some circumstances, it makes sense to embed a table into a presentation, especially when you require greater functionality in the table. The tables provided by Impress do have a limited functionality.

Several predefined table designs are available in the *Table Design* subsection of the Sidebar (Figure 59).

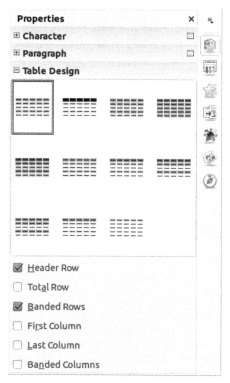

Figure 59: Sidebar Table Design subsection

Creating a table

When working with tables, it is useful to know the number of rows and columns needed as well as the appearance. The parameters can be adjusted later, but this is more laborious than setting the correct table dimensions from the beginning.

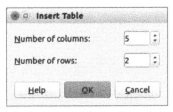

Figure 60: Insert Table dialog

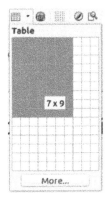

Figure 61: Table graphic insert tool

To insert a table into your slide, proceed as follows:

1) Select the slide which will contain the table and, if necessary, modify the slide layout to create space for the table.

2) Go to **Insert > Table** on the main menu bar or click on the **Table** icon ⊞ on the Standard toolbar to open the Insert Table dialog (Figure 60).

3) Specify the number of columns and number of rows you require for your table.

4) Click **OK** to close the dialog and your table appears in the center of your slide.

Alternatively, click on the small triangle to the right of the **Table** icon ⊞ to open the table graphic insert tool (Figure 61).

5) Using the cursor, select the number of columns and rows required, then click the left mouse button. Your table appears in the center of your slide.

6) Make sure the *Table Design* subsection (Figure 59) in the Sidebar is open.

7) Select one of the predefined styles, which only differ in the color scheme. It is recommended that you select a color scheme similar to the one you want, but you can change table colors later on.

8) Move the table by selecting it and dragging it to a new position, or use the method described in "Position and size" on page 84.

Note	When inserting tables into a slide, the table is inserted with the default style and settings already applied. This table can be modified to your requirements.
	When tables are inserted into a slide, they are given a set of default attributes such as color scheme, banded rows, header row, and so on. Currently these defaults are hard coded in LibreOffice and cannot be changed.

Modifying a table

Once the table is added to the slide, you can control its appearance, size, position, and so on using a combination of the options in the *Table Design* subsection of the Sidebar, the Table toolbar, and the Table properties dialog.

Sidebar options

The following options are available in the *Show* section of Table Design on the Tasks pane:

* *Header Row* – selected by default and adds a first row with a different background from the rest of the table.

* *Total Row* – the opposite of Header Row. If selected, it changes the background of the last row to make it stand out from the other rows.

* *Banded Rows* – selected by default and option colors alternate rows with different backgrounds making it easier to read data presented in rows.

* *First Column* – highlights the first column of the table by allocating a darker background to it.

* *Last Column* – highlights the last column of the table by allocating a darker background to it.

* *Banded Columns* – when selected, alternate columns are colored differently.

Table toolbar

When a table is selected, eight selection handles appear around the edges and the Table toolbar (Figure 62) is displayed. If the Table toolbar is not displayed when a table is selected, go to **View > Toolbars > Table** on the main menu bar. The Table toolbar contains the majority of the tools you need to modify a table.

Table
Creates a new table in the selected slide. Opens the Insert Table dialog (Figure 60) where you can select the required number of rows and columns. Alternatively, click on the small triangle to the right of the Table icon to open a graphic tool for inserting tables (Figure 61). See "Creating a table" on page 79 for more information on inserting tables into your slide.

Line Style
Changes the style of the line of the selected cells. Opens a **Border Style** drop-down list where you can select from a range of predefined line styles.

Line Color (of the border)
Opens a **Border Color** drop-down menu where you can select the color of the borders around the selected cells.

Borders
Opens a **Borders** drop-down menu where you can select a predefined border configuration for the selected cells. If the desired border pattern is not available, you will need to use the Table properties dialog.

Area Style/Filling
In the drop-down menu, select how the selected cells should be filled: *Invisible*, *Color*, *Gradient*, *Hatching*, or *Bitmap*. Depending on the selection, the drop-down menu lists the available fillings for the option selected. Refer to *Chapter 6 Formatting Graphic Objects* for details on how to manage area filling styles.

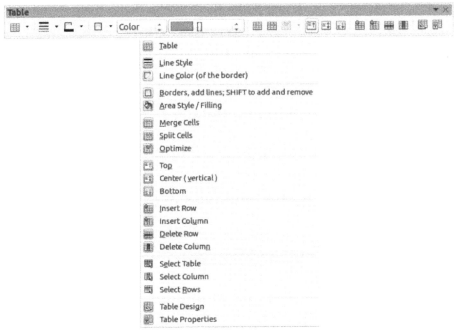

Figure 62: Table toolbar

Merge Cells

Merges the selected cells into one cell. Note that the contents of the merged cells are also merged. You can also right-click on the selected cells and select **Cell > Merge** from the context menu.

Split Cells

Make sure that the cursor is positioned on the cell you want to split, then click to open the Split Cells dialog (Figure 63). Select the number of cells required from the split as well as whether the cell should be split horizontally or vertically. When splitting horizontally, you can select the *Into equal proportions* option to get all cells of equal size. The contents of the split cell are kept in the original cell (the one on the left or top). You can also right-click on the selected cells and select **Cell > Split** from the context menu.

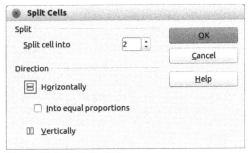

Figure 63: Split Cells dialog

Optimize

Evenly distributes the selected cells either horizontally or vertically. You can also right-click in the selected cells and select **Row > Space Equally** or **Column > Space Equally** from the context menu. If you want to optimize the whole table, you can evenly distribute rows or columns by right-clicking on the table border and select **Row > Space Equally** or **Column > Space Equally** from the context menu.

Top, Center (vertical), Bottom

You can select the vertical alignment of text in a cell by selecting the required cells and choosing the appropriate alignment. You can also right-click in the selected cells, then select **Cell** from the context menu and choose the appropriate alignment. To apply cell alignment to the whole table, right-click on the table border, then select **Cell** from the context menu and choose the appropriate alignment.

Insert Row, Insert Column

Clicking on **Insert Row** or **Insert Column** inserts a single row or column below and to the right of the selected cell. To insert more than one row or column, highlight cells across the number of rows or columns required, then click on **Insert Row** or **Insert Column**. You can also right-click in the selected cells and select **Row > Insert** or **Column > Insert** from the context menu. Select the required number of rows or columns in the dialog that opens and click **OK**.

To insert rows at the beginning of the table and columns at the left of the table, select the table, then right-click on the table border. Select the required number of rows or columns in the dialog that opens and click **OK**.

Delete Row, Delete Column

Clicking on **Delete Row** or **Delete Column** deletes a single row or column below where you have selected a cell. To delete more than one row or column, highlight cells across the number of rows or columns required, then click on **Delete Row** or **Delete Column**. You can also right-click in the selected cells and select **Row > Delete** or **Column > Delete** from the context menu.

Select Table, Select Column, Select Rows

These three icons select the complete table or the columns or rows where you have selected cells. By default these icons are not displayed on the Table toolbar. To display these icons, right-click in a blank area on the toolbar and select **Visible Buttons** from the context menu. Click on the icon you want displayed in the toolbar.

Table Design

This tool no longer functions with Table Design now as a subsection in the Sidebar.

Table Properties

Click the **Table Properties** icon on the Table toolbar, or right-click in the table and select **Table** from the context menu to open the Format Cells dialog (Figure 64), which contains the following pages.

- *Font* – use to select the desired font type, its base attributes (*Italic*, **Bold**, etc.) as well as the size. A sample of the font is displayed in the lower part of the dialog. You can also specify the language. See "Font page" on page 66 for more information on the available options.

- *Font Effects* – use to apply special effects to the text, such as over lining and underlining, color, shadow and so on. A sample of the text is displayed in the lower part of the dialog, providing a quick visual check of the effects applied. See "Font Effects page" on page 66 for more information on the available options.

Figure 64: Format Cells dialog

- *Borders* – use to set advanced properties not available when using the Table toolbar, such as the spacing between the text and the border as well as setting the style of each individual border of the table separately. This page also provides the same options as the **Line Style** and **Line Color** on the Table toolbar.

Note	It is currently not possible to define diagonal borders for Impress tables.

- *Background*: changes the background of the selected cells and provides the same functions as **Area Style/Filling** on the Table toolbar.

Position and size

Impress treats tables just like any other graphic object. You can change table position and size on the slide by using the selection handles and the mouse.

For more accurate control with positioning and table sizing, open the Position and Size dialog (Figure 42 on page 59). With the table is selected, right-click on the border of table and select **Position and Size** from the context menu or go to **Format > Position and Size** on the main menu bar, or press the *F4* key.

Note	Only the Position and Size page in this dialog can be used for tables. For more information on this dialog see *Chapter 6 Formatting Graphic Objects*.

Deleting tables

To delete a table use one of the following methods:

- Click in the slide and drag a selection box over the table to select it, then press the *Delete* key.
- Click on the table border to select the table and press the *Delete* key.

Using fields

Fields allow the automatic insertion of text into the slide. You can think of a field as a kind of formula which is calculated when the document is loaded or printed and the result is written in the document. Fields are commonly used when creating templates and slide masters, as explained in *Chapter 2 Using Slide Masters, Styles, and Templates*.

Inserting a field

To insert a field into a slide, select the slide where the field will be and then select **Insert > Fields** on the main menu bar followed by one of these options:

- **Date (fixed)** – inserts the current date into your slide as a fixed field. The date is not automatically updated.
- **Date (variable)** – inserts the current date into your slide as a variable field. The date is automatically updated each time you open the file.
- **Time (fixed)** – inserts the current time into your slide as a fixed field. The time is not automatically updated.
- **Time (variable)** – inserts the current time into your slide as a variable field. The time is automatically updated each time you open the file.
- **Author** – inserts the first and last names of the author of the presentation. This information is derived from the value recorded in the LibreOffice user data. To modify this information go to **Tools > Options > LibreOffice > User Data**.
- **Page Number** – inserts the page number into the current slide. If you want to add a page number to every slide, go to **View > Master > Slide Master** on the main menu bar and insert the page number field.
- **Page Count** – inserts the total number of slides.
- **File Name** – inserts the name of the file. The file name only appears after you save the file.

Formatting fields

Date and time fields

To format a date or time field:

1) Right-click on the field.
2) Select the desired format from the context menu that opens. The available formats will depend on the language setting in **Tools > Options > Language Settings > Language**.

Page number fields

Formatting the page number fields can be done one of two ways:

- Select the page number field and apply the formatting manually.
- Go to **Format > Page** on the main menu bar and select a format from the list in *Layout Settings* in the Page Setup dialog.

Using hyperlinks

When inserting text (such as a website address or URL) that can be used as a hyperlink, Impress formats it automatically, creating the hyperlink and applying color and underlining. If you do not want Impress to use its default settings, then you have to insert a hyperlink manually.

Inserting hyperlinks

To insert a hyperlink, or customize the appearance of a hyperlink:

1) Select **Insert > Hyperlinks** on the main menu bar or use the keyboard shortcut *Ctrl+K* to open the Hyperlink dialog (Figure 65).

2) On the left hand side, select one of the four types of hyperlinks. The top right part of the dialog changes according to the selection of hyperlink type. A full description of all the choices, and their interactions, is beyond the scope of this chapter. A summary of the most common choices used in a presentation is given below.

3) Create your hyperlink using the dialog, then click **Apply** to insert into your slide.

4) Click **Close** to close the dialog.

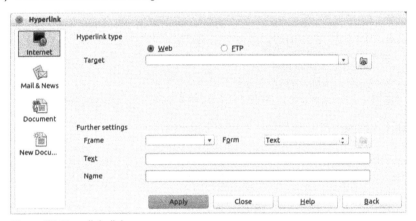

Figure 65: Hyperlink dialog

The options for *Hyperlink type* available are as follows:

• **Internet** – choose whether the link is Web or FTP. Enter the required web address in the *Target* text box.

• **Mail & News** – choose whether the link is an E-mail or news link. Enter the details of the *Recipient* and the *Subject*.

• **Document** – creates a hyperlink to another document or to another place in a document, commonly referred to as a bookmark.

  – Enter the *Path* details in the text box, or click the **Open File** icon to open a file browser. Leave this blank if you want to link to a target in the same presentation.

  – Optionally, you can specify a target (for example a specific slide). Click on the **Target in Document** icon to open a dialog where you can select the target. If you know the name of the target, you can type it into the *Target* text box.

- **New Document**: – creates a hyperlink to a new document. Select whether to edit the newly created document immediately (*Edit now*) or just create it to edit later (*Edit later*). Choose the type of document to create (text, spreadsheet, and so on). The **Select path** icon opens a file browser so that you can choose the directory for the new document.

Note	For navigation within a presentation, it is generally better to use the object interaction menu that you can find either in the Drawing toolbar or in the context menu that opens when right-clicking on an object.

The *Further settings* section on the Hyperlink dialog is common to all the hyperlink types, although some choices are more relevant to some types of links.

- **Frame** – set the value to determine how the hyperlink will open. This applies to documents that open in a web browser.
- **Form** – specifies if the link is to be presented as text or as a button. See "Working with hyperlink buttons" on page 87 for more information.
- **Text** – specifies the text that will be visible to the user.
- **Name** – applicable to HTML documents. It specifies text that will be added as a NAME attribute in the HTML code behind the hyperlink.

Formatting hyperlinks

To format a hyperlink:

1) Select it by dragging a selection across the text. Do not click on the hyperlink because this will open the hyperlink.
2) Right-click on the selected hyperlink.
3) Select the type of formatting you want to change from the options available in the context menu.

Working with hyperlink buttons

A hyperlink button is inserted in the center of the current slide. In most cases, that is not where you want it to appear. To edit the text or size of a hyperlink button, or to move it to another place on the slide:

1) Go to **View > Toolbars > Form Controls** on the main menu bar to open the Form Controls toolbar (Figure 66).

Figure 66: Form Controls toolbar

2) Click the **Design Mode On/Off** icon . All the icons on the Form Controls toolbar become active.
3) Select the hyperlink button you want to edit or move.
4) Drag the hyperlink button to another position, or right-click to open a context menu where you can change the text on the button, the size of the button, and other properties.

5) When you have finished editing the button, click the **Design Mode On/Off** icon again to make the icons inactive. For a detailed description of the properties and how to work with Form Controls, refer to the *Writer Guide*.

LibreOffice
The Document Foundation

Chapter 4
Adding and Formatting
Pictures

Introduction

Images are often used in presentations as they can convey a large amount of information more quickly than the written word. You can also give a more professional look to your presentation by adding a company logo. Also, you may want to use Impress to create a presentation consisting only of images, such as a slideshow of holiday snapshots to share with friends.

This chapter describes how to insert and format images.

Inserting images

This section describes several ways to insert an image from an external source into the presentation. Once the image has been inserted, it can be formatted extensively.

Inserting an image from a file

Inserting an image from a file is quick and easy. First choose a slide layout, as described in *Chapter 1 Introducing Impress*. Most layouts include a set of icons for inserting objects, but you can insert an image into any slide.

Whether you are using an AutoLayout for the placement of the image, or you are just inserting an image, follow these steps:

1) Go to **Insert > Image > From file** on the menu bar or, if you have inserted a slide, click on the **Insert Image** icon (Figure 67) and the Insert Image dialog opens (Figure 68).

2) Navigate to the directory containing the desired image and select the file. LibreOffice recognizes a large number of image types. If the **Preview** option is selected, a thumbnail of the selected file will be displayed in the preview pane on the right.

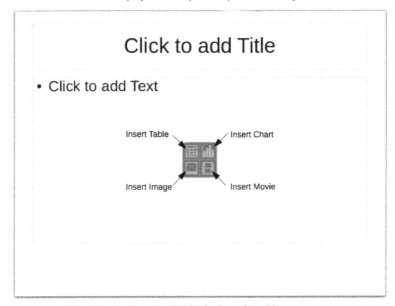

Figure 67: Slide showing the placeholder for inserting objects

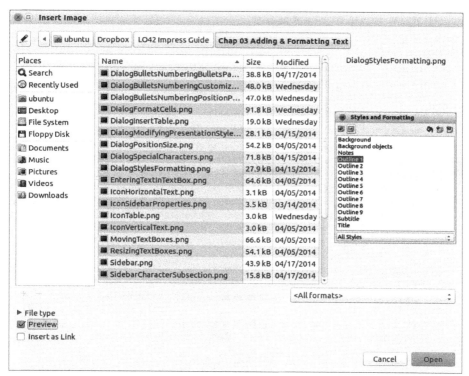

Figure 68: Insert Image dialog

3) Click **Open** to place the image on the current slide and it is displayed on the slide with selection handles displayed around the image border.

Note	The Insert Image dialog has two options: **Link** and **Preview**. The position of these options is determined by the operating system, but they are normally in the bottom-left part of the dialog.

Select the **Link** option to insert the image as a link to a file rather than embedding the file itself. In general it is preferable to embed images so that the presentation can be copied for use on other computers. On some occasions, however, it makes sense to link the image rather than embed it. These include:

- When the image file is quite large and linking rather than embedding will dramatically reduce the size of the presentation file.
- When the same image file is used in many presentations. For example, when using the same background image for all the presentations created.
- When the linked file will be available when loading the presentation. For example, if the presentation is a slide show of holiday photographs.

Inserting an image from a scanner

Inserting an image from a scanner is normally a simple process if one or more than one of the following are valid.

- The scanner software driver has been installed on the computer.
- The scanner is supported by the SANE system if the computer operating system is Linux or other UNIX-like operating system.
- The scanner is TWAIN compatible and the computer is operating Windows or Mac OS.
- The scanner is configured on the computer with LibreOffice software installed.

The following scanning procedure is only an example to demonstrate how to insert an image from a scanner. The actual procedure you use on your computer will depend on the operating system, the type of scanner being used and the scanner driver software installed.

1) Prepare the image for the scanner and make sure that the scanner is switched on.
2) Go to **Insert > Image > Scan > Select Source** on the main menu bar to open the Scanner dialog (Figure 69). If you have previously used your scanner, then go to **Insert > Image > Scan > Request** on the main menu bar to open the Scanner dialog.
3) If you have more than one scanner connected, select the scanner from the *Select Source* or *Device Used* drop-down list.
4) If available, click **Create Preview** or **Preview** to carry out a preview scan of the image and place it in the preview area.
5) If necessary crop the scanned image to what you require and make any necessary scanning adjustments.
6) Click **Scan** and, when the image has been scanned, Impress places it into the selected slide. At this point it can be edited as any other image using the available Impress tools.

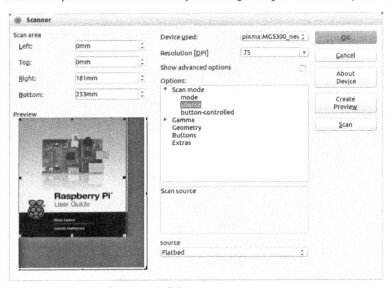

Figure 69: Example of a Scanner dialog

Inserting an image from the Gallery

The Gallery contains a collection of images that you can use in a presentation. You can also add your own images to the Gallery, making it an essential tool for creating presentations quickly and with a consistent look. The Gallery is available in all components of LibreOffice. For an introduction to the Gallery, see the *Getting Started Guide Chapter 11 Graphics, the Gallery, and Fontwork*.

1) Go to **Tools > Gallery** on the main menu bar or click the **Gallery** icon ![icon] on the Drawing toolbar to open the Gallery dialog (Figure 70). The Gallery displays the available themes with images that are available for each theme.
2) Select a theme from the left pane and then scroll through the right pane to find a suitable image.
3) Click on the image and drag it onto the workspace.
4) Release the mouse button and the image will be placed into your slide. If necessary, resize the image as described in "Resizing images" on page 96.

Figure 70: Inserting an image from the Gallery

Positioning the Gallery

To expand the Gallery, position the cursor over the line that divides it from the top of the workspace. When the cursor changes shape, click and drag downward. The workspace will resize in response.

By default, the Gallery is docked above the Impress workspace. To undock it, hold down the *Ctrl* key and double-click on the upper part of the Gallery next to the View icons. Double-click in the same area again to dock it in its default position at the top of the workspace.

When the Gallery is docked, to hide it and view the full Impress workspace, click the **Hide/Show** button in the middle of the thin bar separating the Gallery from the workspace (highlighted in Figure 70). The **Hide/Show** button lets you keep the Gallery open for quick access while you create your slide show, yet out of the way when you are no longer using the Gallery.

Managing Gallery themes

Graphics in the Gallery are grouped by themes, such as Arrows, Backgrounds, Bullets, and so on. The left pane of the gallery window lists the available themes. Click on a theme to see its images displayed in the right pane of the Gallery dialog.

The default themes are read-only; no images or graphics can be added to or deleted from these themes. The default themes are easily recognizable by right-clicking on each category and the only available option in the pop-up menu is **Properties**.

In a default installation of LibreOffice, any themes that you create are the only themes that are customizable and allow you add or delete your own images. You can also create new theme categories where you can add or delete your own images, as explained below.

Creating new themes

To add a new theme to the list of themes in the Gallery:

1) Open the Gallery.
2) Click **New Theme** above the list of themes and the Properties of New Theme dialog opens (Figure 71).
3) Click the **General** tab and type a name for the new theme in the text box.
4) Click the **Files** tab and follow the procedure in "Adding images to your themes" below.
5) Click **OK** and the new theme will now be displayed in the list of themes in the Gallery.

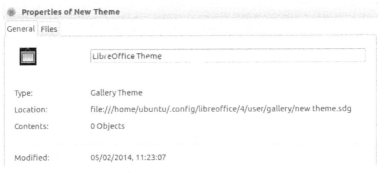

Figure 71: Creating a new theme

Note	If you wish, you can rename a new theme by right-clicking on the theme name and selecting **Rename** from the context menu.

Adding images to your themes

You can only add images to themes that you have created.

1) Right-click on a theme name that you created in the list of themes and select **Properties** from the context menu to open the Properties of New Theme dialog.
2) Click on the **Files** tab (Figure 72).
3) Click **Find Files** to open the **Select Path** dialog.
4) Browse to the folder that contains the images you want to use.

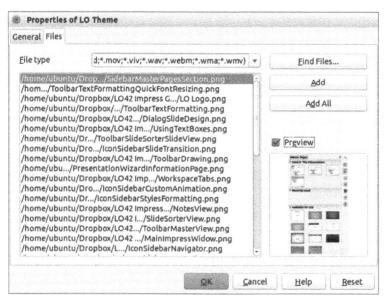

Figure 72: Properties of My Theme dialog – Files page

5) Click **OK** to select the files contained in the folder and the **Select Path** dialog closes. The list of files contained in the folder now appear in the Properties of New Theme dialog.

6) Select the files you want to use in your new theme and click **Add**. The added files will disappear from the file list and the images will appear in the Gallery.

7) If you want to add all the files in the list, then click **Add All**. All the files will disappear from the list and the images will appear in the Gallery.

8) Click **OK** when finished and the Properties of New Theme dialog will close.

Deleting images from the Gallery

You can only delete images from themes that you have created.

1) Open the Gallery and select a theme that you created.

2) Right-click on the image in the Gallery window.

3) Select **Delete** from the context menu.

4) A confirmation message appears, asking if you want to delete this object. Click **Yes**.

Note	Images are linked files and are deleted from the Gallery only. The original image files are not deleted.

Updating themes

All images in the Gallery are linked files. You may wish to update a theme occasionally, to make sure that all the files are still there.

1) Open the Gallery.

2) Right-click on the theme where you added at least one file.

3) Select **Update** from the context menu.

Formatting images

Moving images

1) Click on an image to select it and display the selection handles.
2) Move the cursor over the image until it changes shape. The cursor shape depends on the computer operating system, for example a four headed arrow or a hand.
3) Click and drag the picture to the desired position.
4) Release the mouse button.

For a more accurate placement of images, use the Position and Size dialog described in *Chapter 6 Formatting Graphic Objects*.

Resizing images

1) Click on an image to select it and display the selection handles.
2) Position the cursor over one of the selection handles. The cursor changes shape giving a graphical representation of the direction of the resizing.
3) Click and drag to resize the image.
4) Release the mouse button when satisfied with the new size.

For more accurate resizing of an image, use the Position and Size dialog described in *Chapter 6 Formatting Graphic Objects*.

Note	The corner selection handles resize both the width and the height of the graphic object simultaneously, while the other four selection handles only resize one dimension at a time.

Tip	To retain the original proportions of the graphic, *Shift+click* one of the corner selection handles and then drag. Make sure to release the mouse button **before** releasing the *Shift* key.

Tip	Be aware that re-sizing a bit-mapped (raster) image will adversely affect the resolution causing some degree of blurring. It is better to use a specialized graphics program to correctly scale the picture to the desired size before inserting it into your presentation. LibreOffice recommend you use a tool such as Gimp (http://www.gimp.org/).

Rotating images

As with the position of the image on the page, rotation of an image can be done manually or using a dedicated dialog. The Rotation dialog is described in *Chapter 6 Formatting Graphic Objects*.

Manually rotate an image as follows:

1) Select the image to display the selection handles.
2) Click the **Rotate** icon on the Line and Filling toolbar or click again on the selected image and the selection handles change shape and color (Figure 73). The color change depends on the computer operating system and how your computer has been setup.

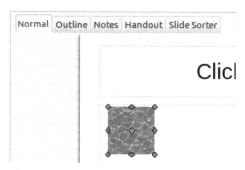

Figure 73: Rotating images

Note	The icons representing the functions in the toolbars depend on the computer operating system used and how the computer has been setup, or whether LibreOffice has been customized or not. When in doubt, hover the mouse over the icons and wait for the tooltip to appear showing the name of the button.

3) A circle or circle with crosshairs (depending on computer system) appears in the center of the picture indicating the rotation point. The center of the picture is the normal rotation point, but this rotation point can be moved to change the rotation center to a corner or to a point outside the picture. To do this, click on the rotation point and drag it to the desired position before applying the rotation.

4) The selection handles in each corner are the rotation handles and the cursor shape will change when moved over one of them. Click the mouse and move in the direction in which you want to rotate the picture.

5) When satisfied, release the mouse button.

Tip	To restrict the rotation angles to multiples of 15 degrees, press the *Shift* key while rotating the graphic. This is very handy to rotate pictures of right angles, for example from portrait to landscape or from landscape to portrait.

Formatting using the Picture toolbar

When an image is selected, the Picture toolbar becomes available. This toolbar provides a number of formatting options which are described in this section. If the Picture toolbar does not appear when an image is selected, display it by selecting **View > Toolbars > Picture** from the menu bar (Figure 74).

Figure 74: Picture toolbar

Applying filters

The graphic filters available on the Picture toolbar apply various filters to the selected picture. The best way to judge if a filter works for your picture is to try it. Table 2 below describes briefly each of the available graphic filters and their effects. See the *Draw Guide* for more information and examples of the effects.

1) Select an image so that the selection handles are displayed and the Picture toolbar becomes available.
2) Click on the **Filter** icon 🖝 to show the different graphic filters that are available.
3) Select the filter you wish to apply. To show the name of the filter, hover the cursor over the icon and wait for the tooltip to appear.
4) If you are not satisfied with the effect obtained or you want to try a different filter and before doing anything else, click the **Undo** icon 🖝 on the Standard toolbar or select **Edit > Undo: Bitmap Graphic Filter** on the main menu bar or use the keyboard combination *Ctrl+Z*.

Table 2: Graphic filters and their effects

Icon	Name	Effect
🖝	Invert	Inverts the color values of a color image, or the brightness values of a grayscale image. Apply the filter again to revert the effect.
🖝	Smooth	Softens or blurs the image by applying a low pass filter.
🖝	Sharpen	Sharpens the image by applying a high pass filter.
🖝	Remove noise	Removes noise by applying a median filter.
🖝	Solarization	Opens a dialog for defining solarization. Solarization refers to an effect that looks like what can happen when there is too much light during photo development. The colors become partly inverted. *Parameters* – specifies the degree and type of solarization. *Threshold Value* – specifies the degree of brightness, in percent, above which the pixels are to be solarized. *Invert* – specifies to also invert all pixels.
🖝	Aging	All pixels are set to their gray values, and then the green and blue color channels are reduced by the amount you specify. The red color channel is not changed. *Aging Degree* – defines the intensity of aging, in percent. At 0% you see the gray values of all pixels. At 100% only the red color channel remains.
🖝	Posterize	Opens a dialog to determine the number of poster colors. This effect is based on the reduction of the number of colors. It makes photos look like paintings. *Poster Colors* – specifies the number of colors to which the image is to be reduced.
🖝	Pop Art	Converts an image to a pop-art format.
🖝	Charcoal sketch	Displays the image as a charcoal sketch. The contours of the image are drawn in black, and the original colors are suppressed.
🖝	Relief	Displays a dialog for creating reliefs. You can choose the position of the imaginary light source that determines the type of shadow created, and how the graphic image looks in relief. *Light Source* – specifies the light source position. A dot represents the light source.

Icon	Name	Effect
	Mosaic	Joins small groups of pixels into rectangular areas of the same color. The larger the individual rectangles are, the fewer details the graphic image has. *Width* – defines the width of the individual tiles. *Height* – defines the height of the individual tiles. *Enhance edges* – enhances, or sharpens, the edges of the object.

Changing graphics mode

Click on **Graphics mode** on the Picture toolbar (Figure 74) to open a drop-down list and change the graphic mode using one of the following options.

- **Default** – the view of the graphic object is not changed.
- **Grayscale** – the graphic object is shown in grayscale. A color graphic object can become monochrome in grayscale. You can also use the color sliders to apply a uniform color to a monochrome graphic object.
- **Black/White** – the graphic object is shown in black and white. All brightness values below 50% will appear black, all brightness values over 50% will appear white.
- **Watermark** – the graphic object is raised in brightness and reduced in contrast so that it can be used in the background as a watermark.

Adjusting color

Click on the **Color** icon in the Picture toolbar (Figure 74) to open the Color toolbar (Figure 75). Use this toolbar to modify the individual color components of the image (red, green, blue) as well as the brightness, contrast, and gamma of the image. Increasing the gamma value of an image makes it more suitable to be used as a background or watermark as it will interfere less with a dark text.

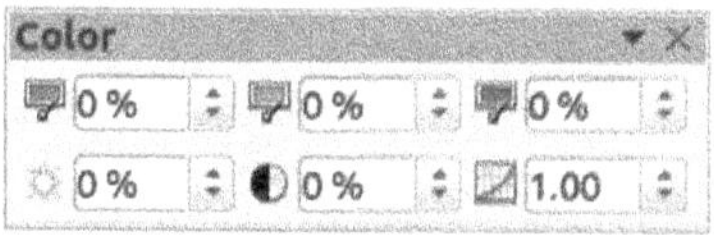

Figure 75: Color toolbar

To adjust colors more accurately, delete, edit or add colors. go to **Format > Area** on the main menu bar to open the Area dialog, then click on the **Colors** tab (Figure 76). This dialog page provides the following options when working with color.

- **Name** – specifies the name of a selected color. You can also type a name in this field when defining a new color.
- **Color** – contains a list of available colors. To select a color, choose one from the list.
- **Color table** – to modify colors, select the color model: Red-Green-Blue (RGB) or Cyan-Magenta-Yellow-BlacK (CMYK). LibreOffice uses only the RGB color model for printing in color. The CMYK controls are provided only to ease the input of color values using CMYK notation.

  If you select RGB, the initials of the three colors will appear and you can set the color from 0 to 255 with the spin button.

  If you select CMYK, the initials of the four colors will appear and you can set the color from 0 to 255 with the spin button.

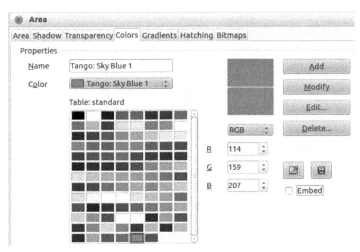

Figure 76: Colors page in Area dialog

- **Add** – adds a new color.
- **Modify** – changes the current color. Note that the color is overwritten without a confirmation.
- **Edit** – define your own colors using the two-dimensional graphic and numerical gradient chart.
- **Delete** – deletes the selected element or elements after confirmation.
- **Load Color List** – this icon ![icon] opens a file dialog, which allows you to select a color palette.
- **Save Color List** – this icon ![icon] opens the Save As dialog, which enables you to save the current color table under a specified name. If you do not choose this command, the current color table will be automatically saved as default and re-loaded the next time you start LibreOffice.
- The preview boxes display the selected color and the new color you are creating.

Setting object transparency

Click on the **Transparency** icon ![icon] on the Picture toolbar (Figure 74) to modify the percentage value and make the image more transparent. As with the gamma value, increasing the transparency of an image makes the image blend more smoothly in the background making the overlay text easier to read.

To adjust the transparency settings applied to an image, go to **Format > Area** on the main menu bar to open the Area dialog, then click on the **Transparency** tab (Figure 77).

- **No transparency** – turns off color transparency. This is the default setting.
- **Transparency** – turns on color transparency. Select this option and then enter a percentage in the box where 0% is fully opaque and 100% is fully transparent.
- **Gradient** – applies a transparency gradient to the current fill color. Select this option, and then set the gradient properties.

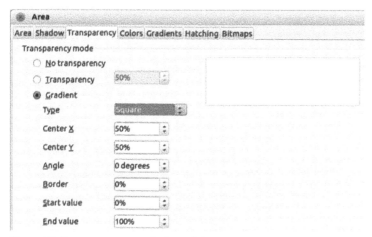

Figure 77: Transparency page in Area dialog

- **Type** – select the type of transparency gradient that you want to apply from *Linear*, *Axial*, *Radial*, *Ellipsoid*. *Quadratic*, or *Square*.
- **Center X** – enter the horizontal offset for the gradient.
- **Center Y** – enter the vertical offset for the gradient.
- **Angle** – enter a rotation angle for the gradient.
- **Border** – enter the amount by which you want to adjust the transparent area of the gradient. The default value is 0%.
- **Start value** – enter a transparency value for the beginning point of the gradient, where 0% is fully opaque and 100% is fully transparent.
- **End value** – enter a transparency value for the endpoint of the gradient, where 0% is fully opaque and 100% is fully transparent.
- Use the preview box to view your changes before you apply the transparency effect to the color fill of the selected object.

Adjusting shadow settings

Click on the **Shadow** icon on the Picture toolbar (Figure 74) to apply a shadow to an image. If a shadow is already applied to the image, clicking on the **Shadow** icon will remove the shadow.

To adjust the shadow settings applied to an image, go to **Format > Area** on the main menu bar to open the Area dialog, then click on the **Shadow** tab (Figure 78).

- **Position** – click where you want to cast the shadow.
- **Distance** – enter the distance that you want the shadow to be offset from the selected object.
- **Color** – select a color for the shadow.
- **Transparency** – enter a percentage from 0% (opaque) to 100% (transparent) to specify the transparency of the shadow.
- Use the preview box to view your changes before you apply the shadow effect to the selected object.

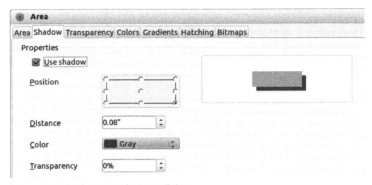

Figure 78: Shadow page in Area dialog

Cropping images

Impress provides two ways to crop an image: using a mouse or using a dialog. Using the mouse is easier, but the dialog provides more precise control.

To crop an image using the mouse:

1) Select the image.

2) Click the **Crop** icon ![icon] on the Picture toolbar (Figure 74). A set of crop marks appears around the picture (Figure 79).

Figure 79: Cropping pictures using the cursor

3) Place the cursor over any of the crop marks, the cursor changes shape. Drag the mark to crop the picture.

4) Click outside the picture to deactivate cropping mode.

5) Press and hold the *Shift* key while working on the crop marks to produce the following effects:

   a) For a corner mark, the two sides of the picture forming the corner are cropped proportionally with the picture anchored to the opposite corner mark.

   b) For a side mark, both dimensions are changed proportionally with the image anchored to the opposite side mark.

To crop an image using a dialog:

1) Select the image.

2) Right-click on the image and select **Crop Picture** from the context menu or go to **Format > Crop Image** on the main menu bar to open the Crop dialog (Figure 80).

3) Crop the picture using the options given in the Crop dialog.

4) Click **OK** when finished to close the dialog.

5) To revert back to the original size of the picture, click **Original Size**.

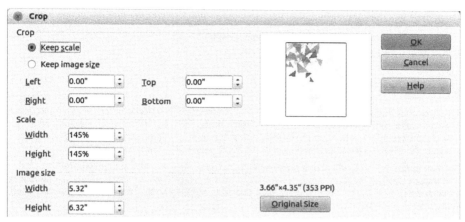

Figure 80: Crop dialog and options available when cropping an image

The Crop dialog has the following options:

- **Keep scale** – maintains the original scale of the graphic when you crop, so that only the size of the graphic changes.

- **Keep image size** – maintains the original size of the graphic when you crop, so that only the scale of the graphic changes. To reduce the scale of the graphic, select this option and enter negative values in the cropping boxes. To increase the scale of the graphic, enter positive values in the cropping boxes.

- **Left** – if the **Keep scale** option is selected, enter a positive amount to trim the left edge of the graphic, or a negative amount to add white space to the left of the graphic. If the **Keep image size** option is selected, enter a positive amount to increase the horizontal scale of the graphic, or a negative amount to decrease the horizontal scale of the graphic.

- **Right** – if the **Keep scale** option is selected, enter a positive amount to trim the right edge of the graphic, or a negative amount to add white space to the right of the graphic. If the **Keep image size** option is selected, enter a positive amount to increase the horizontal scale of the graphic, or a negative amount to decrease the horizontal scale of the graphic.

- **Top** – if the **Keep scale** option is selected, enter a positive amount to trim the top of the graphic, or a negative amount to add white space above the graphic. If the **Keep image size** option is selected, enter a positive amount to increase the vertical scale of the graphic, or a negative amount to decrease the vertical scale of the graphic.

- **Bottom** – if the **Keep scale** option is selected, enter a positive amount to trim the bottom of the graphic, or a negative amount to add white space below the graphic. If the **Keep image size** option is selected, enter a positive amount to increase the vertical scale of the graphic, or a negative amount to decrease the vertical scale of the graphic.

- **Scale** – changes the scale of the selected graphic.
  - *Width* – enter the width for the selected graphic as a percentage.
  - *Height* – enter the height of the selected graphic as a percentage.

- **Image size** – changes the size of the selected graphic.
  - *Width* – enter a width for the selected graphic.
  - *Height* – enter a height for the selected graphic.

- **Original Size** – returns the selected graphic to its original size.

Deleting an image

1) Click on an image to display the selection handles.
2) Press *Delete* key.

Creating an image map

An image map defines areas of the image (called *hotspots*) associated with a URL (a web address or a file on the computer). Hotspots are the graphic equivalent of text hyperlinks. Clicking on a hotspot causes Impress to open the linked page in the appropriate program (for example, default browser for HTML pages; LibreOffice Writer for .ODT files; PDF viewer for PDF files).

You can create hotspots of various shapes, such as rectangles, ellipses, and polygons. You can also include several hotspots in the same image. When you click on a hotspot, the URL opens in a browser window or frame that you have specified. You can also specify the text that appears when your mouse cursor hovers over the hotspot.

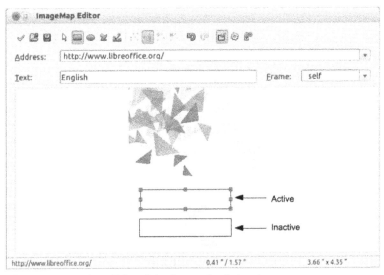

Figure 81: Image Map Editor dialog for creating hotspots

To use the image map tool to create or edit a hotspot:

1) Select the picture on a slide where hotspots are going to be defined.
2) Go to **Edit > ImageMap** on the main menu bar and the ImageMap Editor dialog opens (Figure 81). The main part of the dialog shows the image on which the hotspots will be defined.
3) Active hotspots are indicated by a colored border, while inactive hotspots are indicated by a black or grayed out border.
4) Use the tools at the top of the dialog and the fields to define hotspots and their links.
5) Click the **Apply** icon ✅ to apply the settings.
6) When done, click the **Save** icon 💾 to save the image map to a file, then close the dialog.

The top part of the dialog, from left to right, contains the following tools:

- **Apply** icon – click this icon to apply any changes made.
- **Open, Save,** and **Select** icons.
- **Rectangle**, **Ellipse**, **Polygon** and **FreeForm Polygon** icons – drawing tools hotspot shapes. These tools work in exactly the same way as the corresponding tools in the Drawing toolbar (see *Chapter 5 Managing Graphic Objects*).
- **Edit**, **Move**, **Insert**, **Delete Points** icons – advanced editing tools to manipulate the shape of a polygon hotspot. Select **Edit Points** tool to activate the other tools.
- **Active** icon – toggles the status of the hotspot activating a selected hotspot or deactivating it if active.
- **Undo** and **Redo** icons.
- **Macro** icon – associates a macro with the hotspot instead of a hyperlink.
- **Properties** icon – sets the hyperlink properties and adds the Name attribute to the hyperlink.

Below the toolbar are fields which specify the properties of a hotspot:

- **Address** – the URL address that points to a hyperlink. You can also point to an anchor in a document such as a specific slide number; to do this, write the address in this format: `file:///<path>/document_name#anchor_name`
- **Text** – enter the text that will be displayed when the mouse is moved over the hotspot.
- **Frame** – where the target of the hyperlink will open: _blank (opens in a new browser window), _self (default selection and opens in an active browser window), _top or _parent.

Tip	The value _self for the target frame will work on the vast majority of the occasions. It is not recommended to use the other values unless absolutely necessary.

Chapter 5
Managing Graphic Objects

Introduction

This chapter describes how to manage graphic objects and in particular how to rotate, distort, arrange, and position them on the slide. Though this chapter focuses on the shapes that can be created with the available tools in Impress, some of the techniques described in this chapter are also applicable to images imported into slides.

Drawing toolbar

Default drawing tools

The Drawing toolbar (Figure 82) contains the majority of the tools normally used to create graphic objects. If this toolbar is not visible, select **View > Toolbars > Drawing** from the main menu bar. Table 3 describes the default set of tools that are available on the Drawing toolbar.

To draw a shape, select the desired tool from the toolbar (or from the submenu opened by clicking the triangle to the right of the tool), then place your cursor on the slide and drag the mouse to define an enclosing rectangle. Keep the *Shift* key pressed to obtain a shape where the height and width are equal. Press the *Alt* key to draw a shape from its center.

Figure 82: Drawing toolbar

Note	Your Drawing toolbar may differ from the one shown in Figure 82 as this depends on how many drawing tools have been placed on the toolbar. Right-click on an empty area of the Drawing toolbar, then select **Visible Buttons** from the context menu to display the available tools. From this dialog you can install and remove tools to and from the toolbar. Installed tools are indicated by a border around the icon.

Table 3: Default set of drawing tools on the Drawing toolbar

Tool	Name	Purpose
	Select	Selects objects. To select a group of objects, click above the top left object and drag the mouse below the bottom right object of the intended selection while keeping the mouse button pressed. A "marching ants" rectangle identifying the selection area is displayed. You can also select several objects by pressing and holding the *Shift* key while selecting the individual objects.
	Line	Draws a straight line from the point where you click the mouse to the point where you drag the mouse pointer and release the mouse button. Press the *Shift* key to restrict the angle of the line to multiples of 45°. Press the *Alt* key to draw a line from its center. Press the *Ctrl* key to detach the end point of the line from the grid (see "Snapping objects to grid or snap guides" on page 124).
	Line Ends with Arrow	Draws a straight line ending with an arrowhead. The arrowhead is placed at the end of the line where you release the mouse button. The *Shift, Alt* and *Ctrl* keys have the same effect as for the *Line* tool.

Tool	Name	Purpose
▭	Rectangle	Draws a rectangle when you drag the mouse from the top left to the bottom right corner. Press the *Shift* key to draw a square. Press the *Alt* key to draw a rectangle or square from its center.
⬭	Ellipse	Draws an ellipse. Press the *Shift* key to draw a circle. Press the *Alt* key to draw an ellipse or circle from its center.
T	Text	Creates a text box with text aligned horizontally.
⊨	Vertical Text	Creates a text box with text aligned vertically. This tool is available only when Asian language support has been enabled in **Tools > Options > Language Settings > Languages**.
✐	Curve	Draws a shape depending on the option that has been selected. Click the triangle to the right of the tool icon to show the available options. Actual icon shown will depend on the option that has been selected. Note that the title of this submenu when undocked from the Drawing toolbar is *Lines*.

Lines ▼ ✕ |
| ⚬ | Connector | Draws a connector line between two figures. Click the triangle to the right of the tool icon to show the available options. Actual icon shown will depend on the option that has been selected. Each option is described in "Working with connectors" on page 127.

Connectors ▼ ✕ |
| → | Lines and Arrows | Draws a line ending in an arrow. Click the triangle to the right of the tool icon to show the available options. Actual icon shown will depend on the option that has been selected. Note that the title of this submenu when undocked from the Drawing toolbar is *Arrows*.

Arrows ▼ ✕ |
| ◆ | Basic Shapes | Click the triangle to the right of the tool icon to open a toolbar showing the available options. Actual icon shown will depend on the option that has been selected.

Basic Shapes ▼ ✕ |

Tool	Name	Purpose
	Symbol Shapes	Click the triangle to the right of the tool icon to open a toolbar showing the available options. Actual icon shown will depend on the option that has been selected.
	Block Arrows	Click the triangle to the right of the tool icon to open a toolbar showing the available options. Actual icon shown will depend on the option that has been selected.
	Flowcharts	Click the triangle to the right of the tool icon to open a toolbar showing the available options. Actual icon shown will depend on the option that has been selected.
	Callouts	Click the triangle to the right of the tool icon to open a toolbar showing the available options. Actual icon shown will depend on the option that has been selected.
	Stars	Click the triangle to the right of the tool icon to open a toolbar showing the available options. Actual icon shown will depend on the option that has been selected.
	Points	Edits the individual points that form the shape or line. Select this tool and then select a shape or a line. You can also press the *F8* key to select this tool.
	Glue Points	Edits the glue points of a graphic object. Glue points are the positions where connector lines terminate or start. See "Managing glue points" on page 128 for instructions.
	Fontwork Gallery	Opens the Fontwork gallery. See "Using Fontwork" on page 132 for further information.
	From File	Equivalent to **Insert > Picture > From file** on the main menu bar. See *Chapter 4 Adding and Formatting Pictures* for details.

Tool	Name	Purpose
	Gallery	Opens the gallery. Equivalent to **Tools > Gallery** on the main menu bar. See *Chapter 4 Adding and Formatting Pictures* for details.
	Extrusion On/Off	Switches 3D effects on or off for the selected object. Clicking this button also opens the 3D settings toolbar. See "Working with 3D objects" on page 129 for details.

Additional drawing tools

In addition to the default set of drawing tools available on the Drawing toolbar (Figure 82), you can install additional tools. These additional tools are described in Table 4.

To install additional tools onto the Drawing toolbar:

1) Right-click on an empty area on the Drawing toolbar.
2) Select **Visible Buttons** from the context menu to display a list of the available tools.
3) To install a tool, click on it and the tool will appear in the Drawing toolbar. The list of available tools will close automatically. Installed tools are indicated by a border around the icon.

To remove any additional tools from the Drawing toolbar:

1) Right-click on an empty area on the Drawing toolbar.
2) Select **Visible Buttons** from the context menu to display a list of the available tools.
3) To remove a tool, click on it and the tool is removed from the Drawing toolbar. Uninstalling a tool removes the border around the tool icon. The list of available tools will close automatically.

Table 4: Additional drawing tools

Tool	Name	Purpose
	3D Objects	Click the triangle to the right of the tool icon to open a toolbar showing the available options. Actual icon shown will depend on the option that has been selected. Select the desired 3D shape, then draw it by placing your cursor on the slide and dragging your mouse to define an enclosing rectangle. Keep the *Shift* key pressed to obtain a 3D shape where the height and width are equal. Press the *Alt* key to draw a 3D shape from its center.
	To Curve	Converts the selected object to a Bézier curve.
	To Polygon	Converts the selected object to a polygon (a closed object bounded by straight lines). The appearance of the object does not change. If you want, you can right-click and choose *Edit Points* to view the changes.
	To 3D	Converts the selected 2D object to a 3D object.
	To 3D Rotation Object	Converts the selected 2D object to a 3D rotation object.

Tool	Name	Purpose
	Insert	Inserts a slide, table, from file, movie and sound, formula, or chart into your presentation. Click the triangle to the right of the tool icon to open the **Insert** toolbar showing the available options. Actual icon shown depends on the option that has been selected.
	Controls	Inserts various form controls into your presentation. Click the triangle to the right of the tool icon to open the **Form Controls** toolbar showing the available options.
	Animated Image	Adds animation to a selected object on a slide. Opens the **Animation** dialog.

Creating lines and shapes

Creating shapes and lines is basically the same procedure for all lines and shapes:

1) Click on the triangle to the right of the tool you want to use on the Drawing toolbar and select the desired tool from the available selection. Note that the tools on the Drawing toolbar show the last tool shape selected.

2) Position your cursor on the slide, then click and drag to create the line or shape.

3) Release the mouse button when you have drawn your line or shape. You can then modify and reposition your line or shape using the procedures described later in this chapter.

Regular shapes

When creating shapes that are included in Impress, one or more dots may be displayed in a different color to the selection handles. These dots perform a different function according to the shape they are applied to, as listed below.

Basic Shapes

- *Rounded rectangle* and *rounded square* – use the dot to change the radius of the curve that replaces the angled corners of a rectangle or square.
- *Circle pie* – use the dots to change the size of the filled sector.
- *Isosceles triangle* – use the dot to modify the shape and type of the triangle.
- *Trapezoid*, *parallelogram*, *hexagon*, or *octagon* – use the dot to change the internal angles between the sides.
- *Cross* – use the dot to change the thickness of the four arms of the cross.
- *Ring* – use the dot to change the internal diameter of the ring.
- *Block arc* – use the dot to change both internal diameter and size of the filled area.
- *Cylinder* and *cube* – use the dot to change the perspective.
- *Folded corner* – use the dot to change the size of the folded corner.
- *Frame* – use the dot to change the thickness of the frame.

Symbol Shapes

- *Smiley face* – use the dot to change the smile on the face.
- *Sun*, *moon* and *heart* – use the dot to change the shape of the symbol.
- *Prohibited symbol* – use the dot to change the thickness of the ring and the diagonal bar.
- *Double bracket*, *left bracket*, *right bracket* and *double brace* – use the dot to change the curvature of the bracket.
- *Left brace* and *right brace* – use the dots to change the curvature of the brace and the position of the point.
- *Square bevel*, *octagon bevel* and *diamond bevel* – use the dot to change the thickness of the bevel.

Block Arrows

- *Left arrow, right arrow, up arrow, down arrow, left and right arrow, up and down arrow, striped right arrow* and *notched right arrow* – use the dot to change the shape and thickness of the arrows.
- *Up and right arrow, up, right and down arrow* and *4-way arrow* – use the dots to change the shape and thickness of the arrows.
- *Pentagon* and *chevron* – use the dot to change the angle between the sides and the shape.
- *Right arrow callout, left arrow callout, up arrow callout, down arrow callout, left and right arrow callout, up and down arrow callout, up and right arrow callout* and *4-way arrow callout* – use the dots to change the shape and thickness of the callouts.
- *Circular arrow* – use the dots to change the thickness and area of the arrow.

Callouts

- For all callouts use the dots to change the length, position and angle of the pointer.

Stars

- *4-point star*, *8-point star* and *24-point star* – use the dot to change the thickness and shape of the star points.
- *Vertical scroll* and *horizontal scroll* – use the dot to change the width and shape of the scroll.
- *Doorplate* – use the dot to change the inward curvature of the corners.

Curves, polygons and freeform lines

Figure 83: Lines (curves) toolbar

To draw a curve, polygon, or freeform line, click the **Curve** icon 🖉 on the Drawing toolbar. The default action of this tool is to show the last selected tool and, by default, the last selected tool will be used. To use a different tool, click on the triangle to the right of the icon to open the tools that are available (Figure 83). Note that the title of this tool submenu when undocked from the Drawing toolbar is *Lines*.

If a filled curve, polygon, or freeform line was selected, Impress draws the line connecting the last point to the start point and fills the inside area with the default color.

Curves

1) Select either **Curve filled** or **Curve**.
2) Click and hold the left mouse button to create the starting point of your curve.
3) While holding down the left mouse button, drag from the starting point to draw a line.
4) Release the left mouse button and continue to drag the cursor to bend the line into a curve.
5) Click to set the end point of the curve and fix the line on the page.
6) To continue with the line, drag the mouse cursor to draw a straight line. Each mouse click sets a corner point and allows you to continue drawing another straight line from the corner point.
7) Double-click to end the drawing of your line.

Note	Holding down the *Shift* key when drawing lines with the Curve or Polygon tools will also restrict the angles between the lines to 45 or 90 degrees.

Polygons

1) Select either **Polygon filled** or **Polygon**.
2) Click and draw the first line from the start point with the left mouse button held down. As soon as you release the mouse button, a line between the first and second points is drawn.
3) Move the cursor to draw the next line. Each mouse click sets a corner point and allows you to draw another line.
4) Double-click to end the drawing of your polygon.

Polygons 45°

Select either **Polygon (45°) filled** or **Polygon (45°)** and these polygons are drawn in the same way as polygons above. However, the angles between line segments are restricted to 45 or 90 degrees as you draw your polygon.

Freeform lines

Using the Freeform Line tools is similar to drawing with a pencil on paper.

1) Select either **Freeform line filled** or **Freeform line**.
2) Press and hold the left mouse button and drag the cursor to the line shape you require.
3) When you finished drawing your freeform line, release the mouse button and the drawing is completed.

Grouping objects together

It is often convenient to group objects together so that they are treated as a single object by Impress. A group of objects can be formatted as if it was a single object, moved, rotated, deleted, and so on.

This section gives only a brief introduction to grouping of objects. For more information on working with grouped objects, see the *Draw Guide Chapter 5 Combining Multiple Objects*.

Grouping

To group objects together:

1) Select the objects to be grouped using the selection tool on the Drawing toolbar and draw a rectangle around the objects to be grouped, or hold down the *Shift* key and click on each object. To select all the objects, go to **Edit > Select All** on the main menu bar or use the keyboard combination *Ctrl+A*.

2) When the selection handles are displayed, go to **Format > Group > Group** on the main menu bar or use the keyboard combination *Ctrl+Shift+G* or right-click on an object within the selected group and select **Group** from the context menu.

Editing or formatting groups

To edit or format a group of objects:

1) Click on any one of the objects in the group to select the group. Any editing or formatting is then carried out on all the objects within the group.

2) To edit an individual object within a group:

  a) After selecting the group, press the *F3* key or go to **Format > Group > Enter Group** on the main menu bar or right-click and select **Enter Group** from the context menu.

  b) Select individual objects within the group for editing or formatting.

  c) When you have finished editing or formatting, use the keyboard combination *Ctrl+F3* or go to **Format > Group > Exit group** on the main menu bar or right-click and select **Exit Group** from the context menu. The whole group then becomes selected.

Ungrouping

To ungroup objects:

1) Click on any one of the objects in the group to select the group.

2) When the selection handles are displayed, go to **Format > Group > Ungroup** on the menu bar or use the keyboard combination *Ctrl+Alt+Shift+G* or right-click on the group and select **Ungroup** from the context menu.

Tip	If you use the group and ungroup commands often, why not add them to one of the toolbars shown by default so that the commands are readily available? To do so, you will need to customize the selected toolbar. See *Chapter 11 Setting Up and Customizing Impress*.

Positioning graphic objects

Using a mouse

To position a graphic object using a mouse:

1) Click on a graphic object or a group of objects to display the selection handles.

2) Move the cursor over a selected graphic object until the cursor changes shape. For example, on most operating systems, the cursor associated with moving objects is a clenched hand or a four-headed arrow.

3) Click and drag the graphic object to the desired position. You can also use the arrow keys to move the selected object or group to a new position.

4) Release the mouse button.

> **Tip**
>
> By default Impress makes the objects snap to the grid. If you need to position the object between two points of the grid, hold down the *Ctrl key*, then click on the object and move it to the desired position. Alternatively, you can turn off this snap function or modify the grid resolution by going to **Tools > Options > LibreOffice Impress > Grid**.

Using the Position and Size dialog

For a more accurate placement of the graphic object, use the Position and Size dialog (Figure 84):

1) With the object selected and the selection handles displayed, press *F4* or go to **Format > Position and Size** on the main menu bar, or right-click on the selected object and select **Position and Size** from the context menu.

2) Click on the **Position and Size** tab.

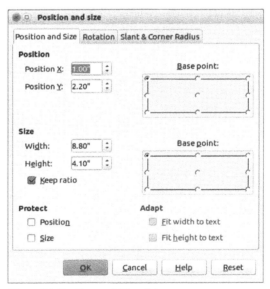

Figure 84: Position and Size dialog

3) Use the *Position* section of the dialog to specify the X (horizontal) and Y (vertical) position of the graphic object. The values represent the distance of the base point selected on the right hand side of the dialog. The default selection for base point is relative to the top left corner of the slide.

4) To prevent accidental modification of the position of the graphic object, select the *Position* option in the **Protect** section of the dialog.

5) Click **OK** when satisfied and to close the dialog.

Note	The units of measurement for this dialog and other dialogs in Impress are set in **Tools > Options > LibreOffice Impress > General**.

Using the Sidebar

You can use the *Position and Size* subsection on the Sidebar to position a graphic object. After selecting the graphic object, click on the **Properties** icon  on the Sidebar and then click on the plus (+) sign next to the title to open the *Position and Size* subsection (Figure 85).

Use the **Horizontal** and **Vertical** text boxes and enter the values you want to use for the X (horizontal) and Y (vertical) position of the graphic object. The values represent the distance of the selected base point and the default position is the top left corner of the slide.

Note	Clicking on the **More Options** icon on the *Sidebar Position and Size* subsection will open the Position and Size dialog.

Figure 85: Sidebar – Position and Size subsection

Resizing graphic objects

Using a mouse

To resize a graphic object using a mouse:

1) Click on a graphic object or a group of objects to display the selection handles.
2) Position the pointer over one of the selection handles. The pointer changes shape giving a graphical representation of the direction of the resizing. The corner handles resize both the width and the height of the graphic object simultaneously, while the other four handles resize only one dimension at a time.
3) Click and drag to resize the graphic object.
4) Release the mouse button to complete resizing.

Tip	To retain the original proportions of the graphic, *Shift*+click one of the corner handles, then drag. Release the mouse button **before** releasing the *Shift* key.

Using the Position and Size dialog

For more accurate resizing of the graphic object, use the Position and Size dialog (Figure 84):

1) With the object selected and the selection handles displayed, press *F4* or go to **Format > Position and Size** on the main menu bar, or right-click on the selected object and select **Position and Size** from the context menu.
2) Click on the **Position and Size** tab.
3) Select as the base point the part of the graphic object that you would like to anchor to the page. The default selection of top left corner means, that when resizing, the position of the top left corner of the object will not change.
4) Now modify either the *Width* value or the *Height* value of the object in the **Size** section.
5) To maintain the proportions between width and height, select the **Keep ratio** option before modifying any value. When **Keep ratio** is selected, changes to one dimension results in an automatic change to the other with the ratio between width and height maintained.
6) To prevent accidental modifications of the size, select the *Size* option in the **Protect** section of the dialog.
7) Click **OK** when satisfied and to close the dialog.

Using the Sidebar

You can use the *Position and Size* subsection on the Sidebar to resize a graphic object. After selecting your graphic object, click on the **Properties** icon [image] on the Sidebar and then click on then click on the plus (+) sign next to the title to open the *Position and Size* subsection (Figure 85).

Use the **Width** and **Height** text boxes and enter the values for the width and height of the graphic object. To maintain the ratio between width and height of a graphic object, select the **Keep ratio** option.

Note	Clicking on the **More Options** icon on the *Sidebar Position and Size* subsection will open the Position and Size dialog.

Applying special effects

As well as the basic actions of moving and resizing an object, a number of special effects can also be applied to objects in Impress. Several of these effects are readily available in the Mode toolbar (Figure 86). If the Mode toolbar is not showing, select it from **View > Toolbars > Mode**.

This section describes how to rotate, flip, distort and two ways of setting an object in a circle. The transparency and gradient tools are more specific to formatting and are discussed in *Chapter 6 Formatting Graphic Objects*.

Figure 86: Mode toolbar

Rotating graphic objects

Rotation of an object can be carried out either using your mouse, using a dedicated dialog, or using the Sidebar. This is similar to changing position and size of an object.

Using a mouse

To rotate a graphic using a mouse:

1) Click on a graphic object and the selection handles will show.

2) Click the **Rotate** icon ☺ on the Line and Filling or Mode toolbars or click again on the graphic object. The square selection handles change shape and also change color (Figure 87). Also, a pivot point indicating the rotation center appears in the center of the object.

3) Move the mouse over one of the corner handles and the mouse cursor shape will change.

4) Click the mouse and move in the direction in which you want to rotate the graphic object. Only the corner selection handles are active for rotation.

5) When satisfied with the rotation, release the mouse button.

6) To change the rotation center of the object, click and drag the pivot point to the desired position before rotating. The pivot point can be moved to any position on the slide, even outside of the object boundaries.

7) To restrict the rotation angles to multiples of 15 degrees, press and hold the *Shift* key while rotating the graphic. This is very handy for rotating pictures through a right angle, for example from portrait to landscape. Remember to release the *Shift* key before releasing the mouse button.

Note	The icons representing the functions in the toolbars may be different depending on the operating system used and on whether LibreOffice has been customized. When in doubt, hover the mouse over an icon and wait for the tooltip to appear showing the name of the icon.

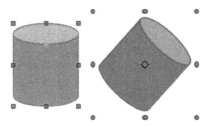

Figure 87: Object selected for rotation

Using the Position and Size dialog

Instead of rotating a graphic object manually, you can use the **Rotation** page of the Position and Size dialog (Figure 88) to accurately rotate an object in degrees:

1) With the object selected and the selection handles displayed, press *F4* or go to **Format > Position and Size** on the main menu bar, or right-click on the selected object and select **Position and Size** from the context menu.

2) Click on the **Rotation** tab.

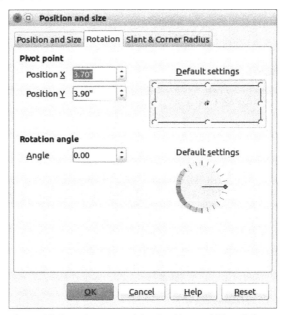

Figure 88: Rotation page of the Position and Size dialog

3) In the **Pivot point** section, select the position of the pivot point. The default position of the pivot point is the center of the object.

4) In the **Rotation angle** section, enter the degrees in the *Angle* text box by which to rotate the graphic object.

5) Alternatively, in *Default settings*, click on the *Rotation Angle* indicator and drag it to a new angle. The angle of rotation is displayed in the *Angle* text box.

6) Click **OK** when satisfied and to close the dialog.

Using the Sidebar

You can use the *Position and Size* subsection on the Sidebar to rotate a graphic object. After selecting your graphic object, click on the **Properties** icon 🔳 on the Sidebar and then click on then click on the plus (+) sign next to the title to open the *Position and Size* subsection (Figure 85).

In *Rotation*, either, click on the **Rotation Angle** indicator and drag it to a new angle, or enter the rotation angle in *Rotation* text box, or select an angle setting from the drop-down list.

Note	Clicking on the **More Options** icon on the *Sidebar Position and Size* subsection will open the Position and Size dialog.

Flipping objects

Using the context menu

The quickest and easiest method to flip an object horizontally or vertically is as follows:
1) Click on a graphic object to display the selection handles.
2) Right-click on the selected object and select **Flip > Horizontally** or **Flip > Vertically** from the context menu to flip the selected object so it faces the other direction.

Using the Flip tool

The Flip tool on the Drawing or Mode toolbar can also be used. Using this tool also allows you to change the position and angle that the object flips over (Figure 89).
1) Click on a graphic object and the selection handles will show.
2) Click on the **Flip** icon 🔳 on the Drawing or Mode toolbar and the *axis of symmetry* appears as a dashed line through the center of the object. The object will be flipped about this axis of symmetry.
3) Click and drag the axis of symmetry to a new position, or position the cursor in one of the circles at each end of the axis of symmetry and drag with your mouse cursor to change the angle.
4) Place the mouse cursor over one of the object selection handles until it changes shape.
5) Click and drag your cursor across the axis of symmetry to flip the object. The new position of the object is shown faintly until the mouse is released.
6) Release the mouse button and the object will appear flipped over. Angle and position of the flip will depend on the angle and position of the axis of symmetry.

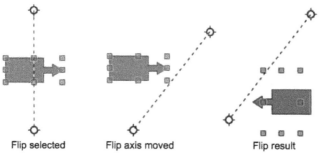

| Flip selected | Flip axis moved | Flip result |

Figure 89: Using the Flip tool

Note	If you press the *Shift* key while moving the axis of symmetry, it will rotate in 45-degree increments.

Using the Sidebar

You can use the *Position and Size* subsection on the Sidebar to rotate a graphic object. After

selecting your graphic object, click on the **Properties** icon 📇 on the Sidebar and then click on then click on the plus (+) sign next to the title to open the *Position and Size* subsection (Figure 85).

In *Rotation*, click on the **Flip Vertical** icon ⬒ to flip the selected object vertically about its central axis or click on the **Flip Horizontal** icon ⬓ to flip the selected object horizontally about its central axis.

Note	Clicking on the **More Options** icon on the *Sidebar Position and Size* subsection will open the Position and Size dialog.

Mirror copies

Impress does not include a mirror command. However, mirroring an object can be emulated by flipping the object:

1) Select the object you want to make a mirror copy of and copy the object to the clipboard.
2) Flip the object using one of the methods in "Flipping objects" above, then move the flipped object to one side.
3) Click on an empty area of the page to deselect the object.
4) Paste from the clipboard to put a copy of the object into your slide.
5) Select both images, then right-click and select **Alignment** from the context menu.
6) Select the type of alignment you want to use. **Top**, **Center**, or **Bottom** if you are creating a horizontal mirror copy. **Left**, **Centered**, or **Right** if you are creating a vertical mirror copy.

Distorting images

Three tools on the Mode toolbar (Figure 86 on page 119) let you drag the corners and edges of an object to distort the image. The **Distort** icon ▱ distorts an object in perspective, the **Set to Circle** (slant) icon ◡ and **Set in Circle (perspective)** icon ◡ both create a pseudo three-dimensional effect. Note that when using these tools, you have to transform an object to a curve before distorting.

Distort tool

1) Select an object and click on the **Distort** icon ▱ on the Mode toolbar.
2) Click **Yes** to convert the object to a curve. If the object is already a curve, this dialog does not appear.
3) Click and drag a corner selection handle to distort the object using the opposite corner selection handle as an anchor point for the distortion (Figure 90).
4) Click and drag the vertical selection handles to distort the object using the opposite vertical side as an anchor point for the distortion.
5) Click and drag the horizontal selection handles to distort the object using the opposite horizontal side as an anchor point for the distortion.

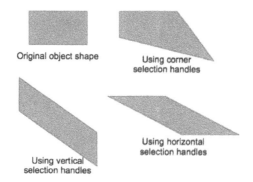

Original object shape

Using corner
selection handles

Using horizontal
selection handles

Using vertical
selection handles

Figure 90: Distorting an object

Set in circle (perspective) tool

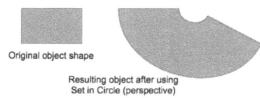

Original object shape

Resulting object after using
Set in Circle (perspective)

Figure 91: Setting an image to a circle with perspective

1) Select an object and click on the **Set in Circle (perspective)** icon 🔲 in the Mode toolbar.
2) Click **Yes** to convert the object to a curve. If the object is already a curve, this dialog does not appear.
3) Click and drag one of the selection handles to give a pseudo three-dimensional perspective using the opposite side as an anchor point (Figure 91). A ghosted image appears as you drag to give you and indication of the resulting object will look.

Set to circle (slant) tool

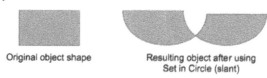

Original object shape

Resulting object after using
Set in Circle (slant)

Figure 92: Setting an image to a circle with slant

1) Select an object and click on the **Set to Circle (slant)** icon 🔲 in the Mode toolbar.
2) Click **Yes** to convert the object to a curve. If the object is already a curve, this dialog does not appear.
3) Click and drag one of the selection handles to give a pseudo three-dimensional perspective using the opposite side as an anchor point (Figure 92). A ghosted image appears as you drag to give you and indication of the resulting object will look.

Note	Transforming an object into a curve is a safe operation, but it cannot be reversed other than by using the **Undo** function.

Aligning objects

Use the alignment tools to adjust the relative position of an object compared to another object. These alignment tools are only available if two or more objects are selected.

Figure 93: Align Objects toolbar

1) Select the objects you want to align.

2) Click on the triangle to the right of the **Alignment** icon ![icon] in the Line and Filling toolbar or go to **View > Toolbars > Align Objects** on the main menu bar to open the **Align Objects** toolbar (Figure 93). The **Alignment** icon shown on the Line and Filling toolbar will depend on the alignment option that had been previously selected.

3) Alternatively, right-click on the group of selected objects and select **Alignment**, then one of the alignment options from the context menu.

The alignment options are as follows:

- **Left**, **Centered**, **Right** – determines the horizontal alignment of the selected objects.
- **Top**, **Center**, **Bottom** – determines the vertical alignment of the selected objects.

Snapping objects to grid or snap guides

Sometimes it is important to align objects to specific points of the page or to make sure that objects that appear on multiple slides are placed in exactly the same position. For this purpose Impress provides two mechanisms: **Grid** and **Snap Lines**.

Using the grid

Options for the grid are available by right-clicking on an empty part of the page in Normal view and choosing **Grid** or by selecting **View > Grid** from the menu bar. The options available from the context menu that opens are:

- **Display Grid** – displays the grid.
- **Snap to Grid** – the anchor points of an object will be placed on a grid when the object is moved or resized.
- **Grid to Front** – displays the grid in the foreground.

To set up the grid spacing and snapping options, go to **Tools > Options > LibreOffice Impress > Grid** on the menu bar.

Using snap lines

Options for the guides are available by right-clicking on an empty part of the page in Normal view and choosing **Snap Lines** or by selecting **View > Snap Lines** from the menu bar. The options available from the context menu that opens are:

- **Display Guides** – the guides are shown on the slide.
- **Snap to Snap Lines** – the anchor points of the objects snap to the guides when the object is moved or resized.
- **Snap Lines to Front** – displays the guides in the foreground.

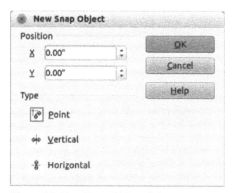

Figure 94: New Snap Object dialog

Creating a new snap point/line

1) Right-click on an empty part of the work area and select **Insert Snap Point/Line** from the context menu to open the **New Snap Object** dialog (Figure 94).
2) Specify the type of snap object. Depending on the choice made determines which field becomes active:
    - **Point** both *X* and *Y* fields become active.
    - **Vertical** only *X* field becomes active.
    - **Horizontal** only *Y* field become active.
3) Enter the position of the snap point/line.
4) Click **OK** to close the dialog.

Tip	When positioning the Snap Lines, it is useful to display the rulers. To do so, select **View > Rulers**. Drag a Snap Line directly onto the slide by clicking on the ruler and then dragging onto the slide.

Editing snap points/lines

1) Right-click next to or on the guide to be edited.
2) Select **Edit Snap line** from the context menu.
3) Enter a new value in the X or Y field for the line position and click **OK.**

Deleting guides

1) Right-click next or on the guide to be deleted.
2) Select **Delete Snap line** from the context menu.

Arranging objects

Impress organizes objects in a stack so that the objects on the top level of the stack cover the objects on lower levels if any overlapping occurs. The stack level of each object can be changed by arranging shapes on a slide or page.

To change the stack level of an object, select an object or objects and then click the small triangle on the side of the **Arrange** icon  on the Line and Filling toolbar to open the **Position** toolbar (Figure 95). The **Arrange** icon shown on the Line and Filling toolbar will depend on the arrange option that had been previously selected.

Alternatively, right-click on your selected objects and select **Arrange**, then select an arrange option from the context menu.

The first four tools determine the stack level of a selected object:

- **Bring to front**: – the selected object is moved in front of all other objects.
- **Bring forward** – the selected object is moved one level up in the stack.
- **Send backwards** – the selected object is moved one level down in the stack.
- **Send to back** – the selected object is moved behind all other objects.The other three tools determine the relative positions of the selected objects:
- **In front of object** – moves the first selected object in front of the second selected object.
- **Behind object** – moves the first selected object behind the second selected object.
- **Reverse** – swaps the stacking order of two selected objects.

Figure 95: Position toolbar

To use the **In front of object** and **Behind object** tools:

1) Select the first object by clicking on it.
2) Select **In front of object** or **Behind object** from the context menu and the mouse cursor changes to a pointing hand.
3) Click on the second object and the objects swap positions.

Working with connectors

Connectors are lines that can be anchored to *glue points* and by default are positioned on the border of an object. When an object with a connector attached is moved or resized, the connector automatically adjusts to the change. When creating a flowchart, organization chart, schematics, or diagrams, it is highly recommended to use connectors instead of simple lines.

When a connector is drawn or selected Impress displays selection handles which are not shown for normal lines. The termination points of a connector are square at the start of a connector and round at the end of a connector. The selection handles on a connector are used to modify the routing of a connector where applicable.

Impress offers a wide variety of predefined connectors, which differ in the termination shape (none, arrow, custom) and in the way the connector is drawn (straight, line, curved).

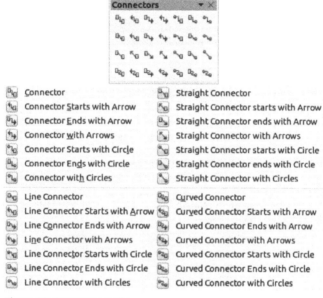

Figure 96: Connector toolbar

Drawing connectors

A simple method of drawing is as follows. For more information on how to format a connector, refer to *Chapter 6 Formatting Graphic Objects*.

1) Click on the triangle next to the **Connector** icon on the Drawing toolbar and select the type of connector you want to use. The **Connector** icon shown on the Drawing toolbar will depend on the connector that had been previously selected and used (Figure 96).

2) Move the mouse cursor over one of the objects to be connected and small crosses appear around the object edges which are the glue points to which a connector can be attached (Figure 97).

3) Click on the required glue point to attach one end of the connector, then hold the mouse button down and drag the connector to another object.

Figure 97: Example of using a connector

4) When the cursor is over the glue point of the target object release the mouse button and the connector is drawn.

5) The selection handles that appear on the connector are used to adjust the path of the connector so that the connector does not cover another object in its path.

Managing glue points

A glue point is the attachment point for a connector on an object. Each object shape has a number of predefined glue points, but it is possible to define new ones, as well as edit them, using the Gluepoints toolbar.

1) Click on the **Gluepoints** icon 🖉 on the Drawing toolbar or go to **View > Toolbars > Gluepoints** on the main menu bar to open the toolbar (Figure 98).

2) Select an object on your slide.

3) To insert a new glue point onto the selected object, click on the **Insert Glue Point** icon.

4) If you want to fix the direction a connector uses when connecting to a glue point, click on one of the exit direction icons. This is useful if you have multiple connectors terminating on one side of an object or the position of the default glue point is not satisfactory.

5) Move the cursor to the position you require on the selected object, then click the mouse button to insert the glue point.

6) Make sure that the **Glue point relative** icon is selected to maintain the relative position of a glue point when resizing the object.

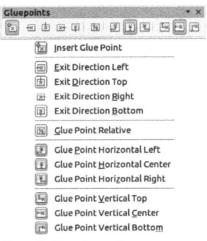

Figure 98: Gluepoints toolbar

7) Deselecting the **Glue point relative** icon activates the remaining six icons on the toolbar. Use these tools to fix the position of the glue point during the resizing of the object.

8) To delete a glue point you have inserted, select it with the cursor and press the *Delete* key. The default glue points on an object cannot be deleted.

9) To move a glue point you have inserted, select it with the cursor and drag the glue point to a new position. The default glue points on an object cannot be moved.

Tip	Glue points are placed by default on the grid (see "Snapping objects to grid or snap guides" on page 124 for information). However it is sometimes necessary to fine tune the position of a glue point depending on the shape of the object. To do this, press the *Ctrl* key to display guide lines and keep the *Ctrl* key pressed while dragging the glue point to the new position.

Working with 3D objects

Although Impress offers advanced functions to manipulate 3D objects, this guide describes only the 3D settings applicable to an object. For additional information on how to use advanced 3D effects such as geometry and shading, refer to the *Draw Guide*.

3D objects can be created in Impress in any of the following ways:

- Click on the triangle to the right of the **3D Objects** icon on the Drawing toolbar and select a 3D object from the options. After selection, draw your 3D object on your slide as you would with any object. The **3D Objects** icon shown on the Drawing toolbar will depend on the 3D object that had been previously selected and used.

- Go to **View > Toolbars > 3D-Objects** on the main menu bar to open the 3D-Objects toolbar (Figure 99). The selection and drawing of 3D objects is the same as clicking on the **3D Objects** icon on the Drawing toolbar.

- Right-click on an object already on your slide and select **Convert > To 3D** or **To 3D Rotation Object** from the context menu. **To 3D** adds thickness to the object to create a 3D object. **To 3D Rotation Object** creates a 3D object by rotating the object around an axis.

Figure 99: 3D-Objects toolbar

- Select an object and click on the **Extrusion on/off** icon on the Drawing toolbar to apply a basic 3D effect and open the 3D-Settings toolbar. Select one of the options on the 3D-Settings toolbar to apply a different 3D effect (Figure 100 and Table 5).

Figure 100: 3D-Settings toolbar

Table 5: 3D-Settings tools and their purpose

Tool	Name	Purpose
	Extrusion On/Off	Adds thickness to an object and activates the 3D properties.
	Tilt Down	Tilts the object downwards around a horizontal axis.
	Tilt Up	Tilts the object up around a horizontal axis.
	Tilt Left	Tilts the object left around a vertical axis.
	Tilt Right	Tilts the object right around a vertical axis.
	Depth	Determines the thickness of the shape. An extended toolbar opens where some default values are given. If none of the values are satisfactory, select **Custom** and then enter the desired thickness.
	Direction	Opens an extended toolbar that lets you pick the direction of the perspective as well as the type (parallel or perspective).
	Lighting	Opens an extended toolbar that lets you specify the direction and intensity of light.
	Surface	Choose between Wire frame (useful when manipulating the object), Matt, Plastic, or Metal.
	3D Color	Selects the color of the object thickness.

Note	Most of the Fontwork shapes (see "Using Fontwork" on page 132) have 3D properties and can be manipulated with the 3D-Settings toolbar.

Converting objects to different types

You can convert an object into a different type. Right-click on the object and select **Convert** from the context menu to display the following options:

- **To Curve** – converts the selected object to a Bézier curve. Click on the **Points** icon on the Drawing toolbar to edit the points after conversion to a Bézier curve.

- **To Polygon** – converts the selected object to a polygon. Click on the **Points** icon to edit the object after conversion to a polygon. A polygon always consists of straight segments.

- **To Contour** – for basic shapes, this is equivalent to converting to polygon. For more complex shapes (or for text objects) this conversion creates a group of polygons that you can then manipulate by pressing *F3* to enter the group.

- **To 3D** – converts the selected object to a 3D object.

- **To 3D Rotation Object** – creates a three-dimensional shape by rotating the selected object around its vertical axis.
- **To Bitmap** – converts the selected object to a bitmap.
- **To Metafile** – converts the selected object to Windows Metafile Format (WMF), containing both bitmap and vector graphic data.

Note	In most cases the conversion to a different type does not produce immediately visible results.

Tip	**To Curve**, **To Polygon**, **To 3D**, and **To 3D Rotation Object** can be added to the Drawing toolbar as additional tools by right-clicking in an empty area on the toolbar and selecting **Visible Buttons**.

Setting up interaction with an object

You can associate an object to an action that is performed when it is clicked and this is called an interaction:

1) Select the object for which an interaction will be created.
2) Click on the **Interaction** icon 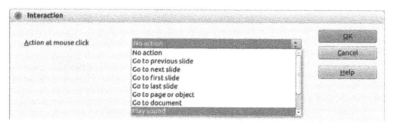 on the Line and Filling toolbar or right-click on the object and select **Interaction** from the context menu to open the **Interaction** dialog (Figure 101).
3) Select the interaction type and the parameters (if applicable). The interactions are explained in Table 6 and the Interaction dialog changes depending on the type of interaction selected.
4) Click **OK** to close the dialog.
5) To remove an interaction from a graphic object follow Steps 1 to 2 and then select **No action** as the interaction type at Step 3.

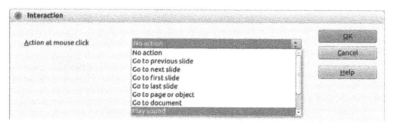

Figure 101: Interaction dialog

Table 6: Interaction types and their parameters

Interaction	Parameters
Go to previous slide	No parameters.
Go to next slide	No parameters.
Go to first slide	No parameters.
Go to last slide	No parameters.
Go to page or object	Specify the target from the list in the Target box. You can search for a specific target in the Slide/Object box at the bottom of the screen.

Interaction	Parameters
Go to document	Select the document in the Document box. Use the Browse button to open a File Open dialog. If the document to be opened is in Open Document Presentation format, the target list will be populated allowing selection of the specific target.
Play sound	Select the file containing the sound to be played. Use the Browse button to open a File Open dialog.
Run program	Select the program to execute. Use the Browse button to open a File Open dialog.
Run macro	Select a macro that will run during the presentation. Use the Browse button to open the Macro Selector dialog.
Exit presentation	When the mouse is clicked over the object, the presentation will terminate.

Using Fontwork

Use Fontwork to obtain special text effects. For more about this topic, see the *Getting Started Guide Chapter 11 Graphics, the Gallery, and Fontwork*.

To start using Fontwork:

1) Click on the **Fontwork Gallery** icon 🄰 on the Drawing toolbar or on the Fontwork toolbar to open the Fontwork Gallery dialog (Figure 102).

Figure 102: Fontwork Gallery

2) Select the preferred style from the Fontwork Gallery dialog and click **OK**. The text *Fontwork* in the selected style appears on the slide. You can modify its shape and properties after it has been placed on the slide.

3) Double-click the object to edit the Fontwork text. Type your own text to replace the word *Fontwork* that appears over the object.

4) Press the *Esc* key or click outside the area with the selection handles to exit.

Using the Fontwork toolbar

Make sure that the Fontwork toolbar (Figure 103) is visible on the workspace. If not, select **View > Toolbars > Fontwork** from the main menu bar.

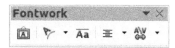

Figure 103: Fontwork toolbar

In addition to the Fontwork Gallery icon, this toolbar contains the following tools:

- **Fontwork Shape** – changes the shape of the selected object. Shapes are selected from the options that become available when you click on the icon.

- **Fontwork Same Letter Heights** – changes the height of characters in the selected object. Toggles between normal height where characters have different heights to where all characters are the same height.

- **Fontwork Alignment:** – specifies the text alignment within the frame from the options available.

- **Fontwork Character Spacing** – selects the desired spacing between characters and whether kerning pairs should be used. For custom spacing, input a percentage value: 100% is normal spacing; less than 100% is tight spacing; more than 100% is expanded spacing.

Modifying Fontwork as an object

It is possible to treat Fontwork text as an object and therefore to apply to it all the formatting that has been described in this chapter. Assign line properties only to Fontwork which does not have a 3D effect, otherwise the changes will not be visible.

You can modify some of the Fontwork shapes just as you modify the angles of trapezoid and parallelogram basic shapes by moving the dot that is displayed along with the selection handles.

Animations

Animated slide transitions can be added between slides to give your presentation a more professional look when you change to the next slide (see *Chapter 9 Slide Shows* for more information on transitions). However, Impress also allows you to add animations onto the slides to create more interest in your presentation.

An animation consists of a sequence of images or objects called frames that are displayed in succession when the animation runs. Each frame may contain one or more objects. For example, make bullet points appear one by one; make pictures, shapes or other objects appear singly or as a group onto a slide. Animations can be controlled using the keyboard or mouse click or automatically in a timed sequence.

Custom Animation

The *Custom Animation* section (Figure 104) is located in the Sidebar to the right of the Workspace in Impress. It is used to add an animation effect to an object on a slide, or change the animation effect of an object. To open the *Custom Animation* section, click on the **Custom Animation** icon on the Sidebar, or right-click on a selected object and select **Custom Animation** on the context menu, go to **Slide Show > Custom Animation** on the main menu bar.

Custom animation options

The available options on the Custom Animation section on the Sidebar allows you to control how the animation is animated on your slide.

Figure 104: Sidebar Custom Animation

- **Add Effect** – click on this icon to open the Custom Animation dialog (Figure 105) and add an animation effect to an object on a slide.
- **Remove Effect** – click on this icon to remove any selected animation effects from an object.

- **Modify Effect** 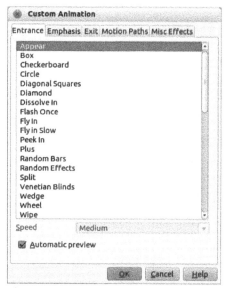 – click on this icon to open the Custom Animation dialog (Figure 105) and modify an animation effect applied to an object on a slide.

- **Move Up** ⇧ – click on this icon to move the selected animation effect up the order of animation effects that have been applied to an object.

- **Move Down** ⇩ – click on this icon to move the selected animation effect down the order of animation effects that have been applied to an object.

- **Preview Effect** – click on this icon to preview the selected animation effect applied to an object.

- **Start** – select from the drop-down list how an animation effect starts when running an animation:

    - *On click* – the animation stops at this effect until the next mouse click.

    - *With previous* – the animation runs immediately.

    - *After previous* – the animation runs as soon as the previous animation ends.

- **Direction** – select from the drop-down list how an animation effect appears on the slide.

- **Speed** – select the speed or duration of the selected animation effect.

- **Automatic preview** – select this option to automatically preview an animation effect as it is selected in the Custom Animation dialog (Figure 105).

- **Effect Options** – click this icon to open the Effect Options dialog (Figure 106) where you can select, adjust and apply options to the animation effect and timing.

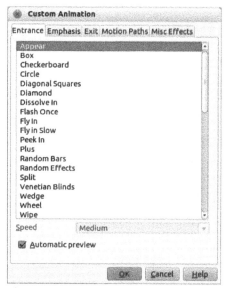

Figure 105: Custom Animation dialog

Custom Animation dialog

The Custom Animation dialog (Figure 105) contains the following tabbed pages for creating animation effects on a selected object:

- **Entrance** – how an animated object appears on the slide.
- **Emphasis** – how an animated object is emphasized when it appears on the slide.
- **Exit** – how an animated object leaves the slide.
- **Motion Paths** – how an object moves on the slide during animation.
- **Misc Effects** – selects media effects from the miscellaneous effects.
- **Automatic preview** – previews any new or edited animation effects on the slide.

Effect Options dialog

The Effect Options dialog (Figure 106) specifies the settings and enhancements on how an animation effect appears on your slide.

Figure 106: Effect Options dialog

The **Effect** page contains the following options:

- **Direction** – specifies the direction for the effect and is the same option that is displayed in the *Custom Animation* section on the Sidebar.
- **Sound** – select a sound from the drop-down list when the animation effect is run.
- **After animation** – select from the drop-down list what happens after an animation effect ends.
    - *Dim with color* – after the animation a dim color fills the shape.
    - *Don't dim* – no after-effect runs.
    - *Hide after animation* – hides the shape after the animation ends.
    - *Hide on next animation* – hides the shape on the next animation.
- **Dim color** – select a dim color.
- **Text animation** – select the animation mode for the text of the current shape:
    - *All at once* – animates the text all at once.

- *Word by word* – animates the text word by word.
- *Letter by letter* – animates the text letter by letter.
- **Delay between characters** – specifies the percentage of delay between animations of words or letters.

The **Timing** page contains the following options:
- **Start** – displays the start property of the selected animation effect. The following start properties are available:
  - *On click* – the animation stops at this effect until the next mouse click.
  - *With previous* – the animation runs immediately.
  - *After previous* – the animation runs as soon as the previous animation ends.
- **Delay** – specifies an additional delay in seconds until the effect starts.
- **Speed** – specifies the duration of the effect.
- **Repeat** – specifies whether and how to repeat the current effect. Enter the number of repeats, or select from the list:
  - *none* – the effect is not repeated.
  - *Until next click* – the animation is repeated until the next mouse click.
  - *Until end of slide* – the animation repeats as long as the slide is displayed.
- **Rewind when done playing** – specifies whether to let the animated shape return to its starting state after the animation ends.
- **Animate as part of click sequence** – specifies whether to let the animation start in the normal click sequence.
- **Start effect on click of** – specifies whether to let the animation start when a specified shape is clicked. Select the shape by its name from the drop-down list.

Creating an animation

To create an animated object or objects using *Custom Animation*:
1) Select an object on a slide.
2) Open the *Custom Animation* section (Figure 104) in the Sidebar, or go to **Slide Show > Custom Animation** on the main menu bar.
3) Click on **Add** in *Custom Animation* to open the Custom Animation dialog (Figure 105).
4) Select an effect category and the type of effect you want to apply to the selected object.
5) Select how the effect starts, the direction, and the speed (if available) of the effect from the various options included on the drop-down lists.
6) Click **Effect Options** icon ⬚ to open the Effect Options dialog (Figure 106) to set the effect options for the animation, then click **OK** to close the dialog.
7) If necessary, change the appearance order of the objects in the animation using the **Move Up** ⬆ and **Move Down** ⬇ icons.
8) Click **Preview Effect** ▶ icon to check the animation effect.
9) When you are satisfied, run the slide show to check your presentation.

Inserting animated images

You can create an animated image and then insert it into your presentation by going to **Insert > Animated Image** on the main menu bar to open the Animation dialog (Figure 107). The animation controls are explained in Table 7.

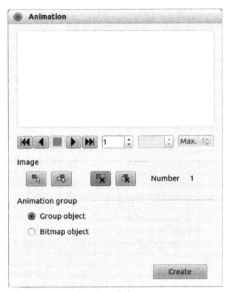

Figure 107: Animation dialog

Table 7: Animation dialog controls

Control	Control Name	Purpose
⏮	First image	Jumps to the first image in the animation sequence.
◀	Backwards	Plays the animation backwards.
⏹	Stop	Stops playing the animation.
▶	Play	Plays the animation.
⏭	Last image	Jumps to the last image in the animation sequence.
2 ⇕	Image number	Indicates the position of the current image in the animation sequence. If you want to view another image, enter its number or click the up and down arrows.
0.00 ⇕	Duration	Enter the number of seconds to display the current image. This option is only available if you select *Bitmap object* in **Animation group**.
Max. ⇕	Loop count	Sets the number of times that animation will play. If you want the animation to play continuously, select **Max**. This option is only available if you select *Bitmap object* in **Animation group**.
🖺	Apply Object	Adds selected object or objects as a single image.

Control	Control Name	Purpose
	Apply Objects Individually	Adds an image for each selected object. If you select a grouped object, an image is created for each object in the group.
		You can also select an animation, such as an animated GIF, and click this icon to open it for editing. When you are finished editing the animation, click **Create** to insert a new animation into your slide.
	Delete Current Image	Deletes the current image from the animation sequence.
	Delete All Images	Deletes all images in the animation.
	Number	Total number of images in the animation.
	Group object	Assembles images into a single object so that they can be moved as a group. You can still edit individual objects by double-clicking the group in the slide.
	Bitmap object	Combines images into a single image.
	Create	Inserts the animation into the current slide.

Creating an animation

To create an animation using **Insert > Animated Image** on the menu bar:

1) Create the object you intend to animate, using the drawing tools.
2) Go to **Insert > Animated Image** on the menu bar to open the Animation dialog (Figure 107 and Table 7).
3) Select the object and click on **Apply Object** icon to add it as the first frame of the animation.
4) Apply a transformation or change to the object; for example, rotation, change color, add or remove characters, and so on.
5) When you are ready, create the second frame of the animation and click **Apply Object** again to add another frame to the animation.
6) Repeat steps 3, 4, and 5 until you have created all the desired frames of the animation.
7) Select *Bitmap object* in **Animation group** to customize the timing of each of the frames and the number of repetitions for the animation.
8) Set the duration of each frame in the animation in *Duration* and the number of repetitions in *Max* to create a loop for your animation. Selecting *Max* creates a continuous loop.
9) Click **Create** and the animated image is placed in the center on your slide.
10) Adjust the position of your animated object on your slide.

Note	If the image to be copied consists of several objects, you can choose to treat each object as a separate frame. In this case, click on **Apply objects individually** icon. Remember that each object will be centered in the animation.

Chapter 6
Formatting Graphic Objects

Formatting objects

This chapter describes how to format the graphic objects created with the available drawing tools.

The format of each graphic object, in addition to its size, rotation and position on the slide, is determined by a number of attributes that define the line, text and area fill of each object. These attributes (among others) also contribute to a *graphics style.* Although this chapter discusses mainly the manual formatting of objects, it concludes by showing how to create, apply, modify and delete graphics styles.

Formatting lines

In LibreOffice the term *line* indicates both a freestanding segment and the outer edge of a shape. In most cases the properties of the line you can modify are its style (solid, dashed, invisible, and so on), its width and its color. Select the line you need to format and then use the controls on the Line and Filling toolbar to select your desired options (highlighted in Figure 108).

Figure 108: Common line options on the Line and Filling toolbar

For more control when changing the appearance of a line, go to **Format > Line** on the main menu bar, or right-click on the line and select **Line** from the context menu, or select the **Line** icon on the Line and Filling toolbar to open the Line dialog (Figure 109) where you can set line properties. This dialog consists of four pages: *Line, Shadow, Line Styles,* and *Arrow Styles.*

You can also use the Line section on the Sidebar to change the appearance of a line. See "Sidebar Line section" on page 147 for more information.

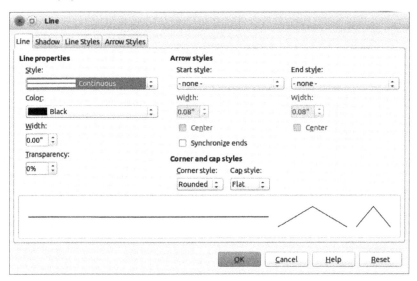

Figure 109: Line dialog – Line page

Line page

The Line page on the Line dialog is where you can set the basic parameters of the line. The page is divided into four sections: *Line properties*, *Arrow styles*, *Width*, and *Corner and cap styles*. At the bottom of the page is a preview of the applied styles for a line and two different corners, so you can evaluate the corner and cap style selections.

Line properties

The *Line Properties* section on the left side allows you to set the following parameters:

- **Line style** – several line styles are available from the drop-down list, but more line styles can be defined if necessary.
- **Color** – choose from the predefined colors in the drop down list or refer to "Custom colors" on page 151 to create a new color.
- **Width** – specifies the thickness of the line.
- **Transparency** – sets the transparency of a line. Figure 110 illustrates the effects of different percentages of transparency to lines when placed over an object.

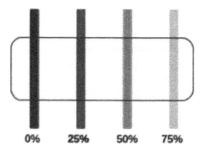

Figure 110: Line transparency effect

Arrow styles

The *Arrow styles* section is only applicable to individual lines and is not used for lines that form the borders of an object. To create a new arrow style, see "Arrow styles page" on page 145.

- **Style** – sets the style of the two ends of a line. The left drop down menu is for where you start the line and the right drop down menu is for where you end the line.
- **Width** – specifies the thickness of the arrow endings
- **Center** – moves the center of the arrow endings to the end point of the line. Figure 111 shows the effects of selecting this option.
- **Synchronize ends** – makes the two line ends identical.

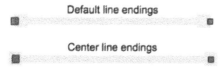

Figure 111: Line arrow endings

Arrowheads

A quick way to set the arrowheads for a selected line is to click on the **Arrow Style** icon in the Line and Filling toolbar (Figure 108) to open the Arrowheads toolbar (Figure 112). Use this toolbar to select one of the many predefined arrowhead styles for the start and ending of a selected line.

Figure 112: Arrowheads menu

Corner and cap styles

Corner and cap styles determine how the connection between two segments of a line looks. There are four available options for corner styles (*none*, *Rounded*, *Mitered*, *Beveled*) and three cap styles (*Flat*, *Round*, *Square*). To appreciate the difference between corner and cap styles, choose a thick line style and observe how the preview changes as you select each option.

Shadow page

Use the *Shadow* page of the *Line* dialog to add and format the line shadow. The settings on this page are the same as those for shadows applied to other objects and are described in Formatting shadows on page 159.

A quicker way to apply a shadow to a line is using the **Shadow** icon on the Line and Filling toolbar (Figure 108). The main disadvantage of using the **Shadow** icon is that the shadow appearance will be constrained by the shadow settings of the default graphics style.

Line styles page

Use the *Line Styles* page (Figure 113) of the Line dialog to create new line styles as well as loading previously saved line styles. It is recommended to create new styles when necessary than to modify the predefined styles.

To create a new line style:

1) Choose **Format > Line** from the menu bar, or right-click on the line and select **Line** from the context menu, or select the **Line** icon from the Line and Filling toolbar.

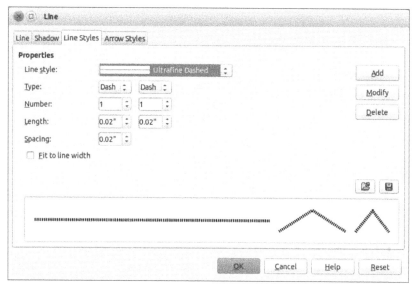

Figure 113: Line dialog – Line Styles page

2) Click on the **Line Styles** tab.

3) Select from the **Line style** drop-down menu a style similar to the style you want to create.

4) Click **Add**. On the pop-up dialog, type a name for the new line style and click **OK**.

5) Now define the new style. Start by selecting the line type for the new style. To alternate two line types (for example, dashes and dots) within a single line, select different types in the two **Type** boxes.

6) Specify the **Number** and **Length** (not available for dot style) of each of the types of line selected.

7) Set the **Spacing** between the various elements

8) If necessary, select **Fit to line width** so that the new style fits the width of the selected line.

9) The new line style created is available only in the current document. If you want to use the line style in other presentations, click the **Save Line Styles** icon ▣ and type a unique filename in the *Save as* dialog that opens. Saved styles have the file extension of .sod.

10) To use previously saved line styles, click the **Load Line Styles** icon ▨ and select a style from the list of saved styles. Click **Open** to load the style into your presentation.

11) If necessary, click on the **Modify** button to change the name of the style.

Arrow styles page

Use the *Arrow Styles* page (Figure 114) of the Line dialog to create new arrow styles, or modify existing arrow styles, or load previously saved arrow styles.

Note	The arrowhead created must be convertible to a *curve*. A curve is something you can draw without lifting a pencil. For example, ☆ can be converted to a curve, but ☺ cannot.

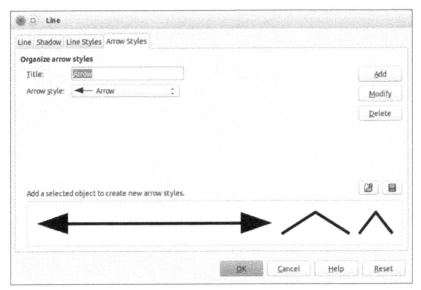

Figure 114: Line dialog – Arrow Styles page

1) First draw a curve in the shape you want to use for the arrowhead or create a shape and convert to a curve. The top of the shape must face upward, as shown in Figure 115, because this becomes the point of the arrow.

> **Note** The arrowhead created must be convertible to a *curve*. A curve is something you can draw without lifting a pencil. For example, ☆ can be converted to a curve, but ☺ cannot.

Figure 115: Using a pentagon shape for arrow styles

2) Select the shape and, if necessary, right click and choose **Convert > To Curve** from the context menu to convert the shape to a curve. If the shape is already a curve, **To Curve** will not be available.

3) With the selection handles showing, select **Format > Line** from the menu bar, or right-click and choose **Line** from the context menu.

4) Go to the *Arrow Styles* page (Figure 114), click the **Add** button, type a name for the new arrow style and click **OK**. The new arrowhead style will be shown in the preview.

5) Now you can access the new style from the Arrow style list. When you select the name of the new style, it is shown at the bottom of the dialog.

6) The new arrowhead style created is available only in the current document. If you want to use this arrowhead style in other presentations, click the **Save Line Styles** icon 🖫 and type a unique filename in the *Save as* dialog that opens. Saved styles have the file extension of .sod.

7) To use previously saved arrowhead styles, click the **Load Line Styles** icon 🗁 and select the style from the saved list of styles. Click **Open** to load the style into your presentation.

8) If necessary, click on the **Modify** button to change the name of the style.

Sidebar Line section

The Line section (Figure 116) on the Sidebar allows you to quickly change the appearance of a line and this section only becomes active when a graphical object is selected. You can change the *Width, Color, Transparency, Style, Arrow, Corner style* and *Cap style* of a selected graphical object and these options are described in "Line page", "Line styles page" and "Arrow styles page" above.

Clicking on the **More Options** icon in the right corner of the title bar will open the Line dialog (Figure 113) giving you more control over the appearance of lines.

Figure 116: Sidebar Line section

Formatting area fills

The term **area fill** refers to the inside of an object that has an unbroken border, for example a rectangle, circle, star, pentagon and so on. An area fill can be a uniform color, gradient, hatching pattern, or bitmap (Figure 117). An area fill can also be made partly or wholly transparent and can throw a shadow.

The Line and Filling toolbar has several tools normally used to quickly format graphic objects. If this toolbar is not visible, go to **View > Toolbars > Line and Filling** on the menu bar. You can also use the Area dialog to quickly format objects, see "Using Area dialog" on page 148 for more information.

Once you have decided on a predefined or custom fill, you can further refine it by adding a shadow or transparency. See "Formatting shadows" on page 159 and "Formatting transparencies" on page 160 for more information.

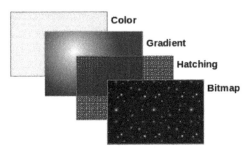

Figure 117: Different types of area fill

Using Line and Filling toolbar

Figure 118: Common area fill options highlighted

To quickly format an area fill of an object using the Line and Filling toolbar (Figure 118):

1) Select the object you wish to edit.

2) On the Line and Filling toolbar, click the left **Area Style/Filling** button and select the type of area fill (*Invisible*, *Color*, *Gradient*, *Hatching* or *Bitmap*) you want to use from the options listed in the drop-down list.

3) On the Line and Filling toolbar, click the right **Area Style/Filling** button and select the color or type of area fill you want to use from the options listed in the drop-down list. The available options change depending on the type of area fill selected. This button is not available when *None* is selected for the area fill.

Note	If you do not require an area fill for an object, select *None* from the options available when you click the left **Area Style/Filling** button on the Line and Filling toolbar.

Using Area dialog

To quickly format an area fill of an object using the Area dialog, use the following procedure. You can also use the Area dialog to create your own area fill.

1) Select the object you wish to edit.

2) Go to **Format > Area** on the menu bar, or click the **Area** icon on the Line and Filling toolbar, or right-click on the object and select **Area** from the context menu to open the Area dialog.

Note	If you do not require a fill for an object when using the Area dialog, select *None* from the options available.

3) For color area fills, select **Color** from the drop down list and then select your required color from the list of available colors (Figure 119).

4) Click **OK** and the color will appear as an area fill in the selected object.

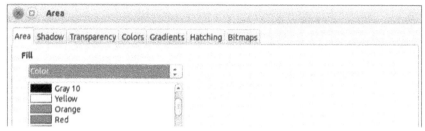

Figure 119: Area color dialog

5) For gradient area fills, select **Gradient** from the drop down list and then select your required gradient from the list of available gradients (Figure 120).

6) To override the number of steps (increments) that are applied to the gradient transition in a gradient fill, deselect **Automatic** in *Increments* and then enter the number of steps required in the text box.

7) Click **OK** and the gradient will appear as an area fill in the selected object.

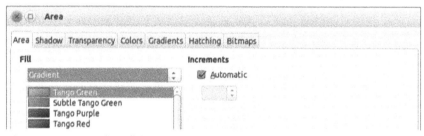

Figure 120: Area gradient dialog

8) For hatching area fills, select **Hatching** from the drop down list and then select your required hatching from the list of available hatchings (Figure 121).

9) Select **Background color** and select a background color for the hatching from the drop down list.

10) Click **OK** and the hatching will appear as an area fill in the selected object.

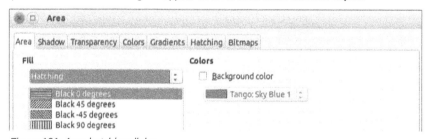

Figure 121: Area hatching dialog

11) For bitmap area fills, select **Bitmaps** from the drop down list and then select your required bitmap from the list of available bitmaps (Figure 122).

12) Set the **Size**, **Position** and **Offset** options as necessary. See Table 8 for more information on bitmap options.

13) Click **OK** and the bitmap will appear as an area fill in the selected object.

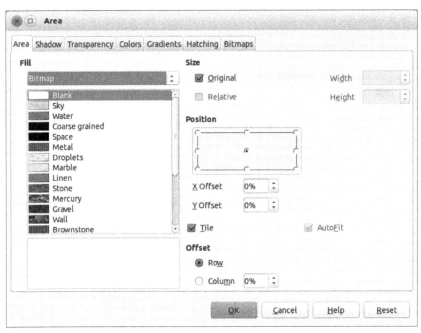

Figure 122: Area bitmap dialog

Table 8: Bitmap options

Option	Meaning
Size – Original	Retains the original size of the bitmap when filling the selected object. To resize the bitmap, clear this checkbox
Size – Relative	When selected, *Relative* rescales the bitmap relative to the size of the bitmap by percentage values entered in the *Width* and *Height* boxes. Clear this checkbox to resize the bitmap using the linear measurements entered in the *Width* and *Height* boxes.
Size – Width	Enter a width for the bitmap. When *Relative* is selected 100% means that the original bitmap width will be resized to occupy the whole fill area width; 50% means that the width of the bitmap will be half that of the fill area.
Size – Height	Enter a height for the bitmap. When *Relative* is selected 100% means that the original bitmap height will be resized to occupy the whole fill area height; 50% means that the height of the bitmap will be half that of the fill area.
Position – Anchor Point	Click in the position grid to specify an anchor point for the offset for tiling the bitmap.
Position – X offset	When *Tile* is selected, enter a horizontal offset from the anchor point for the bitmap in percentage values.
Position – Y offset	When *Tile* is selected, enter a vertical offset from the anchor point for the bitmap in percentage values.
Position – Tile	Tiles the bitmap to fill the selected object. The size of the bitmap used for the tiling is determined by the **Size** options.

Option	Meaning
Position – Autofit	Stretches the bitmap to fill the selected object. To use *Autofit*, uncheck the *Tile* option. Selecting *Autofit* disables all size settings.
Offset – Row	When *Tile* is selected, offsets the rows of tiled bitmaps by the entered percentage value so that each row is offset from the previous row.
Offset – Column	When *Tile* is selected, offsets the columns of tiled bitmaps by the entered percentage value so that each column is offset from the previous column.

Sidebar Area section

The Area section (Figure 123) on the Sidebar allows you to quickly change the appearance of the fill in an object and this section only becomes active when a graphical object is selected. You can change the *Fill* and *Transparency* of a selected graphical object and these options are described in "Using Area dialog" above.

Clicking on the **More Options** icon in the right corner of the title bar will open the Area dialog giving you more control over the appearance of the object fill.

Figure 123: Sidebar Area section

Creating new area fills

The following sections describe how to create new fills and how to apply them.

Although you can change the characteristics of an existing fill and then click the **Modify** button, it is recommended that you create new fills or modify custom fills rather than the predefined area fills, as these predefined area fills may be reset when updating LibreOffice.

Custom colors

On the *Colors* page of the Area dialog (Figure 124), you can modify existing colors or create your own. You can specify a new color either as a combination of the three primary colors Red (R), Green (G), and Blue (B), (RGB notation) or by percentages of Cyan (C), Magenta (M), Yellow (Y) and Black (K) (CMYK notation).

Creating new colors

1) Enter a name for the color you want to create in the *Name* box.
2) Select whether to define the color in RGB or CMYK. For RGB, specify the RGB components on a 0 to 255 scale. For CMYK, specify the CMYK components from 0% to 100%.
3) Click the **Add** button. The color is now added to the *Color* drop down list.

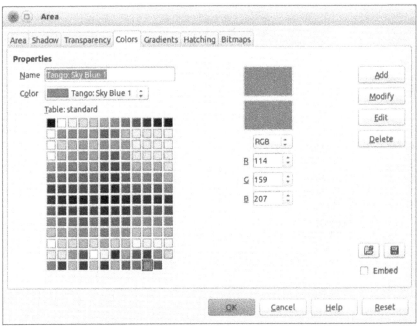

Figure 124: Area dialog – Colors page

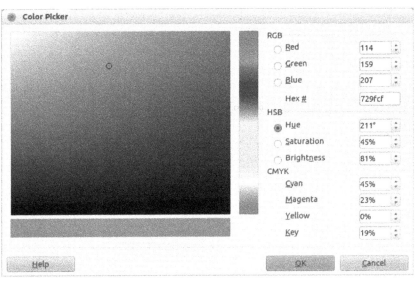

Figure 125: Color Picker dialog

Modifying colors

1) Select the color you want to modify from the *Color* drop down list.
2) Select either RGB or CMYK and enter the new values to define the color.
3) If necessary, type a new name in the *Name* box.
4) Click **Modify** and the modified color is saved.

Editing colors

1) Click **Edit** to open the Color Picker dialog (Figure 125).
2) Modify the color components as required using either RGB, CMYK or HSB (Hue, Saturation, Brightness) values.
3) Click **OK** to close the Color Picker dialog.
4) Click the **Modify** button on the Color dialog.
5) Click **OK** to save the changes and close the Area dialog.

Saving and using custom colors

Any new color created or modified is available only in the current document. If you want to use this color in other presentations, click the **Save Color List** icon 🖫 and type a unique filename in the **Save as** dialog that opens. The file created for a list of saved colors has the file extension of .soc.

To use a previously saved color list , click the **Load Color List** icon 🖼 and select the file used for a custom color list from the file open dialog. Click **Open** to load the saved color list into Impress.

Tip	You can also add custom colors using **Tools > Options > LibreOffice > Colors**. This method makes the color available to all components of LibreOffice. Colors created using the above procedures are only available for Impress.

Custom gradients

On the *Gradients* page of the Area dialog (Figure 126), you can modify existing gradients or create your own gradient. Several types of gradients are predefined in LibreOffice and changing the *From* and *To* colors could be sufficient to obtain a satisfactory result.

Creating or modifying gradients

1) Select a gradient type from the *Type* drop down list: *Linear, Axial, Radial, Ellipsoid,* or *Square.*
2) Alternatively, select one of the predefined gradient types shown in the preview box.
3) Adjust the option settings as necessary. The options used to create a gradient are summarized in Table 9. Depending on the gradient type selected, some options will not be available.
4) Click **Add** to add the newly created gradient to the list.
5) It is recommended to type a memorable name for the new gradient instead of using the default name of Gradient 1, Gradient 2 and so on.
6) Click **OK** to save the new gradient.
7) Click **OK** to close the Area dialog.

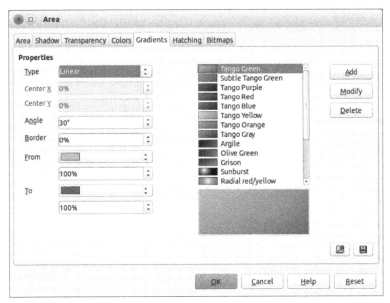

Figure 126: Area dialog – Gradients page

Table 9: Gradient options

Option	Meaning
Center X	For Radial, Ellipsoid, Square and Rectangular gradients, modify these values to set the horizontal offset of the gradient center.
Center Y	For Radial, Ellipsoid, Square and Rectangular gradients, modify these values to set the vertical offset of the gradient center.
Angle	For all the gradient types, specifies the angle of the gradient axis.
Border	Increase this value to make the gradient start further away from the border of the object.
From	The start color for the gradient. In the edit box below enter the intensity of the color: 0% corresponds to black, 100% to the full color.
To	The end color for the gradient. In the edit box below enter the intensity of the color: 0% corresponds to black, 100% to the full color.

Saving and using custom gradients

Any new gradient created or modified is available only in the current document. If you want to use this gradient in other presentations, click the **Save Gradients List** icon and type a unique filename in the **Save as** dialog that opens. The file created for a list of saved gradients has the file extension of .sog.

To use a previously saved gradients list, click the **Load Gradients List** icon and select the file used a custom gradient list from the file open dialog. Click **Open** to load the saved gradients list into Impress.

Advanced gradient controls

Gradient properties can be configured using the options given in Figure 126 and Table 9. Impress provides a graphical interface for modifying these gradient options using only the mouse as follows.

1) Select an object that has a gradient and open the **Mode** toolbar by going to **View > Toolbars > Mode** (Figure 127).

Figure 127: Mode toolbar

2) Open the Gradients page of the Area dialog, see "Creating or modifying gradients" above.

3) Click on the **Gradient** icon 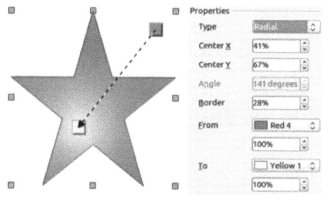 in the Mode toolbar to display a dashed line connected to squares at each end of the dashed line. The colors displayed in the two squares show the **From** and **To** colors used for the selected gradient (Figure 128).

Figure 128: Using mouse to change gradient options

4) The gradient used for area fill in the object is adjusted as follows depending on the type of gradient:

Linear gradients – move the square corresponding to the *From* color to change where the gradient starts (border value). Move the square corresponding to the *To* color to change the orientation (angle value).

Axial gradients – only the *To* color can be moved to change both the angle and border properties of the gradient.

Radial gradients – move the *From* color to modify the border property to set the width of the gradient circle. Move the *To* color to change the point where the gradient ends (*Center X* and *Center Y* values).

Ellipsoid gradients – move the *From* color to modify the border property to set the size of the gradient ellipsoid. Move the *To* color to change the angle of the ellipsoid axis and the axis itself.

Square gradients – move the *From* color to modify the border to set the size of the gradient square and the angle of the gradient shape. Move the *To* color to change the center of the gradient.

5) When you are satisfied with the changes, click anywhere outside the selected object to deselect it.

Note	Moving the squares will have different effects depending on the type of gradient. For example, for a linear gradient, the start and end squares of the gradient will always be situated to either side of the center point of the object.

Custom hatching patterns

To create new hatching patterns or modify existing hatching patterns, select the *Hatching* tab of the Area dialog (Figure 129). The options that can be set for a hatching pattern are explained in Table 10.

Creating or modifying hatching patterns

1) Select one of the predefined gradient types shown in the preview box
2) Modify the options of the lines forming the pattern. A preview is displayed in the window below the available patterns.
3) Click **Add** to add the newly created hatching pattern to the list.
4) It is recommended to type a memorable name for the new gradient instead of using the default name of Hatching 1, Hatching 2 and so on.
5) Click **OK** to save the new hatching pattern.
6) Click **OK** to close the Area dialog.

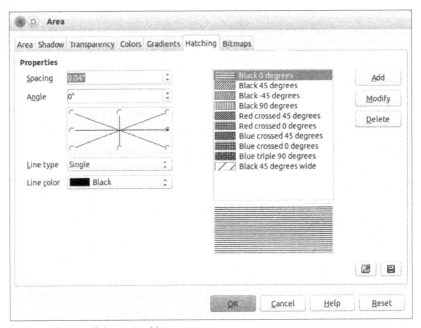

Figure 129: Area dialog – Hatching page

Table 10: Hatching pattern options

Option	Meaning
Spacing	Determines the spacing between two lines of the pattern. As the value is changed the preview window is updated.
Angle	Use the mini map below the numerical value to quickly set the angle formed by the line to multiples of 45 degrees. If the required angle is not a multiple of 45 degrees, just enter the desired value in the edit box.
Line type	Set single, double or triple line for the style of the pattern.
Line color	Use the list to select the color of the lines that will form the pattern.

Saving and using custom hatching patterns

Any new hatching pattern created or modified is available only in the current document. If you want to use this hatching pattern in other presentations, click the **Save Hatches List** icon ⊞ and type a unique filename in the **Save as** dialog that opens. The file created for a list of saved hatching patterns has the file extension of .soh.

To use a previously saved hatching patterns list, click the **Load Hatches List** icon ⊡ and select the file used for a custom hatching patterns list from the file open dialog. Click **Open** to load the saved hatching patterns list into Impress.

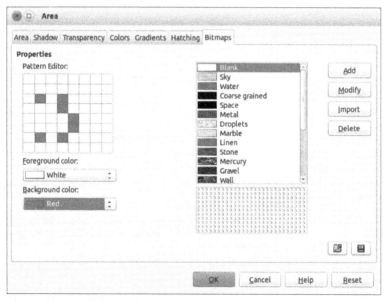

Figure 130: Area dialog – Bitmaps page

Custom bitmap fills

Creating bitmap fills

1) Select **Blank** as the bitmap type from the preview list on the **Bitmap** page of the Area dialog to activate the *Pattern Editor* (Figure 130).

2) Select the *Foreground* and *Background* colors you want to use for your bitmap from the drop down lists.

3) Start creating the pattern by clicking in the squares (pixels) that you want in the foreground color. The background color will automatically fill the grid used for the *Pattern Editor* when you select the color.

4) Check the preview window to see the effect being achieved as you click the mouse button in a square.

5) When satisfied with your bitmap, click **Add** to save the bitmap.

6) Enter a memorable name for your bitmap in the Name dialog that opens. It is recommended not to use the default names of Bitmap 1, Bitmap 2 and so on if you want to reuse the bitmap you have just created.

7) Click **OK** and your bitmap is added to the preview list and is used as an area fill for your selected object.

Modifying bitmaps

Modifying a bitmap that you created creates a copy of the bitmap so that you can edit the bitmap pattern.

1) Select a bitmap pattern that you created from the preview list on the **Bitmap** page of the Area dialog (Figure 130).

1) Click **Modify** and type a new name for the bitmap in the Name dialog that opens.

2) Click **OK**.

3) Select the newly named bitmap from the preview list and modify the pattern. See "Creating bitmap fills" above for more information.

Importing bitmaps

1) Click **Import** on the **Bitmap** page of the Area dialog (Figure 130).

2) Browse to the directory containing the bitmap file you want to import and select it.

3) Click **Open and** type a name for the imported bitmap.

4) Click **OK** and your imported bitmap is added to the preview list and is used as an area fill for your selected object.

Note	Bitmaps generally have an extension .bmp or .png. If you create a bitmap image with Draw, select **File > Export**, choose **PNG** from the pull-down list of file formats, give the file a name and save it.

Saving and using custom bitmaps

Any new bitmap created or modified is available only in the current document. If you want to use a custom bitmap in other presentations, click the **Save Bitmap List** icon and type a unique filename in the **Save as** dialog that opens. The file created for a list of saved bitmaps has the file extension of .sob.

To use a previously saved hatching patterns list, click the **Load Bitmap List** icon and select the file used for a bitmaps list from the file open dialog. Click **Open** to load the saved bitmap list into Impress.

Formatting shadows

Shadows can be applied to objects such as lines, shapes and text. In Impress you can quickly apply a default shadow or apply a customized shadow.

Default shadows

Default shadows use the Impress default settings and cannot be customized.

1) Select the object.
2) Click on the **Shadow** icon in the Line and Filling toolbar and a shadow is applied to the object.

Customizing shadows

To apply a customized shadow to an object, you have to use the Shadow on the Area dialog.

An alternative method for using customized shadows is to apply a style that uses a shadow See "Working with image styles" on page 164 for additional information on using styles.

1) Select the object and then select **Format > Area** on the main menu bar, or right click on the object and select Area from the context menu to open the Area dialog.
2) Click on the **Shadow** tab to open the Shadow page (Figure 131).

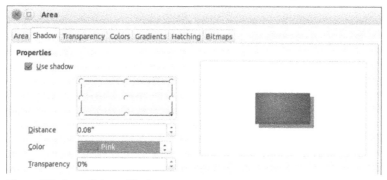

Figure 131: Area dialog – Shadow page

3) Select *Use shadow* and set the shadow options fas follows:
   Position – selects the point determining the direction in which the shadow is cast.
   Distance – determines the offset distance between the object and the shadow.
   Color – sets the color used for the shadow.
   Transparency – determines the amount of transparency for the shadow: 0% opaque shadow, 100% transparent shadow.
4) Click **OK** and the customized shadow is applied to the object.

Formatting transparencies

Transparencies can be applied to objects and to any shadow that has been applied to an object. In Impress two types of transparencies can be applied to an object – uniform transparency and gradient transparency. For more information on gradient transparencies, including an example of combining a color gradient with a gradient transparency, see "Advanced gradient controls" on page 155.

To apply transparencies to lines, refer to "Formatting lines" on page 142 for more information. To apply transparencies to shadows, refer to "Formatting shadows" on page 159 for more information.

1) Select the object and then select **Format > Area** on the main menu bar, or right click on the object and select Area from the context menu to open the Area dialog.

2) Click on the **Transparency** tab to open the Transparency page (Figure 132).

3) To create a uniform transparency, select *Transparency* and then select the percentage of transparency required.

4) To create a gradient transparency so that the area becomes gradually transparent, select *Gradient* and then set the options for the gradient. Refer to Table 11 for a description of the options available for gradient transparencies.

5) Click **OK** and the transparency is applied to the object.

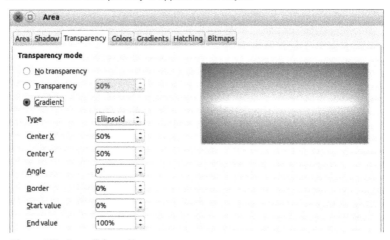

Figure 132: Area dialog – Transparency page

Table 11: Gradient transparency options

Option	Meaning
Type	Select the type of transparency gradient you want to apply.
Center X	Radial, Ellipsoid, Quadratic and Square gradients – modify this value to set the horizontal offset of the gradient center.
Center Y	Radial, Ellipsoid, Quadratic and Square gradients – modify this value to set the vertical offset of the gradient center.
Angle	Linear, Axial, Ellipsoid, Quadratic and Square gradient – specifies the angle of the gradient axis.

Option	Meaning
Border	Increase this value to make the gradient start further away from the border of the object.
Start value	Value for the starting transparency gradient. 0% is fully opaque, 100% is fully transparent.
End value	Value for the ending transparency gradient. 0% is fully opaque, 100% is fully transparent.

Formatting text in objects

Impress provides two dialogs related to text formatting on the main menu bar: **Format > Character** for individual characters and **Format > Paragraph** for paragraphs. However, this section only covers the formatting the appearance of any text which has been added to an object. For more information on formatting text that is used separately on a slide, see *Chapter 3 Adding and Formatting Text*.

Adding text to objects

To add text to an object:
1) Select the object to which text will be added so that the selection handles are showing.
2) Double-click on the object and the cursor becomes an I-beam to indicate text mode.
3) Type your text.
4) When finished, click outside of the object or press *Esc*.

Formatting and editing text in objects

To format text that has been placed into an object:
1) Select the object which contains text.
2) Select the object and go to **Format > Text** on the main menu bar or right-click on the object and select **Text** from the context menu to open the Text dialog (Figure 133).

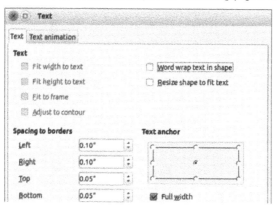

Figure 133: Text dialog

3) Format and edit the text using the available options. Some options will not be available depending on the type of object to which the text has been added.

Fit width to text – expands the width of the object if the text is too long.

Word wrap text in shape – starts a new line automatically when the edge of the object is reached.

Fit height to text – expands the object height whenever it is smaller than the text (set by default for lines).

Resize shape to fit text – expands an object when the text inserted in the object is too large.

Fit to frame – expands the text so that it fills all the available space.

Adjust to contour – makes the text follow a curved line.

Spacing to borders – specify the amount of space to be left between the borders of the object and the text. This is similar to setting indentation and spacing for paragraphs.

Text anchor – used to anchor the text to a particular point within the object.

Full width – when selected, anchors the text in the center of the object and uses the full width of the object before wrapping text.

4) Click **OK** to close the dialog and save the changes to the text.

Text animation

To animate text that has been placed into an object:

1) Select the object which contains text.
2) Select the object and go to **Format > Text** on the main menu bar or right-click on the object and select **Text** from the context menu to open the Text dialog (Figure 133).
3) Click the **Text Animation** tab to open the Text Animation dialog (Figure 134).

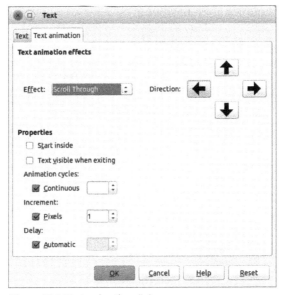

Figure 134: Text animation dialog

4) Select the type of animation required from the *Effects* drop down list as follows:

No animation – default setting.

Blink – the text will blink on the screen.

Scroll through – the text will move into the object and then out following the selected direction.

Scroll back and forth – the text will move first in the selected direction, but will bounce back at the object border.

Scroll in – the text will scroll in towards the given direction starting from the edge of the object and stop in the center.

5) Set the properties for the animation effect as follows:

Direction – use one of the four arrows to set the scroll direction for the text.

Start inside – animation starts from inside the object.

Text visible when editing select to see the text while editing.

Animation cycles – select *Continuous* and the text animates continuously or set a specific number of cycles for the animation.

Increment – sets the amount the animation moves in either *Pixels* or a specific distance. Units of measurement depend on the settings in **Tools > Options > LibreOffice Impress > General**.

Delay – sets the delay time either *Automatically* or a specific length of time before the animation starts.

6) Click **OK** to close the dialog and save the animation effect.

Formatting connectors

Connectors are lines that join two shapes and always start from or finish at a glue point on an object. Refer to *Chapter 5 Managing Graphic Objects* for a description and use of the connectors.

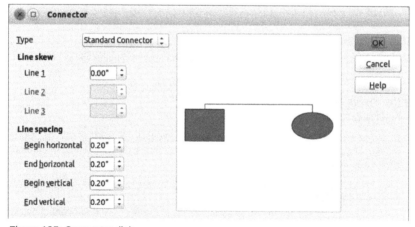

Figure 135: Connector dialog

Connectors are formatted as follows:

1) Right-click on a connector and select **Connector** from the context menu to open the context dialog (Figure 135).

2) Set the type of connector from the *Type* drop down list.

3) Set the *Line skew* for the connector. Line skew is used to set the distance between lines where multiple connectors overlap. You can customize the distance between three different lines.

4) Set the *Line spacing* for the connector. Line spacing is used to set the horizontal and vertical space between the connector and the object at each end of the connector.

5) Click **OK** to close the dialog and save the changes.

Working with image styles

To achieve consistency in styles in slides, or a presentation, or to apply the same formatting to a large number of objects, it is recommended to use image styles.

Image styles are similar to paragraph styles that are used for text. An image style groups all the formatting properties applicable to a graphical object and then associates this group of properties with a name allowing it to be used for other graphical objects. If n image style is modified (for example, changing an area transparency), the changes are automatically applied to all objects that use the same image style.

If you use Impress frequently, a library of well-defined image styles is an invaluable tool for speeding up the process of formatting your work according to any style guidelines you may need to follow (company colors, fonts and so on).

Linked image styles

Image styles support inheritance which allows a style to be linked to another (parent) style so that it inherits all the formatting settings of the parent. This inheritance creates families of styles.

For example, if you require multiple boxes that differ in color, but are otherwise identically formatted, the best way to proceed is to define an image style for the box including borders, area fill, font, and so on and a number of image styles that are hierarchically dependent which differ only in the fill color attribute. If you need to change the font size or the thickness of the border, you only have to change the parent style and all the other styles will change accordingly.

Creating image styles

You can create a new image style either by using the Style and Formatting dialog or from a selection.

Using the Styles and Formatting dialog

1) Select a graphical object.

2) Press the **F11** key, or click on the **Styles and Formatting** icon 🖼 on the Line and Filling toolbar, or select **Format > Styles and Formatting** on the main menu bar to open the Styles and Formatting dialog (Figure 136).

3) Click on the **Image Styles** icon 🖼 on the title bar of the Styles and Formatting dialog to access image styles.

4) Select the style similar to the one you want to use in the Styles and Formatting dialog.

5) Right click and select **New** from the context menu to open the Image Styles dialog (Figure 137). By default, this will link the selected image style with the new image style.

6) To create a image style without linking, select **None** from the *Linked with* drop down menu on the **Organizer** page.

7) Give your new image style a memorable name.

Figure 136: Image Styles and Formatting

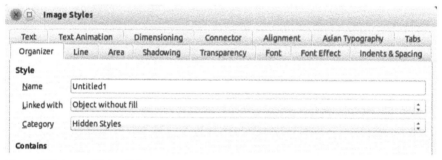

Figure 137: Image Styles dialog

8) Use the various tabs and text boxes in the Image Styles dialog to format and categorize your new style as follows:

Organizer – contains a summary of the style and its hierarchical position.

Font, **Font Effects**, **Indents & Spacing**, **Alignment**, **Tabs** and **Asian Typography** – set the properties of the text inserted in a graphical object.

Dimensioning – used to set the style of dimension lines.

Text, **Text Animation**, **Connector**, **Line**, **Area**, **Shadowing**, and **Transparency** – determine the formatting of a graphical object and are discussed elsewhere in this chapter.

9) Click **OK** when finished to save your new image style.

Note	When styles are linked, changing the font for example will change the font in all linked styles. Sometimes this is exactly what you want; at other times you do not want the changes to apply to all linked styles. It pays to plan ahead.

From a selected object

You can create a new style from an object that has already been formatted. This can be text or graphics:

1) Select the object you want to use to create your new style, then carry out any changes to the object appearance, for example border thickness, fill color and so on.

2) Open the Styles and Formatting dialog and click the **New Style from Selection** icon .

3) In the Create Style dialog (Figure 138) that opens type a name for the new style. The list shows existing custom styles of that are available.

4) Click **OK** to save the new style.

Figure 138: Create Style dialog

Modifying image styles

1) Open the Styles and Formatting dialog.

2) Right-click on the style you want to modify and select **Modify** from the context menu to open the Image Style dialog (Figure 137).

3) Make the required changes to the style and then click **OK** to save the changes.

Updating an image style from a selection

To update a style from changes you have made to a selected object:

1) Select an object that uses the format you want to adopt as a style.

2) Open the Styles and Formatting dialog and select the style you want to update.

3) Click the **Update Style** icon and the style is updated with your changes.

Tip	Any changes you make to a style are effective only in the document on which you are working and do not into change the styles used in the associated template. If you want the changes to apply to more than one document, you need to change the template (see *Chapter 2 Using Slide Masters, Styles, and Templates* for more information).

Applying image styles

Use the following steps to apply an image style to an object.

1) Open the Styles and Formatting dialog (Figure 136) and click on the **Image Styles** icon on the to access image styles.
2) Select the object to which you want to apply an image style.
3) Double-click on the name of the image style you want to apply.

4) Alternatively, click on the **Fill Format Mode** icon and the cursor changes to this icon.
5) Position the icon on the graphic object to be styled and click the mouse button. This mode remains active until you turn it off, so you can apply the same style to several objects.
6) To quit Fill Format mode, click the **Fill Format Mode** icon again or press the *Esc* key.

Note	When Fill Format Mode is active, a right-click anywhere in the document cancels the last Fill Format action. Take care not to accidentally right-click and undo any actions you want to keep.

Tip	At the bottom of the Styles and Formatting window is a drop-down list. You can choose to show all styles or groups of styles such as applied styles or (in the case of image styles) custom styles.

Deleting image styles

You cannot delete any of the predefined styles in Impress, even if you are not using them. You can only delete user-defined (custom) styles. However, before you delete a custom style, make sure the style is not in use. If an unwanted style is in use, replace it with a substitute style.

1) Open the Styles and Formatting dialog (Figure 136) and click on the **Image Styles** icon on the to access image styles.
2) Right-click on a custom graphic style and click **Delete** on the context menu. You can only delete one custom image style at a time.
3) Click **Yes** to confirm the deletion of the image style.

Assigning styles to shortcut keys

LibreOffice provides a set of predefined keyboard shortcuts which allow you to quickly apply styles while working with a document. You can redefine these shortcuts or define your own, as described in *Appendix A Keyboard Shortcuts*.

Chapter 7
Including Spreadsheets,
Charts, and Other Objects

OLE objects

Object Linking and Embedding (OLE) is a software technology that allows embedding and linking of the following types of files or documents into an Impress presentation.

- LibreOffice spreadsheets
- LibreOffice charts
- LibreOffice drawings
- LibreOffice formulas
- LibreOffice text

The major benefit of using OLE objects is that it provides a quick and easy method of editing the object using tools from the software used to create the object. These file types can all be created using LibreOffice and OLE objects can be created from new or from an existing file.

Inserting new OLE objects

When you insert a new OLE object into your presentation, it is only available in your presentation and can only be edited using Impress.

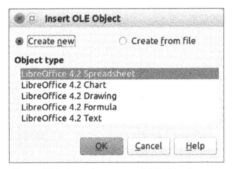

Figure 139: Inserting a new OLE object

To add a new OLE object into your presentation:

1) Go to the slide where you want to insert the OLE object.
2) Select **Insert > Object > OLE Object** from the main menu bar.
3) On the Insert OLE Object dialog (Figure 139), select **Create new.**
4) Select the type of OLE object you want to create and click **OK**.
5) A new OLE object is inserted in the center of the slide in edit mode. The toolbars displayed in Impress will change providing the necessary tools for you to create the new OLE object.

Note	For computers operating Microsoft Windows there is an additional option of **Further objects** in the *Object type* list. Clicking on this option opens another Insert Object dialog allowing you to create an OLE object using other software that is compatible with OLE and LibreOffice. This option is available for new OLE objects and OLE objects from a file.

Inserting OLE objects from files

When you insert an existing file into your slide as an OLE object, by default any subsequent changes that are made to the original file do not affect the copy of the file inserted into your presentation. Similarly, changes to the file copy in your presentation do not change the original file. If you want any changes made to the file, either in the original or in your presentation, to appear in both versions you have to link the original file with your presentation when it is inserted.

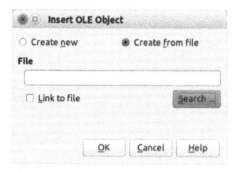

Figure 140: Inserting an OLE object from file

To insert a file into your presentation as an OLE object:
1) Go to the slide where you want to insert the spreadsheet.
2) Choose **Insert > Object > OLE Object** from the menu bar.
3) On the Insert OLE Object dialog, select **Create from file**. The dialog changes to show a File text box (Figure 140).
4) Click **Search** and the Open dialog is displayed.
5) Locate the file you want to insert and click **Open**.
6) Select the **Link to file** option if you wish to insert the file as a live link so that any changes made are synchronized in both the original file and your presentation.
7) Click **OK** to insert the file as an OLE object.

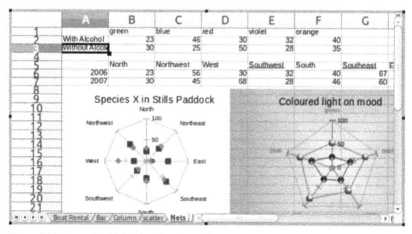

Figure 141: Example OLE object in edit mode

Editing OLE objects

To edit an OLE object after it has been created or inserted from a file:

1) Double-click on the OLE object to open it in edit mode (Figure 141). The toolbars displayed in Impress will change to provide the tools necessary to edit the OLE object (Figure 142).

2) When finished editing the OLE object, click anywhere outside the OLE object to cancel editing.

3) Save your presentation. Any changes made to the OLE object are also saved.

Figure 142: Example toolbars for OLE object editing

Spreadsheets

To include a spreadsheet in an Impress slide, you can either insert an existing spreadsheet file or insert a new spreadsheet as an OLE object. See "OLE objects" on page 170 for more information.

Embedding a spreadsheet into Impress includes most of the functionality of a Calc spreadsheet. Impress is capable of performing complex calculations and data analysis. However, if you plan to use complex data or formulas, it is recommended to perform those operations in a separate Calc spreadsheet and use Impress only to display the embedded spreadsheet with the results.

You may be tempted to use spreadsheets in Impress for creating complex tables or presenting data in a tabular format. However, the Table Design feature in Impress is often more suitable and faster, depending on the complexity of your data; see *Chapter 3 Adding and Formatting Text* for more information.

The entire spreadsheet is inserted into your slide. If the spreadsheet contains more than one sheet and the one you want is not visible, double-click the spreadsheet and then select a different sheet from the row of sheet tabs at the bottom. See "Editing OLE objects" on page 172 for more information on editing the spreadsheet.

Resizing and moving spreadsheets

When resizing or moving a spreadsheet on slides, ignore the first row and first column (easily recognizable because of their light background color) and any horizontal and vertical scroll bars. They are only used for spreadsheet editing purposes and will not be included in the spreadsheet that appears on the slide.

Resizing

When selected, a spreadsheet OLE object is treated like any other object. However, resizing an embedded spreadsheet also changes the spreadsheet area that is visible on a slide.

To resize the area occupied by the spreadsheet on a slide:

1) Double-click the OLE object to enter edit mode, if it is not already active. Note the selection handles visible in the border surrounding the spreadsheet OLE object (Figure 141).

2) Move the mouse over one of the handles. The cursor changes shape to give a visual representation of the effects applied to the area.

3) Click and hold the left mouse button and drag the handle. The corner handles move the two adjacent sides simultaneously, while the handles at the midpoint of the sides modify one dimension at a time.

Moving

You can move a spreadsheet OLE object to change its position within the slide.

1) Select the spreadsheet OLE object so that the object selection handles are displayed.
2) Move the cursor over the object until the cursor changes shape (normally a hand, but this depends on your computer setup).
3) Click and drag the spreadsheet OLE object to the desired position.
4) Release the mouse button.

Note	Do not double click on the spreadsheet OLE object and enter into OLE object editing mode. Moving a spreadsheet OLE object in Impress is the same as moving any other object in Impress.

Editing spreadsheets

When a spreadsheet is inserted into a slide, it is in edit mode ready for inserting or modifying data or modifying the format (example shown in Figure 141). Note the position of the active spreadsheet cell and the small resizing handles on the object border.

When editing a spreadsheet, some of the toolbars change in Impress so that you can easily edit a spreadsheet (Figure 142). One of the most important changes is the presence of the Formula toolbar, just below the Formatting toolbar. The Formula toolbar contains (from left to right):

- The active cell reference or the name of a selected range of cells.
- The **Formula Wizard** icon fx .
- The **Sum** Σ and **Function** $=$ icons *or* the **Cancel** and **Accept** icons, depending on the editing actions taken in the spreadsheet.
- A long edit box to enter or review the contents of the active cell.

If you are familiar with Calc, you will immediately recognize the tools and the menu items. See the *Calc Guide* for more information on how to create and edit spreadsheets in LibreOffice.

Spreadsheet organization

A spreadsheet consists of multiple tables called sheets, which in turn contain cells. However, in Impress, only one sheet can be shown at any one time in a slide when a spreadsheet with multiple sheets is embedded into an Impress slide. The default names for sheets are *Sheet 1*, *Sheet 2*, *Sheet 3* and so on, unless the sheets have been renamed, and the sheet names are shown at the bottom of the spreadsheet area (Figure 141).

Each sheet is organized into *cells*, which are the elementary units of the spreadsheet. They are identified by a row number (shown on the left hand side) and a column letter (shown in the top row). For example, the top left cell is identified as A1, while the third cell in the second row is C2. All data elements, whether text, numbers or formulas, are entered into a cell.

Note	If you have multiple sheets in your embedded spreadsheet, only the active sheet is shown on the slide after exiting edit mode.

Inserting sheets

If required, you can insert sheets to your embedded spreadsheet as follows:

1) Double-click on the embedded spreadsheet to open in edit mode (Figure 141).
2) Right-click on the sheet names and select **Insert > Sheet** from the context menu, or click on the plus sign to the right of the sheet names, or go to **Insert > Sheet** on the main menu bar to open the Insert Sheet dialog (Figure 143).
3) Select the sheet position, quantity of sheets to be inserted, sheet name or which spreadsheet file to use from the options available in the Insert Sheet dialog.
4) Click **OK** to close the dialog and insert the sheet.
5) When finished editing the embedded spreadsheet, click anywhere outside the border to cancel edit mode and save the changes.

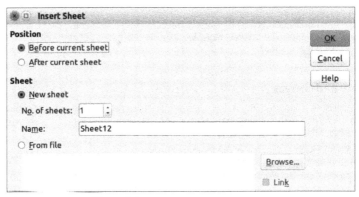

Figure 143: Insert Sheet dialog

Renaming sheets

If required, you can rename sheets in your embedded spreadsheet as follows:

1) Double-click on the embedded spreadsheet to open in edit mode (Figure 141).
2) Click on the sheet tab you want to rename to select the sheet.
3) Right-click on the sheet tab and select **Rename Sheet** from the context menu, or go to **Format > Sheet > Rename** on the main menu bar.
4) When finished editing the embedded spreadsheet, click anywhere outside the border to cancel edit mode and save the changes.

Moving and copying sheets

If required, you can move or copy sheets in your embedded spreadsheet as follows:

1) Double-click on the embedded spreadsheet to open in edit mode (Figure 141).
2) Right-click on the sheet names and select **Move/Copy Sheet** from the context menu, or go to **Edit > Sheet > Move/Copy** on the main menu bar to open the Move/Copy Sheet dialog (Figure 144).
3) Select whether to move or copy the sheet, the sheet location and position, and a new sheet name from the options available in the Move/Copy Sheet dialog.
4) Click **OK** to close the dialog and move or copy the sheet.
5) Alternatively, click on the sheet tab and drag it to a new position in the embedded spreadsheet.

6) When finished editing the embedded spreadsheet, click anywhere outside the border to cancel edit mode and save the changes.

Figure 144: Move/Copy Sheet dialog

Deleting sheets

If required, you can delete sheets and remove them from your embedded spreadsheet as follows:

1) Double-click on the embedded spreadsheet to open in edit mode (Figure 141).
2) Click on the sheet tab you want to delete to select the sheet.
3) Right-click on the sheet tab and select **Delete Sheet** from the context menu, or go to **Edit > Sheet > Delete** on the main menu bar.
4) Click **Yes** to confirm the deletion of the sheet.
5) When finished editing the embedded spreadsheet, click anywhere outside the border to cancel edit mode and save the changes.

Cell navigation

To move around the spreadsheet to select a **cell** to make it active, you can use one of the following methods. By default when open an embedded spreadsheet in Impress, the active cell is A1:

- The keyboard arrow keys.
- Position the cursor in a cell and left click on the mouse.
- *Enter* key to move one cell down and *Shift+Enter* key combination to move one cell up.
- *Tab* key to move one cell to the right and *Shift+Tab* key combination to move one cell to the left.

Note	Other keyboard shortcuts are available to navigate around a spreadsheet. Refer to *Getting Started Guide Chapter 5 Getting Started with Calc* for more information.

Entering data

Data input into a cell can only be done when a cell is *active*. An active cell is easily identified by a thickened and bolder border. The cell reference (or *coordinates*) for the active cell is displayed at the left hand end of the Formula toolbar (Figure 142).

1) Select the cell to make it active and start typing. The data input is also displayed in the large text box on the Formula toolbar making the data entry easier to read.

2) Use the **Formula Wizard** icon f_x, **Sum** icon Σ and **Function** icon $=$ to enter data, formula or function into a cell. If the input is not a formula (for example, a text or date entry), the **Sum** and **Function** icons change to the **Cancel** icon and **Accept** icon.

3) To confirm data input into a cell either select a different cell, or press the *Enter* key, or click on the **Accept** icon.

Formatting cell data

Impress normally recognizes the type of contents (text, number, date, time, and so on) entered into a cell and applies default formatting to it. However, if Impress wrongly recognizes the type of data you have entered into a cell:

1) Select the cell then right-click on the cell and select **Format Cells** from the context menu, or go to **Format > Cells** on the main menu bar, or use the keyboard shortcut *Ctrl+1* to open the Format Cells dialog (Figure 145).

2) Click on the appropriate tab to open the correct page in the dialog and use the options on that dialog page to format the cell data.

3) Click **OK** to close the dialog and save your changes.

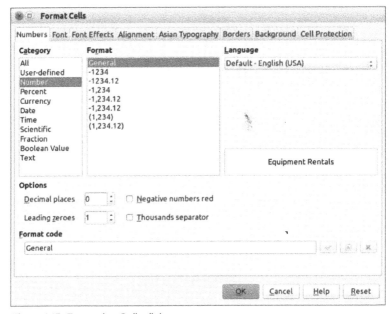

Figure 145: Formatting Cells dialog

Tip	Sometimes it is useful to treat numbers as text (for example, telephone numbers) and to prevent Impress from removing the leading zeros or right align them in a cell. To force Impress to treat numbers as text, type a single quotation mark (') before entering the number.

Formatting spreadsheets

For presentation purposes, it may be necessary to change the formatting of a spreadsheet to match the style used in the presentation.

When working on an embedded spreadsheet, you can also access any cell styles created in Calc and use them. However, if you are going to use styles, it is recommended to create specific cell styles for embedded spreadsheets, as Calc cell styles maybe unsuitable when working within Impress.

Manual formatting

To manually format an embedded spreadsheet:

1) Select a cell or a range of cells. See the *Getting Started Guide Chapter 5 Getting Started with Calc* for more information on selecting ranges of cells.

   a) To select the whole sheet, click on the blank cell at the top left corner between the row and column indexes, or use the keyboard shortcut *Ctrl+A*.

   b) To select a column, click on the column header at the top of the spreadsheet.

   c) To select a row, click on the row header on the left hand side of the spreadsheet.

2) Right-click on a cell and select **Format Cells** from the context menu, or go to **Format > Cells** on the main menu bar, or use the keyboard shortcut *Ctrl+1* to open the Format Cells dialog (Figure 145).

3) Use the various dialog pages to format the embedded spreadsheet so that it matches the style of your presentation.

4) Click **OK** to close the dialog and save your changes.

5) If necessary, adjust the column width by hovering the mouse over the line separating two columns in the header row until the mouse cursor changes to a double-headed arrow; then click the left button and drag the separating line to the new position.

6) If necessary, adjust the row height by hovering the mouse over the line separating two rows in the row header until the mouse cursor changes to a double-headed arrow; then click the left button and drag the separating line to the new position.

7) When you are satisfied with the formatting changes, click outside the spreadsheet area to save your changes and cancel editing.

Using formatting styles

When using styles on an embedded spreadsheet and the spreadsheet is in edit mode, Impress displays the available styles for a spreadsheet in the Styles and Formatting dialog.

If style formatting you want to use is not available, then see the *Writer Guide Chapter 6 Introduction to Styles* on how to create a style. Styles used in an embedded spreadsheet are similar to paragraph styles used in LibreOffice Writer.

To use styles in your embedded spreadsheet:

1) Go to **Format > Styles and Formatting** on the main menu bar or press the *F11* key to open the Styles and Formatting dialog.

2) Select data in a cell and double-click on a style in the Styles and Formatting dialog to apply that style.

Inserting rows, columns or cells

To insert rows, columns, or cells into an embedded spreadsheet:

1) Select the same number of rows, columns or cells on the embedded spreadsheet that you want to insert.

2) Go to **Insert > Rows** or **Insert > Columns** or **Insert > Cells** on the main menu bar or right-click on your selection and select **Insert...** from the context menu.

3) When inserting cells, select the insert option from the Insert Cells dialog that opens and click **OK**.

Deleting rows, columns or cells

To delete rows, columns or cells from an embedded spreadsheet:

1) Highlight the number of rows, columns or cells on the embedded spreadsheet you want to delete.

2) Go to **Edit > Delete Cells** on the main menu bar or right-click on the row or column headers and select **Delete Selected Rows** or **Delete Selected Columns** or **Delete...** from the context menu.

Merging cells

To merge multiple cells into a single cell:

1) Select the number cells to be merged.

2) Go to **Format > Merge cells** on the main menu bar and select either **Merge and Center Cells** or **Merge Cells** from the available options.

3) Alternatively, right-click on the selected cells and select **Merge Cells** from the context menu.

Splitting cells

To split a group of cells that have been merged into a single cell:

1) Select the cell that contains merged cells.

2) Go to **Format > Merge Cells > Split Cells** or right-click on the cell and select **Split Cells** from the context menu.

Charts

A chart is a graphical interpretation of information that is contained in a spreadsheet. More information about charts and the use of charts is described the *Calc Guide Chapter 3 Creating Charts and Graphs*.

Inserting charts

You can insert a chart to your presentation as an OLE object or using the tools within Impress. See "OLE objects" on page 170 for more information on how to insert a chart as an OLE object.

To insert a chart using Impress tools:

1) Go to **Insert > Slide** on the main menu bar, or right-click on the Workspace and select **Slide > New Slide** from the context menu, or right-click on the Slides pane and select **New Slide** from the context menu to insert a new slide into your presentation.

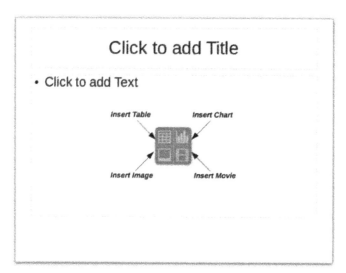

Figure 146: Inserting objects into a slide

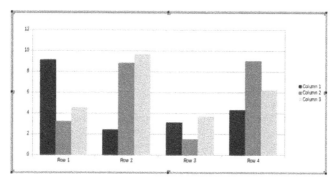

Figure 147: Chart with sample data

2) Select the **Insert Chart** icon on the new slide (Figure 146), or use **Insert > Chart** on the main menu bar, or click the **Chart** icon on the Standard toolbar and a sample chart is inserted into the slide containing sample data (Figure 147). To change chart type, see "Selecting chart type" below and to enter data into the chart, see "Entering chart data" on page 181.

Selecting chart type

Your data can be presented using a variety of different charts. Impress contains several chart types that will help you convey your message to your audience. See "Chart types" on page 180 for an explanation of the different chart types available.

1) Make sure that your chart is selected. The chart has a border and selection handles when selected.

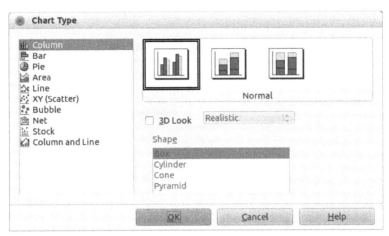

Figure 148: Chart Type dialog showing two-dimensional charts

2) Click the **Chart Type** icon ⊞ on the Formatting toolbar or go to **Format > Chart Type** on the main menu bar, or right-click on the chart and select **Chart Type** from the context menu to open Chart Type dialog (Figure 148).

3) As you change selections in the left-hand list, the chart examples on the right change. If you move the Chart Type dialog to one side, you can see the effect in your chart.

4) As you change chart types, other selections become available on the right-hand side. For example, some chart types have both 3D and 2D variants. When 3D charts are selected, more options become available for selection of shapes for the columns or bars.

5) Choose the chart characteristics you want and click **OK**. The Chart Type dialog closes and you return to the edit window.

6) Continue to format the chart, add data to the chart, or click outside the chart to return to normal view.

Chart types

The following summary of the chart types available will help you choose a type suitable for your data. Column, bar, pie and area charts are available as 2D or 3D types. For more information on charts, see the *Calc Guide Chapter 3 Creating Charts and Graphs*.

Column charts

Column charts displays data that shows trends over time and this the default type of chart used when a chart is inserted into your slide. It is recommended to use column charts where there is a relatively small number of data points. If you have a large time series as your data, it is recommended to use a line chart.

Bar charts

Bar charts give an immediate visual impact for data comparison where time is not important, for example comparing the popularity of products in a marketplace.

Pie charts

Pie charts give a comparison of proportions, for example, when comparing what different departments spent on different items or what different departments actually spent overall. They work best with a small range of values, for example six or less. Using larger range of values, the visual impact of a pie chart begins to fade.

Area charts

Area charts are versions of line or column charts. They are useful when you want to emphasize volume of change. Area charts have a greater visual impact than a line chart, but the type of data you use does make a difference to the visual impact.

Line charts

Line charts are time series with progression. Ideal for raw data and useful for charts with data showing trends or changes over time where you want to emphasize continuity. On line charts, the X-axis is ideal for representing time series data. 3D lines confuse the viewer, so just using a thicker line gives a better visual impact.

Scatter or XY charts

Scatter charts are great for visualizing data that you have not had time to analyze and may be best for data where you have a constant value for comparison: for example weather data, reactions under different acidity levels, conditions at altitude, or any data which matches two numeric series. The X-axis usually plots the independent variable or control parameter (often a time series).

Bubble charts

Bubble charts are used to represent three variables. Two variables identify the position of the center of a bubble on a Cartesian graph, while the third variable indicates the radius of the bubble.

Net charts

Net charts are similar to polar or radar graphs and are useful for comparing data not in time series, but show different circumstances, such as variables in a scientific experiment. The poles of the net chart are the Y-axes of other charts. Generally, between three and eight axes are best; any more and this type of chart becomes confusing.

Stock charts

Stock charts are specialized column graphs specifically used for stocks and shares. You can choose traditional lines, candlestick, and two-column charts. The data required for these charts is specialized with a series for opening price, closing price, and high and low prices. The X-axis represents a time series.

Column and line charts

Column and line charts are a combination of two other chart types. It is useful for combining two distinct, but related data series, for example sales over time (column) and the profit margin trends (line).

Entering chart data

1) Make sure that your chart is selected and you have selected your chart type.

2) Click on the **Chart Data Table** icon ⊞, or select **View** > **Chart Data Table**, or right-click on the chart and select **Chart Data Table** from the context menu to open the Data Table dialog (Figure 149).

3) Type or paste information into the cells within the desired rows and columns to enter data into the Data Table dialog. You can also use the icons in the top left corner of the Data Table dialog to insert, delete or move data.

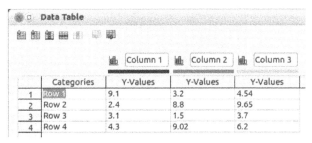

Figure 149: Chart Data Table dialog

Adding or removing chart elements

The specimen chart inserted into a slide only includes two elements: a chart wall and a chart legend (also known as the key). You can add or remove elements to or from a chart as follows:

1) Make sure the chart is selected and in edit mode.

2) Go to **Insert** on the main menu bar and select from the submenu an element that you want to add to the chart, or right-click on the chart wall or a chart element and select an element you want to add from the context menu. Selecting an element opens a dialog where you can specify options for the element.

Note	Right-clicking on a chart element will give you more options to choose from when adding elements to your chart. The number of available insert options in the context menu depends on the type of element selected.

3) To remove an element from a chart, right-click on the chart element you want to remove and select the Delete option from the context menu. The type of element selected for removal will change the delete options in the context menu.

4) Select a chart element and press the *Del* or *Backspace* (←) key to remove it from your chart.

Chart formatting

To change the format of a selected chart:

1) Make sure the chart is selected and in edit mode.

2) Go to **Format** on the main menu bar and select from the submenu an element that you want to format, or right-click on a chart element and select a format option from the context menu. Selecting an element opens a dialog where you can specify format options for the element.

The formatting options available depend on whether the whole chart is selected or which chart element has been selected. For more information on chart formatting, see the *Calc Guide Chapter 3 Creating Charts and Graphs*.

Resizing and moving charts

You can resize or move a chart interactively or by using the Position and Size dialog. You can also use a combination of both methods.

Resizing

To resize a chart interactively:

1) Click on a chart to select it and selection handles appear around the chart.
2) To increase or decrease the height of a chart, click and drag on a selection handle at the top or bottom of the chart.
3) To increase or decrease the width of a chart, click and drag on a selection handle at the left or right of the chart.
4) To increase or decrease both the height and width of a chart at the same time , click and drag on a selection handle in one of the corners of the chart. To maintain the correct aspect ratio between height and width, hold the *Shift* key down while you click and drag.

Moving

To move a chart interactively:

1) Click on the chart to select it and selection handles appear around the chart.
2) Move the cursor anywhere on the chart other than on a selection handle.
3) When it changes shape, click and drag the chart to its new location.
4) Release the mouse button when the chart is in the desired position.

Position and Size dialog

To resize or move a chart using the Position and Size dialog box:

1) Click on the chart to select it and selection handles appear around the chart.
2) Go to **Format > Position and Size** on the menu bar, or right-click on the chart and select **Position and Size** from the context menu, or press *F4* key to open the Position and Size dialog (Figure 150). For more information on the Position and Size dialog and how to use, see *Chapter 6 Formatting Graphic Objects.*

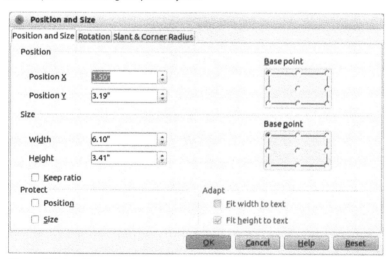

Figure 150: Position and Size dialog

Chart elements

You can move or resize individual elements of a chart element independently of other chart elements. For example, you can move the chart legend to a different position. Pie charts allow individual wedges of the pie to be moved as well as "exploding" the entire pie.

1) Double-click the chart so that it is in edit mode.
2) Click any chart element to select it. Selection handles appear.
3) Move the cursor over the selected element and when the cursor changes shape, click and drag to move the element.
4) Release the mouse button when the element is in the desired position.

Note	If your chart is 3D, round selection handles appear; these control the three-dimensional angle of the chart. You cannot resize or reposition the chart while the round selection handles are showing. *Shift + Click* to get back to the square resizing handles. You can now resize and reposition your 3D chart.

Changing chart area background

The chart area is the area surrounding the chart graphic and includes the (optional) main title and key.

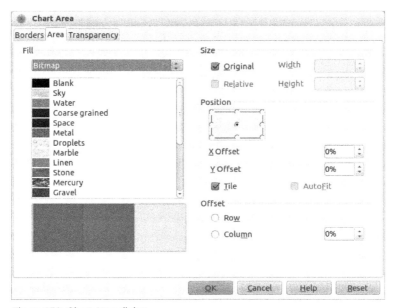

Figure 151: Chart Area dialog

1) Double-click the chart so that it is in edit mode.
2) Go to **Format > Format Selection** on the main menu bar, or right-click in the chart area and select **Format Chart Area**, or double-click in the chart area to open the **Chart Area** dialog (Figure 151).
3) Click on the **Area** tab to open the page containing the area options.

4) Select from the **Fill** drop down list the type of background fill you want to use. The available options will change depending on the type of fill selected.

5) Click **OK** to close the dialog and save your changes.

Changing chart wall background

The chart wall is the area that contains the chart graphic.

1) Double-click the chart so that it is in edit mode.

2) Select **Format > Format Selection** on the main menu bar, or right-click in the chart wall and select **Format Wall**, or double-click in the chart wall to open the **Chart Wall** dialog.

3) Select the **Area** tab from the dialog that opens. This dialog has the same formatting options as described in "Changing chart area background" above.

4) Click **OK** to close the dialog and save your changes.

Movies and sound

Using media files

To insert a media file into your presentation:

1) Click the **Insert Movie** icon on the slide layout (Figure 146) or go to **Insert > Movie and Sound** on the menu bar to open the **Insert Movie and Sound** dialog (Figure 152).

2) Select the media file to insert and click **Open** to place the object on the slide.

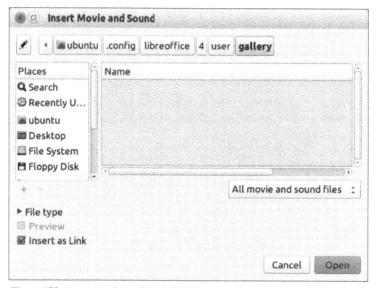

Figure 152: Insert Movie and Sound dialog

Note	Any media file will start playing as soon as the slide is shown during the presentation.

Tip	To see a list of audio and video file types supported by Impress, open the drop-down list of file types. This list defaults to *All movie and sound files*, enabling you to choose unsupported files such as .MOV.

Impress only links media files and does not embed a media file into a presentation. Therefore if a presentation is moved to a different computer, any links will be broken and the media files will not play. To prevent this from happening:

1) Place any media files which are included in a presentation in the same folder where the presentation is stored.
2) Insert the media file in the presentation.
3) Send both the presentation and any media files to the computer which is to be used for the presentation and place both files in the same folder on that computer.

Using the Gallery

To insert media clips directly from the Gallery:

1) If the Gallery is not already open, choose **Tools > Gallery** from the menu bar.
2) Browse to a theme containing media files (for example Sounds).
3) Click on the movie or sound to be inserted and drag it into the slide area.

Media playback

The Media Playback toolbar (Figure 153) is automatically opened when a media file is selected. The default position of the toolbar is at the bottom of the screen, just above the Drawing toolbar. However, this toolbar can be undocked from its fixed position and allowed to float on screen. If the toolbar does not open, go to **View > Toolbars > Media Playback** on the main menu bar.

Figure 153: Media playback toolbar

The Media Playback toolbar contains the following tools from left to right:

- **Movie and Sound** – opens the **Insert Movie and Sound** dialog where you can select a media file to be inserted.
- **Play**, **Pause**, **Stop** – controls media playback.
- **Repeat** – if selected, media will continuously repeat playing until this tool is de-selected.
- **Playback slider** – selects the position to start playing from within the media file.
- **Timer** – displays current position of the media clip and length of media file.
- **Mute** – when selected, the sound will be suppressed.
- **Volume slider** – adjusts the volume of the media file.
- **Scaling drop-down menu** – only available for movies and allows scaling of the movie clip.

Media player

Impress also has a media player so that you can preview any media files that are to be inserted into a presentation. To open it select **Tools > Media Player** on the main menu bar and its tools are the same as that of the Media Playback toolbar (Figure 153).

Formulas

Go to **Insert > Object > Formula** on the main menu bar to create a formula (Math object) in a slide. A formula can also be inserted as an OLE object; see "OLE objects" on page 170 for more information.

When editing a formula, the Math menu becomes available allowing you to create or edit a formula.

When creating formulas, care should be taken about font sizes used to make sure they are similar in size to the font size used in the presentation. To change font attributes of a Math object, go to **Format > Font Size** on the main menu bar. To change font type, go to **Format > Fonts** on the main menu bar.

For information on how to create formulas, see the *Getting Started Guide Chapter 9 Getting Started with Math* or the *Math Guide*.

Note	Unlike formulas in Writer, a formula in Impress is treated as an object and will not be automatically aligned with the rest of the objects on the slide. The formula can be moved around like any other object but cannot be resized.

Drawings, text files, HTML files and other objects

You can insert into a presentation drawings, text files, HTML files and other objects, but only if these objects are compatible for insertion into an Impress presentation.

Go to **Insert > File** on the main menu bar to open a file selection dialog. Only files compatible with Impress will be available for selection.

Drawings, text files, HTML files and other objects can also be inserted as OLE objects; see "OLE objects" on page 170 for more information.

Note	For computers operating Microsoft Windows there is an additional option of **Further objects**. Clicking on this option opens an Insert Object dialog allowing you to create an OLE object using software that is compatible with OLE standards.

Chapter 8
Adding and Formatting Slides,
Notes, and Handouts

Introduction

This chapter describes how to add new slides to the presentation and how to format slides, notes, and handouts. Notes are generally used as prompts for the person giving the presentation. Handouts are normally used for providing a printout of the slides to your audience.

Adding, renaming, and removing slides

Two context menus are available for use when performing operations on slides. One slide context menu is displayed by right-clicking on a slide in the Workspace view and then selecting **Slide** (Figure 154). The other slide context menu is accessed by right-clicking on a slide thumbnail in the **Slides** pane (Figure 155).

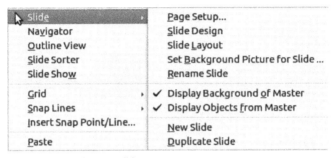

Figure 154: Workspace slide context menu

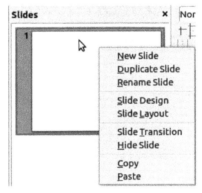

Figure 155: Slide pane context menu

Adding new slides

A new slide is inserted after the current slide or in the position where the mouse was clicked. If multiple slide masters have been used in a presentation, the new slide will use the master of the previous slide in the presentation sequence.

You can add a new slide to a presentation as follows:

1) In Normal, Outline, or Slide Sorter view, go to **Insert > Slide** on the main menu bar.

2) In Normal, Outline, or Notes view, right-click on the Slides pane and select **New Slide** from the context menu.

3) In Slide Sorter view, right click in the main work area and select **New Slide** from the context menu.

4) In Normal view, right-click in the Workspace and select **Slide > New Slide** from the context menu.

Inserting slides from another presentation

Inserting from file

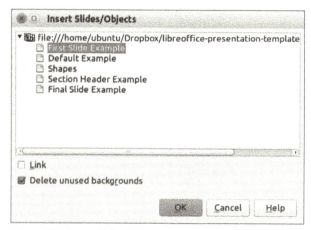

Figure 156: Insert Slides/Objects dialog

1) In Normal view, select the slide in your presentation before the point where you want to insert the new slide.

2) Go to **Insert > File** on the main menu bar to open the Insert File dialog.

3) In the Insert File dialog, locate and select the file containing the slide that you want to insert and click **Open**. This opens the Insert Slides/Objects dialog (Figure 156).

4) Click on the small triangular icon next to the filename to expand the list of slides.

5) Select the slides that you want to insert into your presentation.

6) If required, select the **Link** option to embed the slides as OLE objects.

7) Click **OK**. The slides are inserted after the selected slide in the presentation.

Note	When inserting from a file, you can optionally link the slides instead of copying. This embeds the slides into your presentation using OLE. See *Chapter 7 Including Spreadsheets, Charts, and Other Objects* for more information about OLE.

Tip	Figure 156 shows the importance of giving descriptive names to slides in a presentation. Refer to "Renaming slides" on page 192 for more information.

Copying and pasting between presentations

1) Open the presentations that you want to copy from and paste into.

2) In the presentation containing the slides that you want to copy from, go to **View > Slide Sorter** on the main menu bar or click on the **Slide Sorter** tab in the Workspace so that you can easily locate the slides you want to copy.

3) Select the slides you require and go to **Edit > Copy** on the main menu, or right click and select **Copy** on the context menu, or click the **Copy** icon on the Standard toolbar, or use the keyboard shortcut *Ctrl+C* and the selected slides are copied.

4) Go to the presentation where you want to paste the slides and select **View > Normal** or **View > Slide Sorter** on the main menu bar, click on the **Normal** tab or **Slide Sorter** tab in the Workspace.

5) Select the slide at the point where you want to insert the copied slides after.

6) Go to **Edit > Paste** on the main menu bar, or right click and select **Paste** on the context menu, or click the **Paste** icon on the Standard toolbar, or use the keyboard shortcut *Ctrl+V* and the copied slides are pasted into your presentation.

Dragging and dropping between presentations

1) Open both presentations that you want to use to move or copy slides between and arrange the windows so both presentations are visible.

2) On both presentations, go to **View > Slide Sorter** on the main menu bar or click on the **Slide Sorter** tab in the Workspace.

3) In the presentation containing the slides that you want to move or copy, select the required slides.

4) To move the slides, click and hold down the left mouse button to drag and drop the selected slides into the target presentation.

5) To copy the slides, hold down the *Ctrl* key while dragging and dropping to copy the selected slides into the target presentation.

Duplicating slides

Duplicating a slide is an easy way to add slides if you want a new slide to inherit formatting, layout and animations from a selected slide. To duplicate a slide:

1) Click on the **Normal** tab or **Slide Sorter** tab in the Workspace or go to **View > Normal** or **View > Slide Sorter** on the main menu bar.

2) Select the slide you want to duplicate.

3) Go to **Insert > Duplicate Slide** on the main menu, or right click and select **Duplicate Slide** on the context menu. The duplicated slide is inserted after the original slide.

Tip	Duplicating a slide is a good way of preventing slides being shown with too much information making it difficult for your audience to understand. If a slide becomes crowded with information, try duplicating a "busy" slide then split the information points over two or more slides. All the formatting, backgrounds, and so on will be preserved in each duplicated slide.

Renaming slides

Renaming a slide is as follows:

1) Click on the **Normal** tab or **Slide Sorter** tab in the Workspace or go to **View > Normal** or **View > Slide Sorter** on the main menu bar.

2) In Normal view, right-click on the slide in the Slides pane or Workspace and select **Slide > Rename Slide** from the context menu.

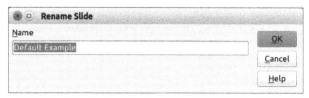

Figure 157: Rename Slide dialog

3) In Slide Sorter view, right-click on the slide and select **Rename Slide** from the context menu.

4) In the Rename Slide dialog (Figure 157), type a new name for the slide and click **OK**.

Expanding slides

Occasionally you may have a slide with too many points to fit in the space available. Instead of reducing the font size or using other methods to squeeze more text onto the slide, it is better to subdivide the contents of the slide into two or more slides.

As mentioned in "Duplicating slides" on page 192, you can duplicate the slide and manually split the points. Alternatively the contents of a slide can be expanded as follows:

1) If necessary, duplicate the slide in case of error and you want to redo expansion of the slide.

2) Select **Insert > Expand Slide** from the main menu to create a new slide for each highest level of the outline. The outline text becomes the title of each new slide. Outline points below the top level on the original slide are moved up one level in the new slides.

3) If required, repeat steps 2 and 3 on any slide where level 2 entries of the outline exist, to expand those as well.

Figure 158 shows a slide with an outline that has been expanded using the **Expand Slide** command. Each expanded slide has been given the slide title of each of the second level points on the original slide.

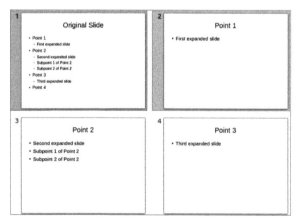

Figure 158: Original slide expanded

Note	For the Expand command to work, ensure that the slide layout contains only one text AutoLayout box. If the layout of the slide is not suitable for expansion, you cannot expand the slide.

Creating summary slides

It is also possible to reverse the Expand operation and create summary slides. The Summary command is useful for creating an agenda for your presentation.

1) Select the slide that will be the first one to appear in the summary.
2) Go to **Insert > Summary Slide** on the main menu bar to create a new slide (Figure 159) at the end of the presentation. All titles of the previous slides are written as bullet points in the body of the slide.
3) If necessary, move this slide to wherever you want it to appear in your presentation.

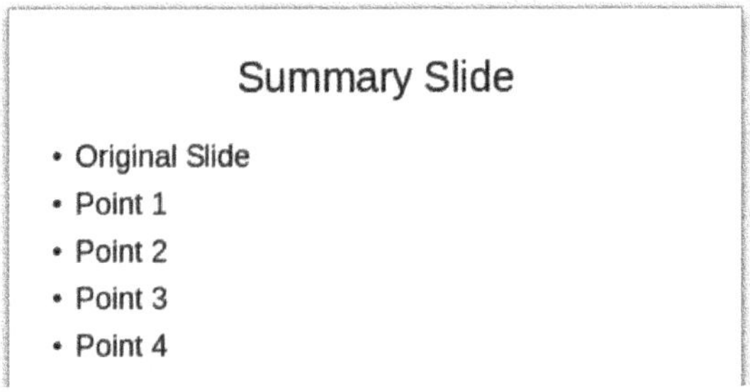

Figure 159: Summary slide

Deleting slides

You can delete a slide or slides from your presentation as follows::

1) In Normal view, go to **Edit > Delete Slide**, or right click in the Workspace and select **Slide > Delete Slide** from the context menu, or press the *Delete* key. This deletes the slide displayed in the Workspace.
2) In Normal or Outline view, select a slide or slides in the Slides pane, then right-click and select **Delete Slide** from the context menu or press the *Delete* key.
3) In Slide Sorter view, select a slide or slides then right-click and select **Delete Slide** from the context menu.

Creating slides from an outline

When planning a presentation it may be useful to develop an outline using LibreOffice Writer. Once the outline is created, you can create one or more separate slides for each of the top level outline elements.

Using a Writer outline

The text document in Writer must contain headings formatted using heading paragraph styles.

1) Open the file in Writer that you want to use to create a presentation from.
2) Go to **File > Send > Outline to Presentation** on the Writer main menu bar to create a new presentation containing the headings as an outline.

3) A new presentation is created and opens in the Impress Outline view (Figure 160) and the heading paragraph styles are converted into the outline styles used in Impress.

4) Some outline levels may have too many points to fit on one slide. You can expand this slide, see "Expanding slides" on page 193, or duplicate the slide and manually change the contents, see "Duplicating slides" on page 192.

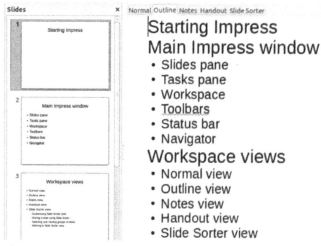

Figure 160: Outline created from a LibreOffice Writer document

Using AutoAbstract

To create a presentation using AutoAbstract and send from Writer to Impress, the text must contain headings formatted with the heading paragraph styles. When using AutoAbstract to copy the headings and subsequent paragraphs to a new presentation, you can specify the number of outline levels as well as the number of paragraphs to be displayed.

1) Open the file in Writer that you want to use to create a presentation from.

2) Go to **File > Send > AutoAbstract to Presentation** on the Writer main menu bar to open the Create AutoAbstract dialog (Figure 161).

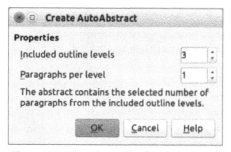

Figure 161: Choosing outline levels for AutoAbstract

3) Select the number of outline levels to be copied to the presentation in **Included outline levels**. For example, if you choose three levels, all paragraphs formatted with heading levels 1 to 3 are included, along with the number of paragraphs specified in **Paragraphs per level**.

4) A new presentation is created and opens in the Impress Outline view and the heading paragraph styles are converted into the outline styles used in Impress.

5) Some outline levels may have too many points to fit on one slide. You can expand this slide, see "Expanding slides" on page 193, or duplicate the slide and manually change the contents, see "Duplicating slides" on page 192.

6) When the presentation is created, some hierarchical structure of the outline may be lost. If necessary, use the **Promote/Demote** icons ⇐ ⇒ on the Text Formatting toolbar to move the outline points to the correct hierarchical levels.

Copying and pasting an outline

Copy and paste an outline into an existing presentation or a new presentation as follows:

1) In Writer, open the file containing the outline you want to use in your presentation.

2) Highlight the outline and select **Edit > Copy** on the main menu bar, or right click on the outline and select **Copy** from the context menu.

3) Create a new presentation in Impress or create a new slide in an existing presentation that you want to use.

4) Select the **Title, Content** layout in the Tasks pane (see "Choosing a slide layout" on page 199).

5) Paste the outline into the text area of the slide. Do not worry if the text does not fit the space on the slide.

6) If the slide contains too much text, either expand the slide, see "Expanding slides" on page 193, or duplicate the slide and manually change the contents, see "Duplicating slides" on page 192.

7) When the presentation is created, some hierarchical structure of the outline may be lost. If necessary, use the **Promote/Demote** icons ⇐ ⇒ on the Text Formatting toolbar to move the outline points to the correct hierarchical levels.

Tip	It may be useful to open the Style and Formatting window of the Presentation styles page to track the outline level of each item.

Modifying slides

Use slide masters to give your presentation a professional look and to avoid manually modifying the formatting of each individual slide. Multiple slide masters can be used in a single presentation to provide the same look for groups of slides and avoid modifying the formatting of each individual slide in a group of slides. See *Chapter 2 Slide Masters, Styles, and Templates* of this guide for more information about using slide masters.

Formatting slides or page area

Note	Any changes to the page format (size, margins, orientation, and so on) apply to *all* slides in the presentation. You can only define one page style in Impress, whereas in Writer or Calc you can define more than one page style. You can change the background of individual slides, see "Changing slide background" on page 199.

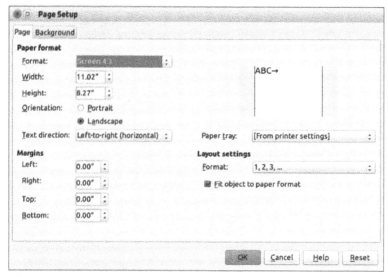

Figure 162: Page Setup dialog

The Page Setup dialog (Figure 162) is used to set up the page and slide layout in Impress for the Normal, Notes or Handouts views.

1) Make sure you are in Normal, Notes or Handout view.
2) Go to **Format > Page on** the main menu bar, or right-click on the slide and choose **Slide > Page Setup** to open the Page Setup dialog (Figure 162).
3) Make your formatting changes using the options given below.
4) Click OK to save your changes and close the dialog.

The options available on the Page Setup dialog are as follows:

- **Paper format** – select from a list of predefined paper sizes, or define a custom paper format. The default value for the screen settings used for slides are for a screen presentation with 4:3 ratio. If your computer uses a wide-screen monitor, you can manually adjust the width and height to fit a wide-screen format.
    - *Format* – select a predefined paper size, or create a custom format by entering the dimensions for the paper in the Height and Width boxes.
    - *Width* – displays the width of the selected paper format. To define a custom format, enter a width here.
    - *Height* – displays the height of the selected paper format. To define a custom format, enter a height here.
    - *Portrait* – displays and prints the current document with the paper oriented vertically.
    - *Landscape* – displays and prints the current document with the paper oriented horizontally.
    - *Text direction* – select the text direction that you want to use in your document. The "right-to-left (vertical)" text flow direction rotates all layout settings to the right by 90 degrees, except for the header and footer.
    - *Paper tray* – select the paper source for your printer. If you want, you can assign different paper trays to different page styles. For example, assign a different tray to the First Page style and load the tray with your company's letterhead paper.

- *Preview field* – displays a preview of the current selection.
- **Margins** – specify the amount of space to leave between the edges of the page and the document text.
  - *Left* – enter the amount of space to leave between the left edge of the page and the document text. If you are using a mirrored page layout, enter the amount of space to leave between the inner text margin and the inner edge of the page.
  - *Right* – enter the amount of space to leave between the right edge of the page and the document text. If you are using a mirrored page layout, enter the amount of space to leave between the outer text margin and the outer edge of the page.
  - *Top* – enter the amount of space to leave between the upper edge of the page and the document text.
  - *Bottom* – enter the amount of space to leave between the lower edge of the page and the document text.
- **Layout settings**
  - *Format* – select the page numbering format that you want to use for the current page style.
  - *Fit object to page format* – resizes the drawing objects so that they fit on the paper format that you select. The arrangement of the drawing objects is preserved.

Selecting slide masters

You can apply a master page to all the slides in a presentation or only selected slides in a presentation. This allows you to use more than one master page in a presentation. For more information on master pages, see *Chapter 2 Slide Masters, Styles and Templates* in this guide. Please note that master pages are also called master slides or slide masters.

Figure 163: Sidebar Master Pages section

1) In the Sidebar, select the **Master Pages** icon ![icon] to show the **Master Pages** section and the available master pages for use in the presentation (Figure 163).

2) To apply a master page to all the slides in the presentation, right click on your selected master page and select **Apply to All Slides** from the context menu.

3) To apply a master page to one slide or several slides, select the slide or slides you want to apply the master page to, then right click on the master page and select **Apply to Selected Slides** from the context menu.

Changing slide background

Tip	For easy maintenance it is recommended that slide masters are used to modify the slide backgrounds by creating any additional slide masters as required.

Note	Applying a background to individual slides is no different from filling the area of a shape. See *Chapter 6 Formatting Graphic Objects* in this guide for more information.

To change the background for all slides or a single slide:

1) Switch to Normal view by clicking the **Normal** tab in the Workspace pane or go to **View > Normal** on the main menu bar.

2) Select a slide in your presentation.

3) Go to **Format > Page** on the main menu bar, or right-click on the slide and select **Slide > Page Setup** to open the Page Setup dialog (Figure 162).

4) Click on the **Background** tab and follow the instructions in *Chapter 6 Formatting Graphic Objects* in this guide to change the background.

5) Click **OK** to save the changes.

6) A pop-up message asks if you want to change the background on all slides. To apply the new background only to the selected slide or slides, click **No**. To apply the new background to all slides used in the presentation, click **Yes**.

Choosing a slide layout

After creating a new slide, you can then decide on what layout is most suitable for the slide contents and your presentation. Impress offers various types of predefined layouts that can be applied to a slide (Figure 164).

If the layouts available in Impress do not fit your presentation style, elements can be rearranged on an individual slide and duplicated as often as required by copying to another presentation or saving it as a template.

All the techniques in *Chapter 3 Adding and Formatting Text* in this guide for working with text boxes can be applied to the title and auto layout text elements of a slide. The placeholder for images can be moved and resized, see *Chapter 4 Adding and Formatting Pictures* in this guide. *Chapter 7 Including Spreadsheets, Charts, and Other Objects* in this guide describes how to include and modify spreadsheets, charts, and other objects.

1) In the Sidebar, select the **Properties** icon ![icon] to open the **Layouts** section and display the various slide layouts available.

2) Hover the cursor over a layout thumbnail to get a summary of the type of layout.

3) If this is the layout you require, click on the selected layout to apply it to the slide.

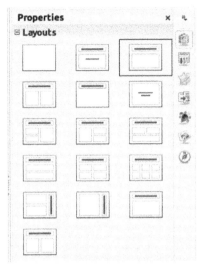

Figure 164: Sidebar Layouts section

Note	If the layout is changed to slide that already contains text and objects, Impress will not delete these, but reposition them according to the selected layout. This may result in some elements overlapping or being out of position.

Comments

Adding comments

When creating a presentation in a collaborative environment, it is often useful to add comments to the presentation for the benefit of the other people working on the presentation.

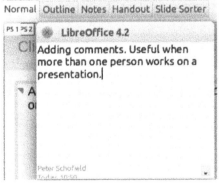

Figure 165: Adding comments

1) Switch to **Normal** view and select the slide where you want the comment to appear.
2) Select **Insert > Comment** on the main menu bar, or use the keyboard shortcut *Ctrl+Alt+C* to display a comment box (Figure 165) in the top left corner of the slide. The size of the comments box is fixed and scroll bars appear when needed.
3) Once you are finished typing your comment, close the comment box by clicking anywhere outside the comment box.
4) Each comment is color coded and marked with the initials of the author as well as a sequential number. This comment indicator is normally shown in the top left corner of the slide in Normal view. Clicking on a comment indicator displays the full text of the comment.
5) To move the comment indicator, click and drag it to a new position on the slide.

Editing, replying and deleting comments

Editing

You can only edit comments that you created and the editing options for comments are limited.

1) Open the comment by clicking on the comment indicator.
2) To change or add more text, simply click in the text and the cursor changes to the text tool.
3) To format the text, right click on the open comment and select the appropriate option from the context menu. Text can also be copied from another source and pasted into a comment.
4) Once you are finished editing your comment, close the comment box by clicking anywhere outside the comment box.

Replying

You can only reply to comments created by another person.

1) Open the comment by clicking on the comment indicator.
2) Click on the small triangle in the bottom right corner of the comment, or right click on the comment and select **Reply** from the context menu. This option is only available if more than one person has made comments.
3) Once you are finished replying to a comment, close the comment box by clicking anywhere outside the comment box.

Deleting

You can delete the current comment that is open, delete all comments from the author of the selected comment, or delete all comments in the presentation.

1) Right click on a comment indicator and select the appropriate option from the context menu.
2) Alternatively, open a comment and click on the small triangle in the bottom right corner of the comment, or right click on the comment and select the appropriate option from the context menu.

Presentation notes

Notes provide a convenient way to create reminders or add extra information to slides in a presentation. Notes are not displayed during a slide show. However, using dual displays, you can display any notes on the second display as a presentation cue. You can also print the notes and use them as handouts.

Adding notes

1) Select the slide to which you want to add notes.
2) Click on the **Notes** tab at the top of the Workspace or go to **View > Notes Page** on the main menu bar to open the Notes view (Figure 166).
3) Click in the text box showing *Click to add notes* and type or paste text or graphics as required.
4) To add notes to another slide, repeat steps 1 to 3.
5) When you have finished entering notes, return to Normal view.

Figure 166: Notes Page view

Formatting notes

It is recommended to use the Notes Master and the Notes Presentation style to format the appearance of notes, rather than formatting notes individually for each slide. All the formatting guidelines given in this section can be applied to either the Notes Master or to the Notes Presentation style.

Formatting Notes page

1) Click on the **Notes** tab at the top of the Workspace or go to **View > Notes Page** on the main menu bar to open the Notes view (Figure 166).
2) Go to **View > Master > Notes Master** on the main menu bar to open the Notes Master layout (Figure 167).
3) Select **Format > Page** from the menu bar, or right-click and choose **Page Setup** to open the Page Setup dialog (Figure 168).

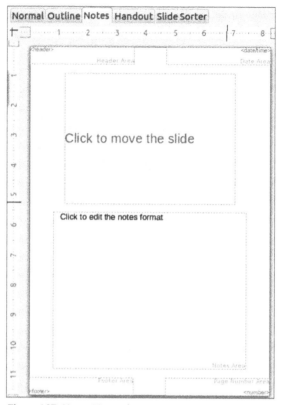

Figure 167: Notes Master layout

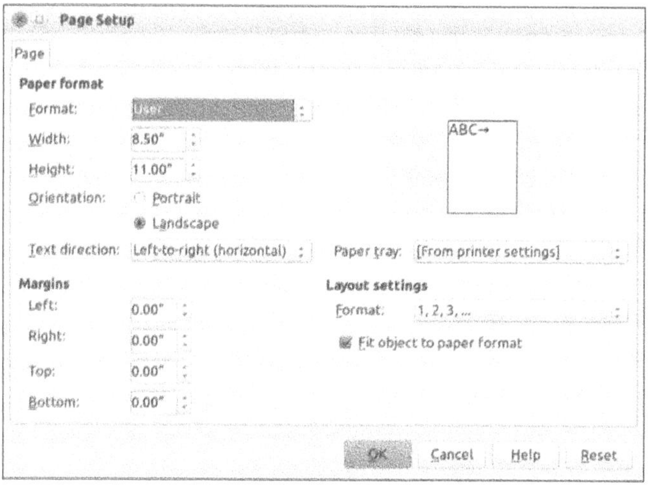

Figure 168: Page Setup dialog for Notes and Handouts

4) Set the desired options for the page. See "Formatting slides or page area" on page 196 for a description of the options available in the Page Setup dialog.

5) Click **OK** save your changes and to close the dialog.

Setting automatic layout options

In Notes, Impress can automatically enter information into four areas on the notes page:

- Header area
- Date and Time area
- Footer area
- Slide or page number area

To setup these fields for automatic layout, proceed as follows:

1) Click on the **Notes** tab at the top of the Workspace or go to **View > Notes Page** on the main menu bar to open the Notes view (Figure 166).

2) Go to **View > Master > Notes Master** on the main menu bar to open the Notes Master layout (Figure 167).

3) Go to **Insert > Page Number** or **Insert > Date and Time** on the main menu bar to open the Header and Footer dialog (Figure 169).

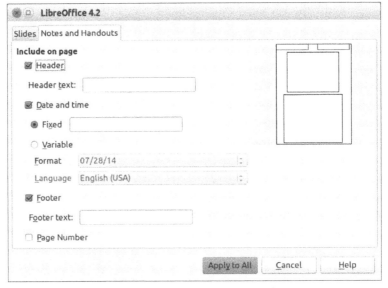

Figure 169: Header and Footer dialog for Notes and Handouts

4) Click on the **Notes and Handouts** tab.

5) If required, check the *Header* option and the text to be included in the header in the text box.

6) If required, check the *Date and Time* option and select whether the date is to be *Fixed* or *Variable*. If the date and time is fixed, enter the date and time that should be displayed in the text box. If the date and time is variable, select the date format and language to be used for the date and time.

7) If required, check the *Footer* option and the text to be included in the footer in the text box.

8) If required, check the *Page number* so that the page number appears on each page. To format the type of numbering, refer to "Formatting Notes page" on page 202 or "Formatting slides or page area" on page 196 for more information.

9) Click **Apply to All** to save your changes and close the dialog.

Text formatting

When text is inserted in the Notes text box, it is automatically formatted using the predefined Notes style that you can find in the Presentation styles. The best way to format the notes text is to modify this style to suit your needs. Refer to *Chapter 2 Slide Masters, Styles, and Templates* of this guide for more information.

If manual formatting is required, for example to highlight a particular section of the notes, refer to *Chapter 3 Adding and Formatting Text* of this guide for more information.

Note	You can move and resize the text box and slide image on the Notes page. Also, you can add more text boxes to the Notes page. Refer to the other chapters in this guide for more information.

Printing notes

1) Click on the **Notes** tab at the top of the Workspace or go to **View > Notes Page** on the main menu bar to open the Notes view (Figure 166).

2) Go to **File > Print** on the main menu bar, or use the keyboard shortcut *Ctrl+P* to open the Print dialog (Figure 170).

3) Click on the **General** tab, select **Notes** from the *Print > Document* drop down list.

4) Make any other necessary changes to the printing options, for example number of copies and print range.

5) Click **OK** to print and close the Print dialog.

For more information on printing slides, notes, and handouts, see *Chapter 10 Printing, E-mailing, Exporting, and Saving Slide Shows* in this guide.

Exporting notes as PDF

1) Click on the **Notes** tab at the top of the Workspace or go to **View > Notes Page** on the main menu bar to open the Notes view (Figure 166).

2) Go to **File > Export as PDF** on the main menu bar to open the PDF Options dialog (Figure 171).

3) Click on the **General** tab.

4) In the *General* section, check the **Export notes pages** option.

5) Make any other necessary changes to the PDF export options and click **OK** to close the PDF options dialog.

6) In the Export dialog that opens, enter a filename and select a folder in which to save the file.

7) Click **Export** to export and save the file, and close the Export dialog.

Note	If your presentation has 10 slides, the PDF will contain 20 pages consisting of 10 pages of individual slides followed by 10 pages with notes formatted for paper. If you want only the Notes pages, you will need to use another program to remove the unwanted pages of slides from the PDF file.

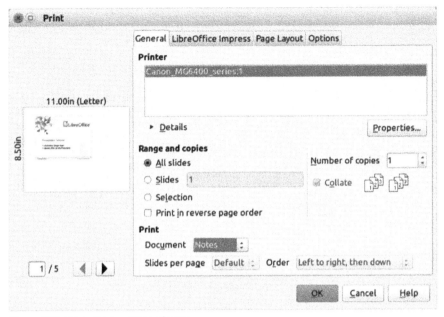

Figure 170: Print dialog – General page

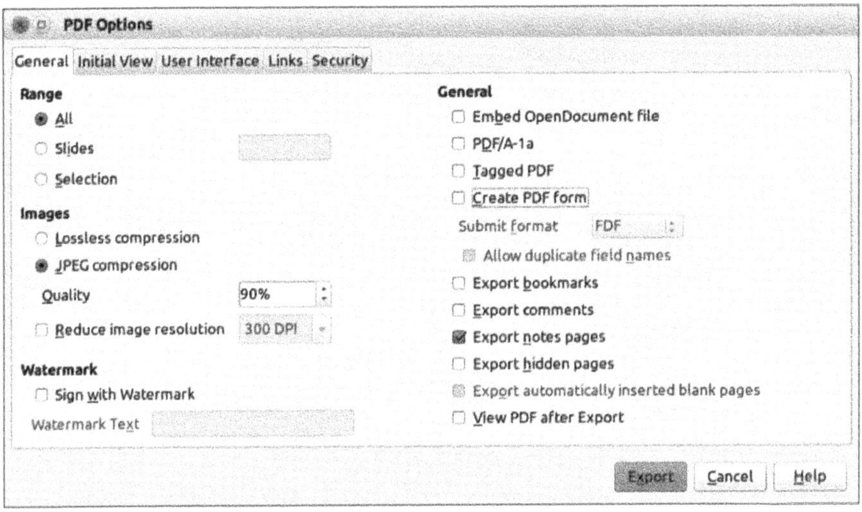

Figure 171: PDF Options dialog – General page

Presentation handouts

A handout is a special view of the presentation suitable for printing and distribution to the audience. Each handout page can contain from one to nine thumbnails of the slides used in the presentation so that the audience can follow what is being presented as well as use the handouts for reference. This section explains how to customize the handout page.

Note that the Handout view consists of only one page regardless of the number of slides in the presentation or the number of pages of slides that will be printed.

Changing layout

When creating handouts, first decide how many slide thumbnails you want printed on each handout page.

1) Click on the **Handout** tab at the top of the Workspace or go to **View > Handout Page** on the main menu bar to open the Handout page (Figure 172).

2) Click on **Properties** icon in the Sidebar to open the **Layouts** section and display the available for handouts (Figure 173).

3) Select the preferred number of thumbnails and the Workspace changes to reflect the selection.

Formatting handouts

You can format several aspects of the handout, from the page style to the elements that appear on the page. You cannot format individual handout pages and any changes apply to all handouts in the presentation file.

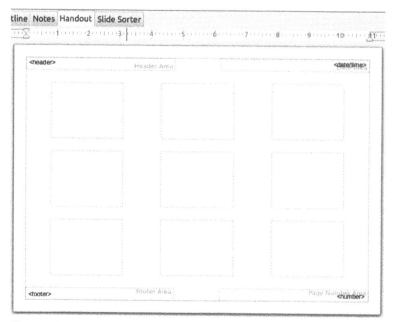

Figure 172: Handout page with nine slide thumbnails

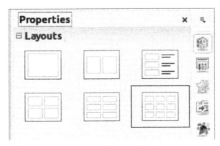

Figure 173: Layouts for handouts

Handout page formatting

1) Click on the **Handout** tab at the top of the Workspace or go to **View > Handout Page** on the main menu bar to open the Handout page (Figure 172).

2) Select **Format > Page** from the main menu, or right-click on the handout and select **Slide > Page Setup** from the pop-up menu to open the Page Setup dialog (Figure 168).

3) Set the paper size, orientation (portrait or landscape), margins, and other print options.

4) Click **OK** to close the Print dialog and print the handouts.

Setting automatic layout options

In Handouts, Impress can automatically enter information into four areas on the handout page. Refer to "Setting automatic layout options" on page 204 for more information on setting the automatic layout options for handouts.

- Header area
- Date and Time area
- Footer area
- Slide or page number area

Note	The information in these areas does not show in Handout view, but does appear correctly on the printed handouts.

Moving thumbnails and adding graphics

You can move (but not resize) the slide thumbnails and add lines, boxes, and other graphic elements to the handouts. See *Chapter 5 Managing Graphic Objects* in this guide for more information on using the graphics tools.

Tip	After designing a handout, you may wish to save it in a template so you can reuse it whenever you want. See *Chapter 2 Slide Masters, Styles, and Templates* in this guide for information on saving templates and starting a new presentation from a template.

Note	If you click on one of the other handout layouts and then return to the one you have reformatted, the slide thumbnails return to their original positions, although any lines or other graphics you have added remain where you put them. You will need to move the thumbnails back to where you want them.

Printing handouts

1) Click on the **Handout** tab at the top of the Workspace or go to **View > Handout Page** on the main menu bar to open the Handout page (Figure 172).

2) Go to **File > Print** on the main menu bar, or use the keyboard shortcut *Ctrl+P* to open the Print dialog (Figure 170).

3) Click on the **General** tab, select **Handouts** from the *Print > Document* drop down list.

4) Make any other necessary changes to the printing options, for example number of copies and print range.

5) Click **OK** to print and close the Print dialog.

For more information on printing slides, notes, and handouts, see *Chapter 10 Printing, E-mailing, Exporting, and Saving Slide Shows* in this guide.

Exporting handouts as PDF

At present there is no way to export handouts to PDF. If you try, then the PDF file only contains slides with one slide per page. However, you can print to a PostScript file, if you have a postscript printer driver installed, and then use another program (for example Ghostscript or Adobe Acrobat) to create a PDF file from a PostScript file.

Chapter 9
Slide Shows

Transitions, animations, and more

Creating a slide show

LibreOffice Impress gives you the tools to organize and display a slide show, including:

- Which slides to show and in what sequence
- Whether to run the show automatically or manually
- Transitions between slides
- Animations on individual slides
- Interactions: what happens when you click a button or link
- A presenter console

Most tasks associated with putting together a slide show are best done in Slide Sorter view. Go to **View > Slide Sorter** on the main menu bar or click the **Slide Sorter** tab at the top of the Workspace pane. All of your slides appear in the workspace.

Basic settings

Basic settings for a slide show include which slide to start from, the way you advance the slides, the type of presentation, and pointer options.

1) Go to **View > Slide Sorter** on the main menu bar, or click on the **Slide Sorter** tab in the Workspace.
2) Go to **Slide Show > Slide Show Settings** on the main menu bar to open the Slide Show dialog (Figure 174).

Figure 174: Slide Show dialog

3) Select the options you want to use for your slide show. See "Slide Show options" on page 213 for more information on options.
4) Click **OK** to save your changes and close the dialog.

Slide Show options

In the *Range* section, select which slides to include in the slide show:

- **All slides** – includes all slides except for those slides marked Hidden (see "Hiding slides" on page 214). Slides are shown in the sequence they occur in the file. To change the sequence, either rearrange the slides in the slide sorter or choose a custom slide show (see below).
- **From** – starts the show at a slide other than the first slide. For example, you might have several slides at the beginning that describe you and your company, but when you present this show to your work colleagues, you may want to skip that introduction.
- **Custom Slide Show** – shows the slides in a different sequence that you have previously set up. This setting is not available until you have set up a custom slide show (see "Showing slides in a different order" on page 215). You can set up as many different custom shows as you wish from one set of slides and they will appear in the drop-down list under this option.

In the *Type* section, select how the slides will be displayed:

- **Default** – shows the slides full screen without the LibreOffice program controls visible and exits the show after the last slide.
- **Window** – runs the slide show in the Impress window and exits the show after the last slide.
- **Auto** – restarts the slide show after the last slide. A pause slide is displayed between the last slide and the start slide. Press the *Esc* key to stop the show. In the box, specify the length of time before the show restarts. If you enter zero, the show restarts immediately without showing a pause slide. The **Show Logo** option shows the LibreOffice logo on the pause slide.

In the *Options* section:

- **Change slides manually** – prevents slides from changing automatically even if an automatic transition has been set up.
- **Mouse pointer visible** – shows the mouse pointer during a slide show. If you do not have a laser pointer or other device to highlight items of interest during the show, this can be useful.
- **Mouse pointer as pen** – enables you to write or draw on slides during the presentation. Anything you write with the pen is not saved when you exit the slide show. The color of the pen cannot be changed.
- **Navigator visible** – displays the Navigator during the slide show. For more information on the Navigator, see *Chapter 1 Introducing Impress* in this guide.
- **Animations allowed** – displays all frames of animated GIF files during the slide show. If this option is not selected, only the first frame of an animated GIF file is displayed. This has nothing to do with the slide animations described in "Using animation effects" on page 219.
- **Change slides by clicking on background** – advances to the next slide when you click on the background of a slide. You can also press the spacebar on the keyboard to advance to the next slide.
- **Presentation always on top** – prevents any other program window from appearing on top of the presentation.

In the *Multiple displays* section:

- You can select which display to use for full screen slide show mode. Only available if the current computer desktop is displayed on more than one monitor.
- If the current desktop is displayed on only one monitor, or if the multiple-display feature is not supported on the current system, you cannot select another display.
- By default the primary display is used for slide show mode.

- **Presentation Monitor** – select a monitor to use for full screen slide show mode. If the system allows to span a window over all available monitors, you can also select *All monitors* and the presentation spans over all available monitors.

Note	The multiple displays setting is not an option saved with the presentation file, but is instead saved as a local setting in the user configuration. This means that if you open the presentation on a different computer the local settings for that computer are applied.

Hiding slides

You may not want to show all of the slides in a particular slide show. You can either hide some of the slides or set up a custom slide show; whichever method suits your requirements. For example, you may have draft slides that you do not want to show until they are finished, or you may have some slides that contain information for yourself, but not your audience.

To hide a slide:

1) In the Slides pane, or in Slide Sorter view, select the slides that you want to hide.

2) Click the **Hide Slide** icon ![icon] on the Slide View toolbar (Figure 175), or right-click and select **Hide Slide** from the context menu, or go to **Slide Show > Hide Slide** on the main menu bar. The slide is now displayed grayed out to indicate that it is hidden (Figure 176). The slide is not deleted and remains in the file. The **Hide Slide** icon is only active when a slide is selected in your presentation.

Figure 175: Slide View toolbar

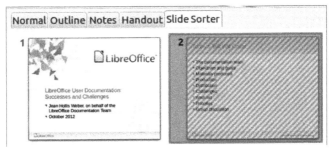

Figure 176: Slide 2 is hidden

To show a hidden slide:

1) In the Slides pane, or in Slide Sorter view, select the hidden slides that you want to show.

2) Click the **Show Slide** icon ![icon] on the Slide View toolbar (Figure 175), or right-click and select **Show Slide** from the context menu, or go to **Slide Show > Show Slide** on the main menu bar. The **Slide Show** icon is only active when the hidden slides are selected in your presentation.

Showing slides in a different order

To show the slides in a different order, you can either rearrange them in the slide sorter, or set up a custom slide show. You can define as many custom slide shows as you require from one set of slides.

In a custom slide show, you can select which slides to include as well as the order in which they are shown. Any hidden slides will not appear in a custom show.

Custom slide show

To set up a new custom slide show:

1) Go to **Slide Show > Custom Slide Show** on the main menu bar to open the Custom Slide Shows dialog (Figure 177).

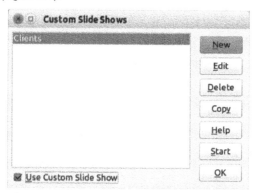

Figure 177: Custom Slide Shows dialog

2) Click on **New** and the Define Custom Slide Show dialog opens (Figure 178).

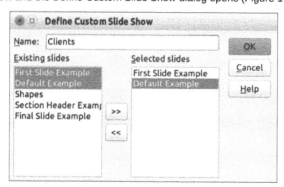

Figure 178: Define Custom Show dialog

3) Type a name for the new custom show in the *Name* text box.

4) In the *Existing slides* list, select the slides to include in the show. Click the **>>** button to include the slides in the *Selected slides* list. In Figure 178, the first two slides have been selected.

5) You can select and include several slides at the same time. Hold down the *Shift* key and click the first and last slide in a group to select that group, or hold down the *Ctrl* key and click on individual slides to select them.

6) When you have finished arranging the order of the slides, click **OK** to save this custom show and return to the Custom Slide Shows dialog.

7) To activate a custom show, select it in the list in the Custom Slide Shows dialog box and then select the **Use Custom Slide Show** option.

Note	If you include several slides at the same time, they are added to the *Selected slides* list in the order they appear in your presentation regardless of the order in which you selected them. To put the selected slides in a different order, either select and include each slide individually or select a slide and drag it up or down in the selected slide list. You can also use the Slide Sorter view to rearrange the order of slides before making your selection.

Tip	Slides are added to the *Selected slides* list after the slide that is currently highlighted in the list. By default, the last slide added is highlighted unless you have selected a different one. For example, in Figure 178, to add the slide *Final Slide Example* after the *First Slide Example* and before *Slide2*, make sure that *First Slide Example* is highlighted before moving *Final Slide Example* into *Selected slides* list.

Editing, deleting, or copying a custom slide show

1) To edit a custom slide show (add, remove, or change the order of slides, or change the name of the show), select it in the Custom Slide Shows dialog (Figure 177) and click **Edit**.

2) To delete a custom slide show, select it in the Custom Slide Shows dialog and click **Delete**. Deletion is immediate and no confirmation message appears.

3) To create a copy of a slide show, select it in the Custom Slide Shows dialog and click **Copy**. You can now edit the copy by renaming and adding, removing, or changing the order of slides in it.

4) You can preview your custom slide show from the Custom Slide Shows dialog if the *Use Custom Slide Show* option is selected. Select the slide show from the list and click on **Start**.

5) When you have finished working with custom slide shows, click **OK** to save all changes and close the Custom Slide Shows dialog.

Using slide transitions

Slide transitions are the effects that take place between slides when slides change in a presentation. Transitions can add a professional look to a slide show, smoothing the change over between slides.

Adding transitions

1) In the Sidebar, select the **Slide Transition** icon ⊞ to open the Slide Transition section (Figure 179).

2) In the Slides pane or Slide Sorter view, select the slides to which you want to apply the transition. If you want the transition to apply to all slides, do not select any slides.

3) In the **Apply to selected slides** list, select a transition.

Figure 179: Sidebar Slide Transition section

4) Modify the selected transition by changing the speed or adding a sound, in the **Modify transition** section. If you decide to play a sound during transitions, select a sound from the **Sound** list.

5) If a sound is selected, the **Loop until next sound** option becomes active. Select this option to play the sound repeatedly until another sound starts. If there are no subsequent sounds in your slide show, the selected sound will play continuously for the remainder of the show.

6) Select how to advance to the next slide: manually (*On mouse click*) or automatically (*Automatically after*). If you select an automatic advance, you can specify how long the slide remains visible before it automatically advances to the next slide.

7) If you want the transition to apply to all slides, click **Apply to All Slides**.

8) To start the slide show from the current slide so you can check your transitions, click **Slide Show**.

9) If the **Automatic preview** checkbox is marked, the effect of a selected transition is immediately displayed in the work area. You can replay the effect at any time by clicking **Play**.

Tip	You can apply a single type of transition to all slides in the presentation or apply a different transition to any single slide in the slide show. While using many different transitions may be fun to do, it may not give your slide show a professional appearance.

Tip	If you want most of the slides in your slide show to have the same transition and only use a few different transitions, you may find it easier to apply one transition to all slides and then change only the ones you want to be different.

Removing transitions

1) Select the slides from where you want to remove the transitions.
2) Select *No Transition* in the **Slide Transition** list on the Tasks pane.

Setting timing of automatic slide changes

You can set up a slide show to run automatically, either unattended or while you speak.

Default timing

To set the default time for slides to be displayed before changing to the next slide:

1) In the Sidebar, select the **Slide Transition** icon to open the Slide Transition section (Figure 179).
2) Leave the transition effect set to **No Transition**.
3) Select **Automatically after** in the *Advance slide* section.
4) Set a time and click **Apply to All Slides**.

Variable timing

To vary the timing for some of the slides in your slide show:

1) Select **Slide Show > Rehearse Timings** from the main menu, or click the **Rehearse Timings** icon on the Slide Show toolbar. The slide show begins in full-screen mode and a timer appears in the lower left corner of the display.
2) When you want to advance to the next slide, click the timer. To keep the default setting for this slide, click the slide and not the timer.
3) Continue until you have set the timing for all slides in your presentation. Impress records the display time for each slide. When you next look at the time set under **Automatically after**, you will see that the times have changed to match what you set when rehearsing.
4) To exit from the rehearsal, press the *Esc* key or right-click on the slide and select **End Show** from the context menu.

Auto repeat

If you want the whole presentation to auto-repeat:

1) Open the Slide Show dialog (Figure 174) by going to **Slide Show > Slide Show Settings** on the main menu bar.
2) Click **Auto** and set the timing for the pause between slide shows.
3) Select **Show logo** if you want the LibreOffice logo to show during the pause between slide shows.

4) Click **OK** to save the settings and close the dialog.

Playing sounds

You can use the Slide Transition pane to select a sound or song that is played throughout your presentation.

1) Select the slide where you want the sound to start.
2) In the Sidebar, select the **Slide Transition** icon to open the Slide Transition section (Figure 179).
3) In the *Modify transition* section, select **Other sound** from the *Sound* drop-down list.
4) Navigate to where the sound file is located in the Open dialog that opens.
5) Select the sound file you want to use and click **Play** to check if the sound file is suitable.
6) If the sound file is suitable, click **Open**.
7) Select **Loop until next sound** if you want the sound to restart once it is finished.

Note	Do not click the **Apply to all** button; otherwise your selected sound will restart at every slide.

Note	The sound file is linked to a presentation rather than embedded. Therefore if you plan to display the presentation on a different computer, remember that you also have to make the sound file available on the computer where the presentation will be played, and re-establish the link to the sound file before starting the slide show.

Using animation effects

Slide animations are similar to transitions, but they are applied to individual elements in a single slide: title, chart, shape, or individual bullet point. Animations can make a presentation more lively and memorable. Just as with transitions, heavy use of animations can be fun, but distracting and even annoying for an audience expecting a professional presentation.

Animation effects are applied from Normal view so that you can select individual objects on a single slide.

Note	At present it is not possible to apply animation effects to the slide master elements. This means that if you want to display the items in a text box one by one, and use the same animation on more than one slide, you need to apply the effects to each slide, or alternatively copy the text box from one slide to another.

Applying animation effects

In Normal view, display the desired slide and then select the text or object you want to animate. An object such as a graphic or an entire text box will have selection handles around it when selected. If you choose only a portion of the text in a text box, you may not see any selection handles.

1) Go to **View > Normal** on the main menu bar, or click on the **Normal** tab in the Workspace.

Figure 180: Sidebar Custom Animation section

2) Select the slide and the object you want to apply the animation effect to.

3) In the Sidebar, select **Custom Animation** icon to open the Custom Animation section (Figure 180).

4) Click **Add** to open the Custom Animation dialog (Figure 181).

5) Select the animation effect types from one of the tabbed pages on the Custom Animation dialog. More than one type of animation effect can be applied to an object.

  a) Use the *Entrance* page to be apply an animation effect when an object is placed on the screen.

  b) Use the *Emphasis* page to apply an animation effect to an object, for example changing font color, or adding special effects such as blinking text.

  c) Use the *Exit* page to apply an animation effect when an object leaves the screen.

  d) If you want the object to move along a line or curve, select an animation effect from the *Motion Paths* page. An example of this type of animation is provided in "Setting up a motion path" on page 226.

6) Select the duration of the animation effect from the *Speed* drop down list.

7) If required, select *Automatic preview* so you can check the animation effect on the object.

Figure 181: Custom Animation dialog

8) Click **OK** to apply the animation effect and close the dialog. Each object that has had an animation effect applied to it appears in the list on the Custom Animation section on the Sidebar.

9) Select an animated object in the list and then select from the **Start** drop list how the animation effect starts.

   a) *On click* – the animation does not start until you click the mouse.

   b) *With previous* – the animation runs at the same time as the previous animation.

   c) *After previous* – the animation runs as soon as the previous animation ends.

10) With the animated object still selected in the list, select a direction on how the object appears on the slide from the **Direction** drop list. The options available in this drop down list may change depending on the type of animation effect being used.

11) If necessary and with the animated object still selected in the list, change the speed of the animation effect using the **Speed** drop list.

12) If necessary, change the order of the animation list by selecting an animated object and click on the **Move Down** or **Move Up** arrows.

13) Click **Play** to check how the animation effect looks on the slide.

14) Click **Slide Show** to check how your presentation runs and looks.

Changing animation effects

1) On the Custom Animation section on the Tasks pane, select the animation effect.

2) Click **Change**, then follow "Applying animation effects" above.

Removing animation effects

1) On the Custom Animation section on the Tasks pane, select the animation effect.
2) Click **Remove**.

Additional options for animation effects

Many animation effects have properties or options that you can set or change. That actual properties or options that will be available will depend on which animation effect you have selected.

1) On the Custom Animation section on the sidebar, select an animated object from the list.
2) Click the **Effect Options** icon 🔲 to the right of the **Direction** drop down list to open the Effect Options dialog.
3) Click on a tab to open the options for the type of effect options you want to change and use.
   a) *Effect* – Specifies the settings and enhancements of the selected animation effect (Figure 182).
   b) *Timing* – specifies the timing for the selected animation effect (Figure 183).
   c) *Text Animation* – specifies how the text is animated for the selected animation effect (Figure 184).
4) Click **OK** to save your changes and close the dialog.

Figure 182: Effect Options dialog – Effect page

Effect page options

Specifies the settings and enhancements for the current effect (Figure 182).

- **Direction** – specifies the direction for the effect.
- **Sound** – select a sound from the drop down list or select one of the special entries.
  - *(No sound)* – no sound is played during animation of the effect.
  - *(Stop previous sound)* – the sound of the previous effect is stopped as soon as the current effect runs.
  - *Other sound* – displays a file open dialog to select a sound file.

- **Play sound** – clicking on this icon ▶ to the right of the **Sound** drop down list to play the selected sound file.

- **After animation** – select a color to be shown after the animation ends, or select another after-effect from the list.
  - *Dim with color* – after the animation a dim color fills the shape.
  - *Don't dim* – no after-effect runs.
  - *Hide after animation* – hides the shape after the animation ends.
  - *Hide on next animation* – hides the shape on the next animation.
- **Dim color** – select the dim color. Only available if *Dim with color* has been selected.
- **Text animation** – select the animation mode for the text of the current shape:
  - *All at once* – animates the text all at once.
  - *Word by word* – animates the text word by word.
  - *Letter by letter* – animates the text letter by letter.
- **Delay between characters** – specifies the percentage of delay between animations if *Word by word* or *Letter by letter* has been selected for text animation.

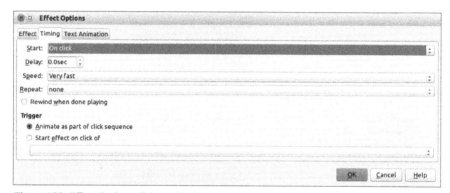

Figure 183: Effect Options dialog – Timing page

Timing page options

Specifies the timing for the current effect (Figure 183).

- **Start** – displays the start property of the selected animation effect.
  - *On click* – the animation stops at this effect until the next mouse click.
  - *With previous* – the animation runs immediately.
  - *After previous* – the animation runs as soon as the previous animation ends.
- **Delay** – specifies an additional delay of n seconds until the effect starts.
- **Speed** – specifies the duration of the effect.
- **Repeat** – specifies whether and how to repeat the current effect. Enter the number of repeats, or select from the list:
  - *none* – the effect is not repeated.
  - *Until next click* – the animation is repeated until the next mouse click.
  - *Until end of slide* – the animation repeats as long as the slide is displayed.
- **Rewind when done playing** – specifies whether to let the animated shape return to its starting state after the animation ends.

- **Animate as part of click sequence** – specifies whether to let the animation start in the normal click sequence.
- **Start effect on click of** – specifies whether to let the animation start when a specified shape is clicked. Select the shape by its name from the list box.

Figure 184: Effect Options dialog – Text Animation page

Text animation page options

Specifies the text animation settings for the current effect (Figure 184).

- **Group text** – specifies how multiple paragraphs are animated:
    - *As one object* – all paragraphs are animated as one object.
    - *All paragraphs at once* – all paragraphs are animated at once, but can have different effects.
    - *By 1st level paragraphs* – the first level paragraphs, including sub-level paragraphs, are animated one after another.
- **Automatically after** – if *By 1st level paragraphs* is selected for **Group text**, the paragraphs are animated one after the other. Enter an additional delay in seconds to animate subsequent paragraphs.
- **Animate attached shape** – deselect this box to animate only the text, not the shape.
- **In reverse order** – animates the paragraphs in reverse order.

Examples of animation effects

Using multiple animation effects

To illustrate how you can set up multiple effects, the following example shows you how to animate list items that fly in one at a time from the bottom of the slide and, as each new item appears, the previous items change to a different color.

1) Go to **View > Normal** on the main menu bar, or click on the **Normal** tab in the Workspace.
2) Select a slide with objects that you want to apply the animation effect to.
3) Select three objects on your selected slide.
4) In the Sidebar, select **Custom Animation** icon 🌟 to open the Custom Animation dialog (Figure 181).
5) Click the **Entrance** tab to open the Entrance page of the Custom Animation dialog.
6) Select the **Fly In** effect and change the speed to **Medium.**
7) Click **OK** and the three objects appear in the **Custom Animation** list on the Sidebar (Figure 185).
8) Select the top object in the **Custom Animation** list and select **From top** from the *Direction* drop down list on the Sidebar.

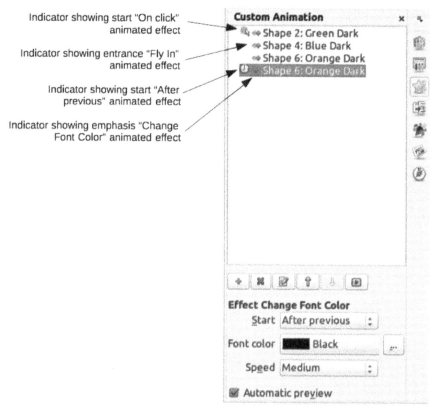

Indicator showing start "On click" animated effect

Indicator showing entrance "Fly In" animated effect

Indicator showing start "After previous" animated effect

Indicator showing emphasis "Change Font Color" animated effect

Figure 185: Example of animated points

9) Select the second object in the **Custom Animation** list and select **From right** from the *Direction* drop down list on the Sidebar.

10) Select the last object in the **Custom Animation** list and select **From bottom** from the *Direction* drop down list on the Sidebar.

11) With the last object still selected, click on the **Add Effect** icon ✛ on the Sidebar to open the Custom Animation dialog (Figure 181).

12) Click the Emphasis tab to open the Emphasis page of the Custom Animation dialog.

13) Select **Change Font Color** and click **OK** to save this animated effect.

14) From the *Start* drop down list on the Sidebar, select **After previous**.

15) From the *Font color* drop list on the Sidebar, select the color you want to use for the emphasis.

16) In Figure 185, the three animation effects are now indicated with icons and these indicator show what type of animated effect has been added to thee objects.

17) To test the animation effects, make sure all the objects are selected and click on the **Preview Effect** icon ▣ on the Sidebar.

Setting up a motion path

A motion path effect moves an object along a path consisting of a combination of straight and curved lines. Several pre-packaged motion paths are provided in LibreOffice, but it is not difficult to create your own custom path as follows. You can also combine a motion path with other animation effects such as spinning or changing of size or colors to create dramatic effects.

1) Select the object you want to animate.
2) Click on the **Add Effect** icon ✚ in the Sidebar to open the Custom Animation dialog (Figure 181).
3) Click the **Motion Paths** tab to open the Motion Paths page of the Custom Animation dialog.
4) Select a pre-packaged motion path animation that is similar to the effect you want to obtain. Alternatively use the **Polygon** or **Curve** animation effect to create a new motion path.
5) Select the object to show the animation path, which is displayed as a thin gray line with triangles showing the end points of the motion path.
6) Click on the animation path so that selection handles are displayed around it. When the selection handles are shown, you can move or resize the path the same way you would perform these operations on an object.

Note	When moving a path, remember to also move the object on that path; otherwise the animation will start with a jump. Currently it is not possible to rotate a path.

7) While the path is selected. select the **Points** icon ⬡ on the Drawing toolbar or press the F8 key to display the Edit Points toolbar (Figure 186). If is not displayed, go to **View > Toolbars > Edit Points** on the main menu bar. The number of icons available in the Edit Points toolbar will depend on the type of motion path and object selected.

Figure 186: Edit Points toolbar and icons

8) Once a point is selected, you can delete the point, move the point, or add another point and so on. For a detailed explanation on how to manipulate the points on a curve, see the *Draw Guide*.
9) When you are satisfied with the shape of the curve and its speed, click anywhere on the screen to deselect the object and continue normal editing.
10) To test the motion path, click **Preview Effect** icon ▶ on the Sidebar to start the animation.

Using interactions

Interactions are things that happen when you click on an object in a slide. They are typically used with buttons or images, but text objects can also have interactions.

To apply an interaction to an object (or change an interaction applied to an object):

1) Select the object, then right-click on the object and select **Interaction** from the context menu, or go to **Slide Show > Interaction** on the main menu bar to open the Interaction dialog (Figure 187).
2) Select an interaction from the **Action at mouse click** drop-down list. With some interactions, the Interaction dialog changes to offer more options.

3) Click **OK** to save your changes and close the dialog.

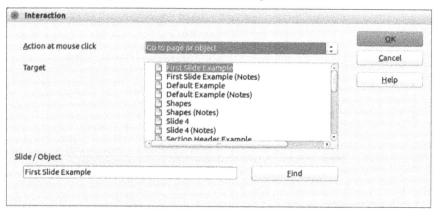

Figure 187: Interaction dialog

> **Tip**   A sound interaction can be also applied using the Effect Options dialog See "Additional options for animation effects" on page 222 for more information.

Slide shows

Running a slide show

To run a slide show:

1) Open your presentation using LibreOffice Impress.
2) Press the *F5* key, or go to **Slide Show > Slide Show** on the main menu bar, or click the **Slide Show** icon on the Presentation toolbar or the Slide Sorter toolbar.
3) If the slide transition is set to *Automatically after x seconds*, let the slide show run by itself.
4) If the slide transition is set to *On mouse click*, press the *down arrow* key, the *right arrow* key, or the *Page Down* key on the keyboard, click the left mouse button, or press the *Spacebar*.
5) To navigate backwards through the slide show one slide at a time, press the *up arrow* key, the *left arrow* key, or the *Page Up* key.
6) For more complex navigation during the slide show, use the right-click navigation (see "Right-click navigation and options" below).
7) When you advance past the last slide, the message **Click to exit presentation...** appears. Click the left mouse button or press any key to exit the presentation.
8) To exit the slide show and return to the Impress workspace at any time, including at the end of the slide show, press the *Esc* key.

> **Note**   Any custom animations on a slide are run in the specified order when performing one of the above actions while running the slide show.

Right-click navigation and options

If your presentation consists of more than one slide, right-clicking anywhere on the screen brings up a context menu. The options are as follows:

- **Next** – moves to the next slide in the defined sequence.
- **Previous** – moves to the previous slide in the defined sequence.
- **Go to Slide** – displays a submenu allowing to quickly select and navigate to any slide in the presentation. Options on the submenu include **First slide**, **Last Slide**, or any slide in the presentation and illustrates why giving the slides meaningful names, rather than leaving them at the default Slide 1, Slide 2, and so on, can be very helpful.
- **Mouse pointer as Pen** – allows you to use the cursor as a pen and draw on a slide to emphasize or explain a point.
- **Pen Width** – adjusts the width of any lines drawn when using the cursor as a pen.
- **Change pen Color** – allows you to change the color of any line when using the cursor as a pen.
- **Erase all ink on Slide** – deletes all lines drawn after you have finished using the cursor as a pen.
- **Screen** – displays a submenu with two options. Each option blanks the screen, showing it as either all black or all white. This can be useful if you want to pause the show for awhile, perhaps during a break or to demonstrate something on another computer.
- **End Show** – ends the presentation and returns you to the Impress workspace. This is the same effect as pressing the *Esc* key.

Using the Presenter Console

Most installations of LibreOffice Impress come with the Presenter Console extension built in. If it is not included, you can also get the extension and install it as described in *Chapter 11, Setting up and Customizing Impress*.

The Presenter Console (Figure 188) provides extra control over slide shows when using dual displays for a slide show, such as a laptop for yourself and large display or projector for your audience.

The view you see on your computer display includes the current slide that can be seen by the audience, the next slide in your presentation, any slide notes, and a presentation timer.

Note	The Presenter Console works only on operating systems that support two displays, and only when two displays are connected (one may be the laptop display).

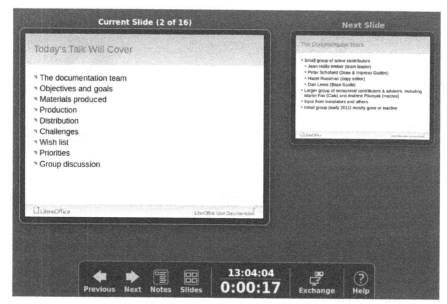

Figure 188: Presenter Console

The Presenter Console provides the following easily changeable views:

- First view, which is the default view, displays the current slide, including the effects, and the upcoming slide. Click on the **Previous** and **Next** arrows to navigate through your presentation.

- Second view shows the notes for the speaker in large, scalable type, plus the current and upcoming slides. Click on the **Notes** icon to switch to this view. Click on the **Notes** icon again to return to the first view.

- Third view is a slide sorter view with the slide thumbnails where you can select a thumbnail to jump to a slide out of sequence. Click on the **Slides** icon to switch to this view. Click on the **Slides** icon again to return to the first view.

- Click on the **Exchange** icon to switch the Presenter Console between displays.

- Click on the **Help** icon to display a list of the controls that are available in the Presenter Console. Click on the **Help** icon again to return to the previous view.

Chapter 10
Printing, E-mailing, Exporting,
and Saving Slide Shows

Introduction

This chapter provides information about printing, exporting, and e-mailing documents from LibreOffice Impress.

Quick printing

Click the **Print File Directly** icon 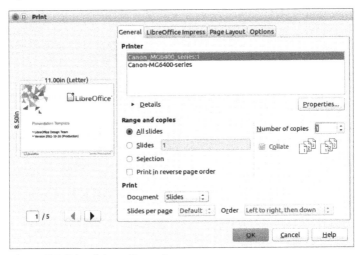 on the Standard toolbar to send the entire document to the default printer defined for your computer.

Note	You can change the action carried out when you click the **Print File Directly** icon. Go to **Tools > Options > Load/Save > General** and select the **Load printer settings with the document** option. When this option is selected, your document will be printed with the settings that have been specified for the document and will not use the default printing options that are specified for your computer.
	Also with this option selected, your document will be printed on the printer specified for your document and not your default printer if you do not change the printer in the Print dialog. For more information, see "Controlling printing" below.

Controlling printing

Impress provides many options for printing a presentation; for example multiple slides on one page, single slide per page, slides with notes, as an outline, with date and time, with page name, and so on.

For more control over printing a presentation, go to **File > Print** on the menu bar, or use the keyboard shortcut *Ctrl+P* to open the Print dialog (Figure 189). The Print dialog has four tabbed pages where you can choose a range of options, as described in the following sections.

Figure 189. Print dialog – General page

General printing

On the **General** page of the Print dialog (Figure 189):

1) Select a printer from the list of printers available.

2) Select the slides to print, the number of copies to print, whether to collate multiple copies and to reverse printing order using the **Range and copies** section.

3) Select whether to print slides, notes, handouts, or an outline of the presentation, slides per page and printing order using the **Print** section.

4) Click **Properties** to display a Properties dialog. Actual printer properties available will depend on the printer being used and type of computer operating system being used.

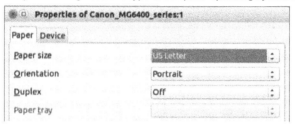

Figure 190: Example of a Properties dialog – Paper page

Figure 191: Example of a Properties dialog – Device page

5) On the **Paper** page, select paper size to use, portrait or landscape orientation, double sided printing (if available) and the paper tray to use. An example is shown in Figure 190.

6) On the **Device** page, select the options you want to use from the list of available options and the value you want to use. An example is shown in Figure 191.

7) Click **OK** to print your presentation and close the dialog.

Example of selecting slides to print

To print an individual slide or several slides:

1) Open the Print dialog and select the **General** page. Then, do one of the following:

   - To print a single slide or a selection of slides, select the *Slides* option in the **Ranges and copies** section and type the slide numbers in the text box. Separate each slide number by a comma, for example 1,3,7,11.

   - To print a range of slides, select the *Slides* option in the **Ranges and copies** section and type the slide numbers in the text box as a range, for example 1-4.

   - To print a selection of slides, select the slides in the Slides pane or Slide Sorter view and then select *Selection* in the **Range and copies section**.

2) Click **OK** to print your slides and close the dialog.

Example of printing handouts

Handouts of slides can be printed using one to nine slides per page. The slides can be printed horizontally (landscape orientation) or vertically (portrait orientation) on the page. To print handouts:

1) Open the Print dialog and select the **General** page.

2) In the **Print** section of the Print dialog, select **Handouts** from the *Document* drop-down list.

3) Select how many slides to print per page and the order in which they are printed.

4) Click **OK** to print your slides and close the dialog.

LibreOffice Impress

On the **LibreOffice Impress** page of the print dialog (Figure 192), you can select how your presentation is printed using the **Contents**, **Color** and **Size** sections. These options will override default printer options in **Tools > Options > LibreOffice Impress > Print** for the current print job.

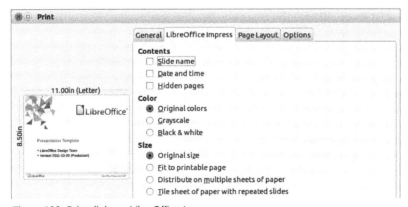

Figure 192. Print dialog – LibreOffice Impress page

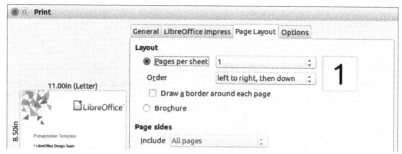

Figure 193. Print dialog – Page Layout page

Page layout

On the **Page Layout** page of the print dialog (Figure 193), you can select how your presentation is printed using the **Layout** and **Page sides** sections.

The following steps give you an example on how you can print multiple pages of a document on one sheet of paper.

1) Open the Print dialog and select the **Page Layout** page.
2) In *Layout*, select from the drop-down list the number of pages to print per sheet. The preview panel on the left shows how the printed document will look.
3) When printing more than two pages per sheet, select the *Order* in which they are printed across and down the paper.
4) Select whether to *Draw a border around each page* that is printed.
5) In the *Page sides* section, select whether to print all pages or only some pages.
6) Click **OK** to print the presentation and close the dialog.

Options

The **Options** page of the Print dialog (Figure 194) allows you to select other options for printing your presentation. These options will override default printer options in **Tools > Options > LibreOffice Impress > Print** for the current print job.

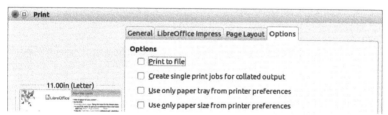

Figure 194: Print dialog – Options page

Selecting default print options

Printing options selected in the Print dialog override any default settings for printing that have been set using **Tools > Options > LibreOffice Impress > Print** and in **Tools > Options > LibreOffice > Print**. Use these settings to specify quality settings for printing, and whether to have Impress warn you if the paper size or orientation of your document does not match the printer settings. See *Chapter 11 Setting Up and Customizing Impress* for more information.

Brochure printing

You can print a presentation with two slides on each side of a sheet of paper, arranged so that when the printed pages are folded in half, the slides are in the correct order to form a booklet or brochure.

Note	The procedures given below are only examples. The actual procedure may differ as this depends on your computer system and type of printer being used. You may have to experiment to find the correct method for brochure printing.

Single sided printing

To print a brochure on a printer that can only print single-sided pages:

1) Go to **File > Print** on the menu bar, or use the keyboard shortcut *Ctrl+P* to open the Print dialog (Figure 189 on page 232).
2) Make sure the Print dialog has the **General** page open.
3) Click **Properties** and check the printer is set to the same orientation (portrait or landscape) as specified in the page setup for your document. Usually the orientation does not matter, but it does for brochures. Click **OK** to return to the Print dialog.
4) Select which slides you want printed as a brochure in the **Range and copies** section. You have to select four or more slides for brochure printing.
5) Select the **Page layout** page in the Print dialog (Figure 193 on page 235).
6) Select the *Brochure* option in the **Layout** section.
7) In the *Page sides* section, select **Back sides / left pages** option from the *Include* drop-down list.
8) Click **OK** to close the Print dialog and print the first page side of selected slides.
9) Take the printed pages out of the printer, turn the pages over, and put them back into the printer in the correct orientation to print on the blank side. You may need to experiment a bit to find out what the correct arrangement is for your printer.
10) Repeat Steps 1 through 6 above.
11) In the *Page sides* section, select **Front sides / right pages** option from the *Include* drop-down list.
12) Click **OK** to close the print dialog and print the second page side of selected slides.

Duplex printing

To print a brochure on a printer that can print double-sided pages (duplex printing):

1) Go to **File > Print** on the menu bar, or use the keyboard shortcut *Ctrl+P* to open the Print dialog (Figure 189 on page 232).
2) Make sure the Print dialog has the **General** page open.
3) Click **Properties** and check the printer is set to the same orientation (portrait or landscape) as specified in the page setup for your document. Usually the orientation does not matter, but it does for brochures.
4) Make sure that duplex or double sided printing is selected and the type of binding you want to use.

5) Click **OK** to return to the Print dialog.

6) Select which slides you want printed as a brochure in the **Range and copies** section. You have to select four or more slides for brochure printing.

7) Select the **Page layout** page in the Print dialog (Figure 193 on page 235).

8) Select the *Brochure* option in the **Layout** section.

9) In the *Page sides* section, select **All pages** option from the *Include* drop-down list.

10) Click **OK** to close the Print dialog and print your selected slides as a brochure.

PDF export

Impress can export presentations to PDF (Portable Document Format). This industry-standard file format for file viewing is ideal for sending the file to someone else to view using Adobe Reader or other PDF viewers.

Quick export

Click the **Export Directly as PDF** icon 📷 on the Standard toolbar to export the entire presentation using the default PDF settings. You are asked to enter the file name and location for the PDF file, but you cannot select a page range or print quality for the PDF file.

Controlling PDF content and quality

For more control over the content and quality of the PDF produced:

1) Go to **File > Export as PDF** on the menu bar to open the PDF Options dialog (Figure 195). This dialog has five pages and the options available are described below.

2) Make your selections and then click **Export**.

3) Enter the location and file name of the PDF to be created.

4) Click **Save** to export the file.

General options

On the General page (Figure 195), you can select which pages (slides) to include in the PDF, the type of compression to use for images (this affects the quality of images in the PDF), and so on.

- **Range** – sets the export options for the slides to be included in the PDF file.
    - *All* – exports the entire document.
    - *Slides* – exports the slide numbers you type in the box. To export a range of slides, use the format 3-6. To export single slides, use the format 7;9;11. You can also export a combination of slide ranges and single slides, by using a format like 3-6;8;10;12.
    - *Selection* – exports the current selection of slides.
- **Images** – sets the PDF export options for images inside your document. EPS images with embedded previews are exported only as previews. EPS images without embedded previews are exported as empty placeholders.
    - *Lossless compression* – selects a lossless compression of images. All pixels are preserved.
- *JPEG compression* – selects a JPEG compression of images. With a high quality level, almost all pixels are preserved. With a low quality level, some pixels get lost and artifacts are introduced, but file sizes are reduced.
- *Quality* – enter the quality level for JPEG compression.

– *Reduce image resolution* – select to resample or down-size the images to a lower number of pixels per inch. Enter the target resolution for the images.

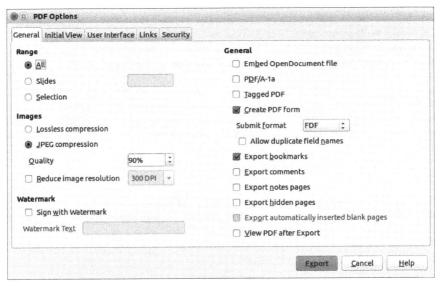

Figure 195: PDF Options dialog – General page

- **General** – sets general PDF export options.

    – *Embed OpenDocument file* – export the document as a PDF file containing two file formats: PDF and ODF. In PDF viewers it behaves like a normal PDF file, but it remains fully editable in LibreOffice.

    – *PDF/A-1a* – convert to the PDF/A-1a format. This is defined as an electronic document file format for long term preservation. All fonts that were used in the source document will be embedded into the generated PDF file. PDF tags will be written.

    – *Tagged PDF* – write PDF tags. This can increase file size by huge amounts. A tagged PDF contains information about the structure of the document contents. This can help to display the document on devices with different screens, and when using screen reader software.

    – *Create PDF form* – create a PDF form, which can be filled out and printed by the user of the PDF document.

    – *Submit format* – select the format of submitting forms from within the PDF file. Select the format of the data that you will receive from the submitter: FDF (Forms Data Format), PDF, HTML, or XML. This setting overrides the URL property that you set in the document.

    – *Allow duplicate field names* – allows you to use the same field name for multiple fields in the generated PDF file. If disabled, field names will be exported using generated unique names.

    – *Export bookmarks* – export bookmarks of Writer documents as PDF bookmarks. Bookmarks are created for all outline paragraphs (**Tools > Outline Numbering**) and for all table of contents entries for which you did assign hyperlinks in the source document.

    – *Export comments* – export comments in Writer and Calc documents as PDF notes.

- *Export notes pages* – export a set of notes as pages after the set of slides.
- *Export hidden pages* – export any hidden pages in your document as part of the PDF.
- *Export automatically inserted blank pages* – if selected, automatically inserted blank pages are exported in the PDF file. This is best if you are printing the PDF file double-sided. For example, in a book a chapter paragraph style is set to always start with an odd numbered page. If the previous chapter ends on an odd page, LibreOffice inserts an even numbered blank page. This option controls whether to export that even numbered page.
- *View PDF after Export* – automatically opens the newly created PDF file after it has been exported.

Initial View options

On the Initial View page (Figure 196), you can select how the PDF file opens by default in a PDF viewer.

If you have Complex Text Layout enabled (in **Tools > Options > Language settings > Languages**), an additional selection is available under *Continuous facing*: **First page is left**. Normally, the first page is on the right when using the *Continuous facing* option.

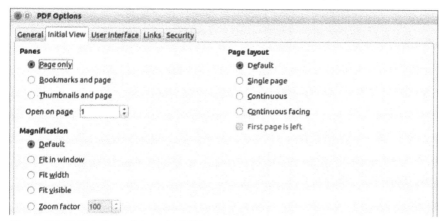

Figure 196: PDF Options dialog – Initial View page

- **Panes**
  - *Page only* – generate a PDF file that shows only the page contents.
  - *Bookmarks and page* – generate a PDF file that shows a bookmarks palette and the page contents.
  - *Thumbnails and page* – generate a PDF file that shows a thumbnails palette and the page contents.
  - *Open on page* – show the given page when the reader opens the PDF file.

- **Magnification**
  - *Default* – generate a PDF file that shows the page contents without zooming. If the reader software is configured to use a zoom factor by default, the page shows with that zoom factor.
  - *Fit in window* – generate a PDF file that shows the page zoomed to fit entirely into the window of the PDF file reader.

- *Fit width* – generate a PDF file that shows the page zoomed to fit the width of the window of the PDF file reader.
- *Fit visible* – generate a PDF file that shows the text and graphics on the page zoomed to fit the width of the window of the PDF file reader.
- *Zoom factor* – select a zoom factor to apply when the reader opens the PDF file.

• **Page layout**

- *Default* – generate a PDF file that shows the pages according to the layout setting of the reader software.
- *Single page* – generate a PDF file that shows one page at a time.
- *Continuous* – generate a PDF file that shows pages in a continuous vertical column.
- *Continuous facing* – generate PDF file that shows pages side by side in a continuous column. For more than two pages, the first page is displayed on the right.
- *First page is left* – generate a PDF file that shows pages side by side in a continuous column. For more than two pages, the first page is displayed on the left. You must enable support for complex text layout in **Tools > Options > Language settings > Languages**.

User Interface options

On the User Interface page (Figure 197), you can choose more settings to control how a PDF viewer displays the file. Some of these options are particularly useful when you are creating a PDF for use in a presentation or kiosk-type display.

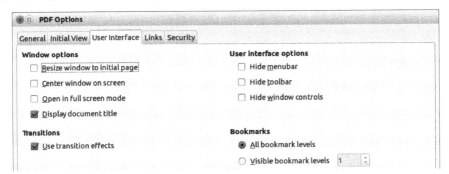

Figure 197: PDF Options dialog – User Interface page

• **Window options**

- *Resize window to initial page* – generate a PDF file that is shown in a window displaying the whole initial page.
- *Center window on screen* – generate a PDF file that is shown in a reader window centered on screen.
- *Open in full screen mode* – generate a PDF file that is shown in a full screen reader window in front of all other windows.
- *Display document title* – generate a PDF file that is shown with the document title in the reader title bar.

• **User interface options**

- *Hide menu bar* – hide the reader's menu bar when the document is active.

- – *Hide toolbar* – hide the reader's toolbar when the document is active.
- – *Hide window controls* – hide the reader's controls when the document is active.

• **Transitions**
- – *Use transition effects* – export Impress slide transition effects to respective PDF effects.

• **Bookmarks**
- – *All bookmark levels* – show all bookmark levels when the reader opens the PDF file.
- – *Visible bookmark levels* – show bookmark levels down to the selected level when the reader opens the PDF file.

Links options

On the Links page (Figure 198), specify how to export bookmarks and hyperlinks in your document.

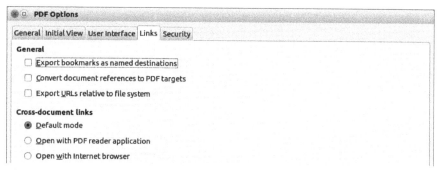

Figure 198: PDF Options dialog – Links page

• **Export bookmarks as named destinations** – bookmarks (targets of references) in PDF files can be defined as rectangular areas. Additionally, bookmarks to named objects can be defined by their names. Enable this option to export the names of objects in your document as valid bookmark targets. This allows to link to those objects by name from other documents.

• **Convert document references to PDF targets** – convert the URLs referencing other ODF files to PDF files with the same name. In referencing URLs the extensions .odt, .odp, .ods, .odg, and .odm are converted to the extension .pdf.

• **Export URLs relative to file system** – export URLs to other documents as relative URLs in the file system.

• **Cross-document links** – specify how to handle hyperlinks from your PDF file to other files.
- – *Default mode* – links from your PDF document to other documents will be handled as specified in your operating system.
- – *Open with PDF reader application* – cross-document links are opened with the PDF reader application that currently shows the document. The PDF reader application must be able to handle the specified file type inside the hyperlink.
- – *Open with Internet browser* – cross-document links are opened with the Internet browser. The Internet browser must be able to handle the specified file type inside the hyperlink.

Security options

On the Security page (Figure 199), you can set PDF export options to encrypt a PDF file so that it can only be opened using a password and also apply digital rights management (DRM) features. You have to set a password before the security options are available. Click **Set passwords** to open the **Set passwords** dialog (Figure 200).

Note	Security settings are effective only if another PDF viewer respects the settings.

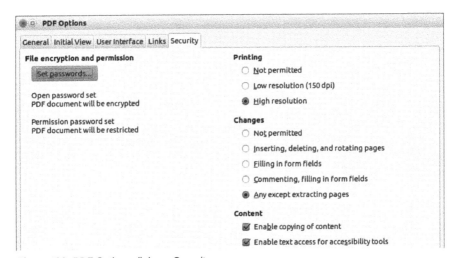

Figure 199: PDF Options dialog – Security page

Figure 200: Set Passwords dialog

- **Set passwords** – click to open the Set passwords dialog. You can enter a password to open the file. You can also enter an optional password that allows readers to edit the document.

- **Printing**
  - *Not permitted* – printing the document is not permitted.
  - *Low resolution (150 dpi)* – the document can only be printed in low resolution (150 dpi). Not all PDF readers honor this setting.
  - *High resolution* – the document can be printed in high resolution.

- **Changes**
  - *Not permitted* – no changes of the content are permitted.
  - *Inserting, deleting, and rotating pages* – only inserting, deleting, and rotating pages is permitted.
  - *Filling in form fields* – only filling in form fields is permitted.
  - *Commenting, filling in form fields* – only commenting and filling in form fields is permitted.
  - *Any except extracting pages* – all changes are permitted, except extracting pages.
- **Content**
  - *Enable copying of content* – select to enable copying of content to the clipboard.
  - *Enable text access for accessibility tools* – select to enable text access for accessibility tools.

Flash file export

Macromedia Flash file format (.swf) was created to store animation for web pages. With most browsers able to play Flash movies these files can be viewed by the majority of users. If a browser cannot play Flash movies, then Adobe Flash Player is available as a free download from Adobe at http://www.adobe.com/products/flashplayer/.

Note	Saving in Flash format does not retain animation and slide transitions.

Using LibreOffice, you can export your Impress slide show as a Flash file in .swf format as follows:
1) Go to **File > Export** on the menu bar.
2) Select the location where you want the file saved and type a name for the file.
3) Under **File Format**, select **Macromedia Flash (SWF) (.swf)** from the drop down list and click **Save.**

Web pages (HTML files) export

You can export presentations as a series of web pages that can be viewed in any browser.

Note	Saving as web pages (HTML format) does not retain animation and slide transitions.

1) Go to **File > Export** on the menu bar and select **HTML Document (Impress) (.html; .htm)** as the file type.
2) Create a folder for the files, then give a name for the resulting HTML file and click **Save** to open the HTML Export wizard (Figure 201).

Figure 201: HTML Export wizard – selecting a design

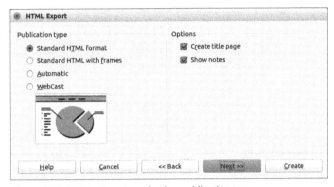

Figure 202: HTML Export – selecting publication type

3) Select a design for all of the pages, either from an existing design or by creating a new one. If you have not previously saved a design, the *Existing Design* choice is not available.

4) Click **Next** to select the type of web pages to create (Figure 202). The available options will change depending on publication type selected.

- *Standard HTML* – one page for each slide with navigation links to move from slide to slide.

- *Standard HTML with frames* – one page with a navigation bar on the left-hand side; uses slide title as navigation links. Click on links to display pages in right-hand side.

- *Automatic* – one page for each slide, with each page set with the refresh meta tag so a browser automatically cycles from one page to the next.

- *WebCast* – generates an ASP or Perl application to display the slides. Unfortunately LibreOffice has no direct support for PHP yet.

5) Click **Next** to decide how the images will be saved (PNG, GIF or JPG) and what resolution to use (Figure 203). When choosing a resolution, consider what the majority of your viewers may have. For example, if you use a high resolution, then a viewer with a medium-resolution monitor will have to scroll sideways to see the entire slide.

6) If *Create title page* was selected in Step 4, supply the information for the title page on the next page that appears after clicking **Next** (Figure 204). The title page contains name of the author, e-mail address and home page, along with any additional information you want to include. This page of the Wizard does not display if *Create title page* was not selected.

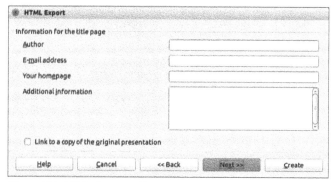

Figure 203: HTML Export – selecting graphics type

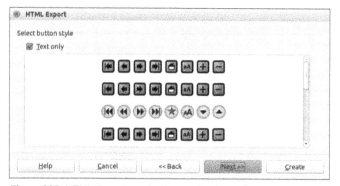

Figure 204: HTML Export – title page information

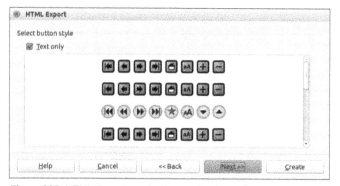

Figure 205: HTML Export – selecting navigation style

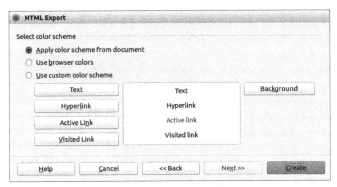

Figure 206: HTML Export – selecting color scheme

7) Click **Next** to select the style of navigation buttons to use when moving from one page to another (Figure 205). If you do not choose a navigation style, LibreOffice will create a text navigator.

8) Click **Next** to select the color scheme for the web pages (Figure 206). Available schemes include the existing scheme for the presentation, one based upon browser colors, and a user-defined scheme. You can save a new scheme so that it will appear on the first page of the HTML export wizard.

9) Click **Create** to generate the HTML files. If this is a new design, a dialog opens so you can save the design. If you want to reuse this design, you can give it a name and save it. Otherwise, click **Do Not Save**.

E-mailing a presentation

LibreOffice provides several ways to quickly and easily send a presentation as an e-mail attachment in one of three formats: ODP (OpenDocument Presentation, the LibreOffice default format), PPT (Microsoft PowerPoint format), or as a PDF file.

- To send the presentation in ODP format, go to **File > Send > Document as E-mail** or **File > Send > E-mail as OpenDocument Presentation** on the menu bar. LibreOffice opens a new e-mail in your e-mail program with the ODP document attached.

- To send the presentation in PPT format, go to **File > Send > E-mail as Microsoft PowerPoint Presentation** on the menu bar. LibreOffice creates a PPT file and then opens a new e-mail in your e-mail program with the PPT file attached. This PPT file is not saved on your computer.

- To send the presentation in PDF format, go to **File > Send > E-mail as PDF** on the menu bar. LibreOffice first creates a PDF using your default PDF settings (similar to using the **Export Directly as PDF** icon in the standard toolbar) and then opens a new e-mail in your e-mail program with the PDF file attached. This PDF file is not saved on your computer.

- In your e-mail program, enter the recipient, subject and any text you want to add, then send the e-mail.

Tip	If you want to keep a copy of the .PPT or .PDF file as well as e-mailing it to someone, first save or export the presentation into the required format, then attach it to an e-mail in the usual way.

Digital signing of documents

To sign a document digitally, you need a personal key, also known as a certificate. A personal key is stored on your computer as a combination of a private key, which must be kept secret, and a public key, which you add to your documents when you sign them. You can get a certificate from a certification authority, which may be a private company or a governmental institution.

When you apply a digital signature to a document, a kind of checksum is computed from the document contents plus your personal key. The checksum and your public key are stored together with the document.

When someone later opens the document on any computer with a recent version of LibreOffice, the program will compute the checksum again and compare it with the stored checksum. If both are the same, the program will signal that you see the original, unchanged document. In addition, the program can show you the public key information from the certificate. You can compare the public key with the public key that is published on the web site of the certificate authority.

Whenever someone changes something in the document, this change breaks the digital signature.

On Windows operating systems, the Windows features for validating a signature are used. On GNU/Linux systems, files that are supplied by Thunderbird, Mozilla, or Firefox are used. For a more detailed description of how to get and manage a certificate, and signature validation, see "About Digital Signatures" and "Applying Digital Signatures" in the LibreOffice Help.

To digitally sign a document:

1) Go to **File > Digital Signatures** on the menu bar.
2) If you have not saved the document since the last change, a message appears. Click **Yes** to save the file and the Digital Signatures dialog opens (Figure 207).
3) Click **Sign Document** to add a public key to the document.
4) In the Select Certificate dialog that opens, select your certificate and click **OK** to close the dialog.
5) If necessary, repeat Steps 3 and 4 to add more certificates.
6) Click **OK** to add the public key to the saved file. When a document is digitally signed, an indicator appears on the status bar. You can double-click the icon to view the certificate.

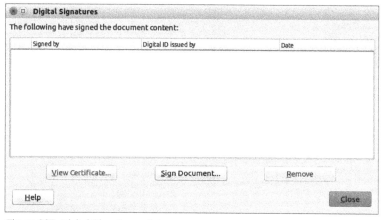

Figure 207: Digital Signatures dialog

Removing personal data

You may wish to ensure that personal data, versions, notes, hidden information, or recorded changes are removed from files before you send them to other people or create PDF files from them.

In **Tools > Options > LibreOffice > Security > Options**, you can set LibreOffice to remind (warn) you when files contain certain information and remove personal information automatically when saving the file or when creating a PDF.

To remove personal and some other data from a file, go to **File > Properties**. On the *General* tab, uncheck **Apply user data** and then click the **Reset** button. This removes any names in the created and modified fields, deletes the modification and printing dates, and resets the editing time to zero, the creation date to the current date and time, and the version number to 1. Make sure you click **OK** to save the changes.

Opening and saving a PowerPoint file

The file format of LibreOffice Impress is highly compatible with the format used by Microsoft PowerPoint. You can open a PowerPoint presentation in Impress, edit it, then save it in its original PowerPoint format or in OpenDocument Presentation format used by Impress. You can also create a new presentation in Impress and save it as a PowerPoint file.

Note	There are some differences between OpenDocument (.odp) and PowerPoint (.ppt, .pptx) files in text and graphics formatting, animations, transitions, and fields. For best results, avoid using features that are not fully supported in both formats.

Saving an Impress file as a PowerPoint file

1) Go to **File > Save As** on the menu bar.
2) Select the location where you want the PowerPoint file saved and type a name for the file.
3) Under *File type*, select a **Microsoft PowerPoint** format (.ppt or .pptx) from the available drop-down list.
4) Click **Save**. If you have the "Warn when not saving in ODF or default format" option set in **Tools > Options > Load/Save > General**, a Confirm file Format dialog (Figure 208) opens. Click on the button showing the Microsoft PowerPoint format to confirm that you want to save the file in that format. You can deselect the *Ask when not saving in ODF format* checkbox to not show the message again unless you re-enable it in the options.

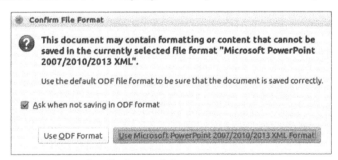

Figure 208: Confirm file Format dialog

Tip	Always save your work in Impress OpenDocument format (.odp) before saving in Microsoft format. Keep the Impress file as your working copy: if you need to change the presentation, change it in the Impress version and then save it again as PowerPoint. You are much less likely to have problems than if you open a file previously saved in PowerPoint format, edit it, and save it again.

Opening a PowerPoint file in Impress

If you receive a file from someone in PowerPoint format and need to edit it in Impress, here is how:

1) In LibreOffice, go to **File > Open** on the menu bar.
2) In **File type**, select *All files (*.*)* or *Presentations* or *Microsoft PowerPoint* from the drop-down list.
3) Navigate to the PowerPoint file, select it, and click **Open.**

The PowerPoint file can now be edited and saved as an Impress file or as a PowerPoint file. To save the file as an Impress file, select **Open Document Presentation (.odp)** as the file type.

Chapter 11
Setting Up and Customizing Impress

LibreOffice options

This section covers some of the settings that apply to all the components of LibreOffice and are of interest to users of Impress. Other general options are discussed in *Getting Started Guide Chapter 2 Setting Up LibreOffice*.

1) Go to **Tools > Options** (**LibreOffice > Preferences** on a Mac) on the main menu bar to open the Options dialog. The list on the left-hand side of the Options dialog varies depending on which component of LibreOffice is open. The illustrations in this chapter show the list as it appears when Impress is open (Figure 209).

2) Click the expansion marker (+ or triangle, depending on computer setup) by **LibreOffice** on the left-hand side. A list of subsections drops down.

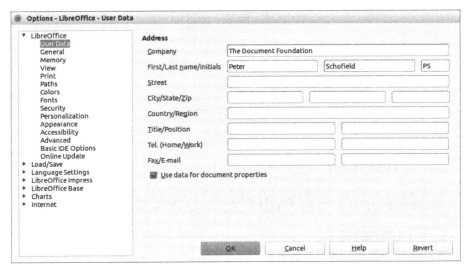

Figure 209: Options – LibreOffice – User Data dialog

Note	The **Revert** button has the same effect on all pages of the Options dialog. It resets the options to the values that were in place when you opened LibreOffice.

User Data options

Impress uses the first and last name stored in the User Data to fill in the *Created by* and *Modified by* fields in document properties, the optional *Author* field used in the footer of a presentation, and the name associated with comments. If you want your name to appear, then do the following:

1) In the Options dialog, click **LibreOffice > User Data** (Figure 209).

2) Fill in the **Address** form with your details and/or amend/delete any existing incorrect information.

Print options

In the Options dialog, click **LibreOffice > Print** (Figure 210) to set the print options that suit your default printer and your most common printing method.

You can change these settings at any time, either through the Options dialog or during the printing process. See *Chapter 10 Printing, E-mailing, Exporting, and Saving Slide Shows* in this guide for more information about the printing options available.

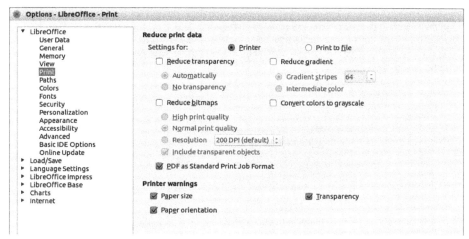

Figure 210: Options – LibreOffice – Print dialog

Color options

In the Options dialog, click **LibreOffice > Colors** (Figure 211) to specify colors used in LibreOffice documents. You can select a color from a color table, edit an existing color, or define new colors. These colors are stored in your color selection palette and are then available in all components of LibreOffice.

You can also define colors within Impress by going to **Format > Area** on the menu bar, or through the Line and Filling toolbar, but those colors will not be available to other components of LibreOffice.

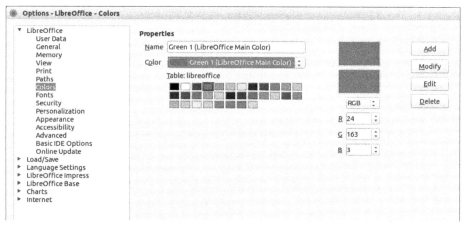

Figure 211: Options – LibreOffice – Colors dialog

Appearance options

In the Options dialog, click **LibreOffice > Appearance** (Figure 212) to specify which items are visible and the colors used to display various elements of the user interface.

The only option specific to Impress (and Draw) is the color of the grid points. Scroll down in the page until you find **Drawing/Presentation**. To change the default color for grid points, click the down-arrow by the color and select a new color from the pop-up dialog.

If you wish to save your color changes as a color scheme, click **Save,** type a name in the *Save scheme* dialog, then click **OK**.

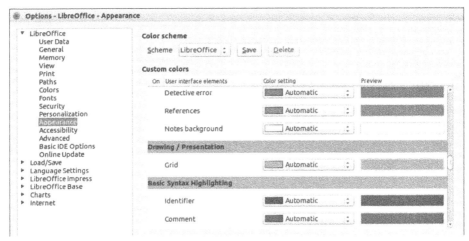

Figure 212: Options – LibreOffice – Appearance dialog

Choosing options for Impress

In the Options dialog, click the expansion marker to the left of **LibreOffice Impress** on the left-hand side. A list of subsections for Impress drops down (Figure 214).

General options

In the Options dialog, click **LibreOffice Impress > General** (Figure 214) to specify the general options for presentation documents.

Text objects

- **Allow quick editing** – if selected, you can edit text immediately after clicking a text object. If deselected, you must double-click to edit text. In a presentation, you can also activate the text editing mode using the **Allow Quick Editing** icon ![ABC] on the Option toolbar (Figure 213).

Figure 213: Options toolbar

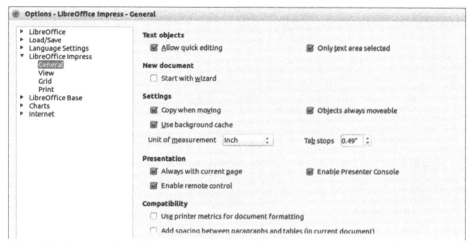

Figure 214: Options – LibreOffice Impress – General dialog

- **Only text area selectable** – specifies whether to select a text frame by clicking the text. In the area of the text frame that is not filled with text, an object behind the text frame can be selected. In a presentation, you can also activate this mode using the **Select Text Area Only** icon ▭ on the Option toolbar.

New document (presentations only)

- **Start with Wizard** – specifies whether to activate the Presentation Wizard when creating a new presentation using **File > New > Presentation** on the menu bar.

Settings

- **Use background cache** – specifies whether to use the cache for displaying objects on the master page. This speeds up the display. Deselect this option if you want to display changing contents on the master page.
- **Copy when moving** – if selected, a copy is created when you move an object while holding down the *Ctrl* key. The same will apply for rotating and resizing the object. The original object will remain in its current position and size.
- **Objects always moveable** – specifies that you want to move an object with the **Rotate** tool enabled. If this option is not selected, the **Rotate** tool can only be used to rotate an object.
- **Unit of measurement** – determines the unit of measurement used for presentations.
- **Tab stops** – defines the spacing between tab stops.

Presentation

- **Always with current page** – specifies that you always want a presentation to start with the current slide. When this option is not selected, a presentation always starts with the first page.
- **Enable remote control** – specifies that you want to enable Bluetooth remote control while Impress is running. Deselect this option to disable remote control.

- **Enable Presenter Console** – when selected, opens the Presenter Console for presentations when using multiple displays.

Compatibility

The settings in this area are valid for the current document only.

- **Use printer metrics for document formatting** – specifies that printer metrics are applied for printing and also for formatting the display on the screen. If this option is not selected, a printer independent layout will be used for screen display and printing. If you set this option for the current document and then save the document, for example, in an older binary format, this option will not be saved. If you later open the file from the older format, this option will be set by default.

- **Add spacing between paragraphs in the current document** – specifies that Impress calculates the paragraph spacing exactly like Microsoft PowerPoint. Microsoft PowerPoint adds the bottom spacing of a paragraph to the top spacing of the next paragraph to calculate the total spacing between both paragraphs. Impress utilizes only the larger of the two spacings.

View options

In the Options dialog, click on **LibreOffice Impress > View** (Figure 215) to specify the available display modes. By selecting an alternative display, you can speed up the screen display while editing your presentation.

- **Rulers visible** – specifies whether to display the rulers at the top and to the left of the work area.

- **Snap Lines when moving** – specifies whether to display guides when moving an object. Impress creates dotted guides that extend beyond the box containing the selected object and which cover the entire work area, helping you position the object. You also can use this function using the **Helplines While Moving** icon ⊞ on the Options toolbar (Figure 213) if a presentation is open.

- **All control points in Bézier editor** – displays the control points of all Bézier points if you have previously selected a Bézier curve. If this option is not selected, only the control points of the selected Bézier points will be visible.

- **Contour of each individual object** – Impress displays the contour line of each individual object when moving this object. This option enables you to see if single objects conflict with other objects in the target position. If you do not select this option, Impress displays only a square contour that includes all selected objects.

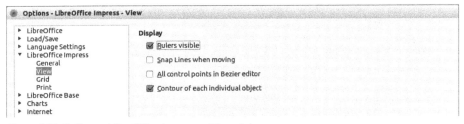

Figure 215: Options – LibreOffice Impress – View dialog

Grid options

In the Options dialog, click **LibreOffice Impress > Grid** (Figure 216) to specify the grid settings for Impress. Using a grid helps you determine the exact position of your objects. You can also set this grid to line up with the snap grid.

If you have activated the snap grid, but wish to move or create individual objects without snap positions, keep the *Shift* key pressed to deactivate this function for as long as needed.

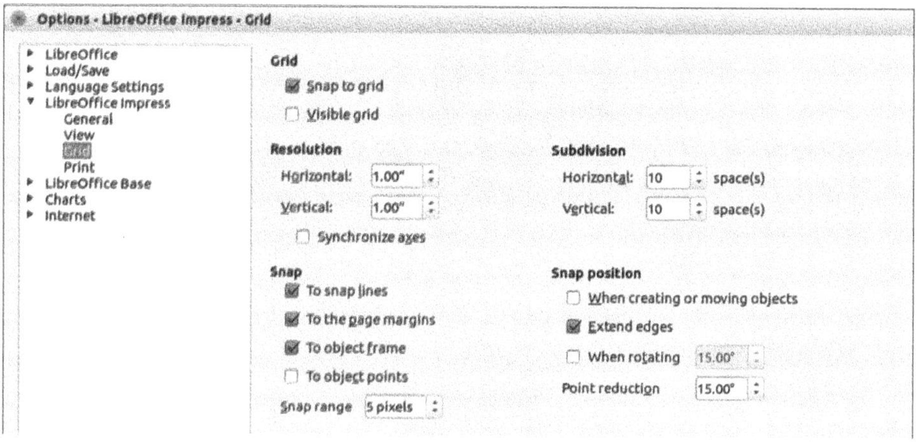

Figure 216: Options – LibreOffice Impress – Grid dialog

Grid

- **Snap to grid** – activates the snap function. If this option is selected, but you want to move or create individual objects without snapping to the grid, press the *Shift* key to deactivate **Snap to grid** whilst moving the individual object. You can also use the **Snap to Grid** icon on the Options toolbar (Figure 213).
- **Visible grid**: displays grid points on the screen. These points will not display or print as part of a presentation.

Resolution

- **Horizontal** – defines the unit of measure for the spacing between grid points on the X-axis.
- **Vertical** – defines the grid points spacing in the desired unit of measurement on the Y-axis.
- **Synchronize axes** – specifies whether to change the current grid settings symmetrically. The resolution and subdivision for the X and Y axes remain the same.

Subdivision

- **Horizontal** – specify the number of intermediate spaces between grid points on the X-axis.
- **Vertical** – specify the number of intermediate spaces between grid points on the Y-axis.

Snap

- **To snap lines** – snaps the edge of an object being dragged to the nearest snap line when you release the mouse. You can also define this setting by using the **Snap to Snap Lines** icon on the Options toolbar (Figure 213).

- **To the page margins** – specifies whether to align the contour of the graphic object to the nearest page margin. The cursor or a contour line of the graphics object must be in the snap range. In a presentation, this function can also be accessed with the **Snap to Page Margins** icon 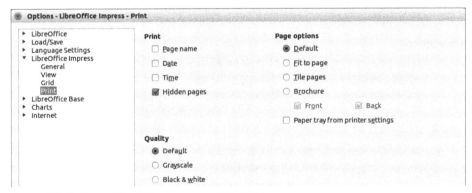 on the Options toolbar.

- **To object frame** – specifies whether to align the contour of the graphic object to the border of the nearest graphic object. The cursor or a contour line of the graphics object must be in the snap range. In a presentation, this function can also be accessed with the **Snap to Object Border** icon on the Options toolbar.

- **To object points** – specifies whether to align the contour of the graphic object to the points of the nearest graphic object. This only applies if the cursor or a contour line of the graphics object is in the snap range. In a presentation, this function can also be accessed with the **Snap to Object Points** icon on the Options toolbar.

- **Snap range** – defines the snap distance between the mouse pointer and the object contour. LibreOffice Impress snaps to a snap point if the mouse cursor is nearer than the distance specified.

Snap position

- **When creating or moving objects** – specifies that graphic objects are restricted vertically, horizontally or diagonally (45°) when creating or moving them. You can temporarily deactivate this setting by pressing the *Shift* key.

- **Extend edges** – specifies that a square is created based on the longer side of a rectangle when the *Shift* key is pressed before you release the mouse button. This also applies to an ellipse (a circle will be created based on the longest diameter of the ellipse). When this option is not selected, a square or a circle will be created based on the shorter side or diameter.

- **When rotating** – specifies that graphic objects can only be rotated within the rotation angle that you selected. If you want to rotate an object outside the defined angle, press the *Shift* key when rotating. Release the key when the desired rotation angle is reached.

- **Point reduction** – defines the angle for point reduction. When working with polygons, you might find it useful to reduce their editing points.

Figure 217: Options – LibreOffice Impress – Print dialog

Print options

In the Options dialog, click on **LibreOffice Impress > Print** (Figure 217) to specify print settings for a presentation. See *Chapter 10 Printing, E-mailing, Exporting, and Saving Slide Shows* for more information about the options available.

Print

- **Page name** – specifies whether to print the page name.
- **Date** – specifies whether to print the current date.
- **Time** – specifies whether to print the current time.
- **Hidden pages** – specifies whether to print the pages that are currently hidden from the presentation.

Page options

- **Default** – specifies that you do not want to further scale pages when printing.
- **Fit to page** – specifies whether to scale down objects that are beyond the margins of the current printer so that they fit on the paper in the printer.
- **Tile pages** – specifies that pages are to be printed in tiled format. If the pages or slides are smaller than the paper, several pages or slides will be printed on one page of paper.
- **Brochure** – select this option to print the document in brochure format. You can also decide if you want to print the front, the back or both sides of the brochure.
- **Front** – select this option to print the front of a brochure.
- **Back** – select this option to print the back of a brochure.
- **Paper tray from printer settings** – determines that the paper tray to be used is the one defined in the printer setup.

Quality

- **Default** – specifies that you want to print in original colors.
- **Grayscale** – specifies that you want to print colors as grayscale.
- **Black & white** – specifies that you want to print the document in black and white.

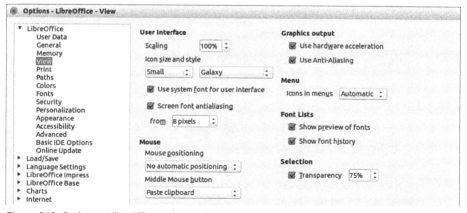

Figure 218: Options - LibreOffice - View dialog

Customizing the user interface

Menu font

If you want to change the menu font from that supplied by LibreOffice to the system font used for your operating system:

1) Go to **Tools > Options > LibreOffice > View** (Figure 218) on the menu bar.
2) Select **Use system font for user interface** and click **OK**.

Menu content

You can customize the menus in Impress by adding and rearranging items on the menu bar, adding items to menus, and other changes.

1) Go to **View > Toolbars > Customize** or **Tools > Customize** on the menu bar to open the Customize dialog (Figure 219).
2) Make sure the **Menus** page is open.

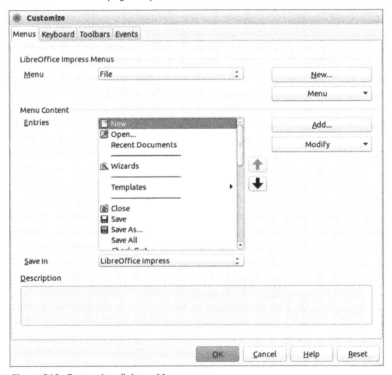

Figure 219: Customize dialog – Menus page

3) In the **Save In** drop-down list, select whether to save this customized menu in LibreOffice Impress or for a presentation.
4) In the section **LibreOffice Impress Menus**, select from the **Menu** drop-down list the menu that you want to customize.

5) To customize the selected menu, click on the **Menu** or **Modify** buttons. You can also add commands to a menu by clicking on the **Add** button. These actions are described in the following sections. Use the up and down arrows next to the **Entries** list to move the selected menu item to a different position.

6) When you have finished making all your changes, click **OK** to save them.

Creating new menus

To create a new menu:

1) On the **Menus** page of the Customize dialog, click **New** to open the Move Menu dialog (Figure 220).

Figure 220: Move Menu dialog

2) Type a name for your new menu in the **Menu name** box to replace the default *New Menu 1* name.

3) Use the up and down arrow buttons to move the new menu into the required position on the menu bar.

4) Click **OK** to save. The new menu now appears on the list of menus in the Customize dialog. It will appear on the menu bar itself after you save your customizations.

5) After creating a new menu, you need to add some commands to it, as described in "Adding menu commands" on page 263.

Moving existing menus

To move an existing menu:

1) On the **Menus** page of the Customize dialog (Figure 219) and select the menu you want to modify from the *Menu* drop down list.

2) Click **Menu** and select **Move** from the drop down list to open the Move Menu dialog (Figure 220).

3) Select the menu you want (for example *File*) from the **Menu position** list.

4) Use the up and down arrow buttons to move the menu into the required position.

5) To move submenus (for example *File | Send*), select the main menu (*File*) in the Menu list and then, in the **Menu Content** section of the Customize dialog (Figure 219), select the submenu *Send* in the **Entries** list and use the arrow keys to move it up or down in the sequence.

6) Click **OK** to save your changes and close the dialog.

Note	If you are moving a default menu only **Move** is available in the list. **Rename** and **Delete** are not available for the default menus within LibreOffice.

Creating keyboard shortcuts

In addition to renaming a menu, you can specify a keyboard shortcut that allows you to select a menu command when you press *Alt* key plus a letter in the name of a menu command. This keyboard shortcut is indicated by underlining the letter in the name of the menu command.

1) Select a menu or menu entry.
2) Click **Modify** in the Customize dialog (Figure 219) and select **Rename**. This opens the Rename dialog with the selected entry in *New name* text box.
3) Add a tilde (~) in front of the letter that you want to use as an accelerator. For example, when the File menu is open, to select the Save All command by pressing *Alt+V*, enter **Sa~ve All**.
4) Click **OK** to save your changes to the name and close the Rename Menu dialog.
5) Click **OK** to save your changes and close the Customize dialog.

Note	Be VERY careful when creating new keyboard shortcuts. In the example above, if the File menu is not already open, then pressing *Alt+V* opens the View menu. If another menu is open, *Alt+V* might activate some other command.

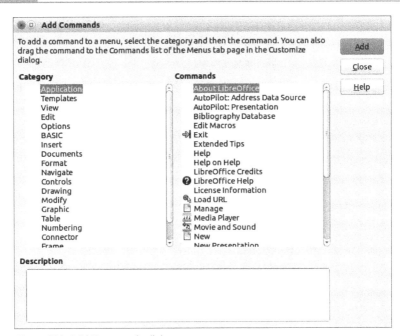

Figure 221: Add Commands dialog

Adding menu commands

You can add commands to menus and to menus you have created.

1) On the **Menus** page of the Customize dialog (Figure 219), select the menu in the Menu list and click **Add**. This opens the Add Commands dialog (Figure 221).

2) Select a category and then the command that you want use.

3) Click **Add**. The dialog remains open, so you can select additional categories and commands.

4) When you have finished adding menu commands, click **Close**.

5) In the Customize dialog, use the up and down arrow buttons to arrange the commands in your preferred sequence.

6) Click **OK** to save your changes and close the dialog.

Modifying menu entries

In addition to changing the sequence of entries on a menu or submenu, you can add submenus, rename or delete the entries, and add group separators.

1) On the **Menus** page of the Customize dialog (Figure 219), select the menu in the Menu list you want to modify.

2) Select an entry in the **Entries** list under Menu Content.

3) Click the **Modify** button and choose the required action from the drop-down list of actions. Most of the actions are self-explanatory. **Add Separator** adds a separator line after the highlighted entry.

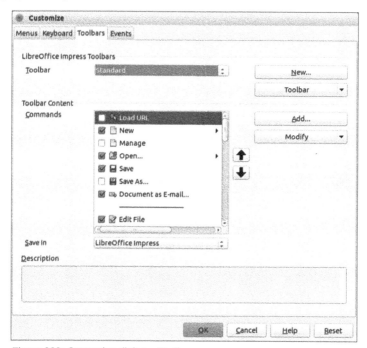

Figure 222: Customize dialog – Toolbars page

Customizing toolbars

You can customize toolbars in several ways, including choosing which icons are visible, and locking the position of a docked toolbar, as described in *Getting Started Guide Chapter 1, Introducing LibreOffice*. This section describes how to create new toolbars and add other icons (commands) to the list of those available on a toolbar.

Customize toolbars

1) Go to **View > Toolbars > Customize** or **Tools > Customize** on the menu bar, or right-click in an empty area on the toolbar and select Customize Toolbar from the context menu, to open the Customize dialog (Figure 222).
2) Make sure the **Toolbars** page is open.
3) In the **Save In** drop-down list, select whether to save this customized toolbar for Impress or for a selected presentation.
4) In the **LibreOffice Impress Toolbars** section, select from the *Toolbar* drop-down list the toolbar that you want to customize.
5) Click **Toolbar** on the right to display a drop-down list of options for customizing the toolbar.
6) Select the option you want to use from the context menu. **Icons Only** is the default setting for toolbars.
7) To display or hide commands, select or deselect the checkboxes in *Commands* in the **Toolbar Content** section.
8) To change the position of commands on a toolbar, select a command and click the up and down arrows to the right of the list.
9) When you have finished customizing a toolbar, click **OK** to save your changes and close the dialog.

Creating new toolbars

To create a new toolbar:

1) Go to **View > Toolbars > Customize** or **Tools > Customize** on the menu bar, or right-click in an empty area on the toolbar and select Customize Toolbar from the context menu, to open the Customize dialog (Figure 222).
2) Make sure the **Toolbars** page is open.
3) Click **New** to open the Name dialog (Figure 223).
4) Type a name for the new toolbar and select from the **Save In** drop-down list where to save this new menu for Impress or for a selected document.
5) Click **OK** and the new toolbar now appears on the list of toolbars in the Customize dialog. After creating a new toolbar, you have to add some commands to it, as described below.

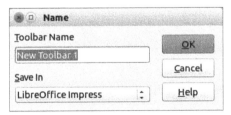

Figure 223: Name dialog for new toolbars

Adding toolbar commands

To add commands to a new toolbar or to customize an existing toolbar:

1) Go to **View > Toolbars > Customize** or **Tools > Customize** on the menu bar, or right-click in an empty area on the toolbar and select Customize Toolbar from the context menu, to open the Customize dialog.
2) Make sure the **Toolbars** page is open (Figure 222).
3) Select the toolbar from the **Toolbar** drop down list.
4) Click **Add** to open the Add Commands dialog (Figure 221 on page 262) and is the same dialog used for adding commands to menus ("Adding menu commands" on page 263).
5) Select a **Category** and then a **Command** from the relevant list.
6) Click **Add**. The Add Commands dialog remains open, so you can select additional commands.
7) When you have finished adding commands, click **Close**. If you insert an item which does not have an associated icon, the toolbar will display the full name of the item; see "Choosing icons for toolbar commands" below on how to choose an icon for a toolbar command.
8) On the Customize dialog, use the up and down arrow buttons to arrange the commands in your preferred sequence.
9) When you have finished making changes, click **OK** to save and close the dialog.

Choosing icons for toolbar commands

Toolbars usually have icons and not words to indicate commands, but not all commands have associated icons.

1) Select the command and click **Modify** and select **Change icon** on the context menu to open the Change Icon dialog (Figure 224).

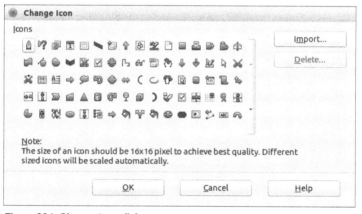

Figure 224: Change Icon dialog

2) Scroll through the available icons and select the one you want to use.
3) Click **OK** to assign it to the command.

Note	To use a custom icon, create it in a graphics program and then import it into LibreOffice by clicking **Import** on the Change Icon dialog. Custom icons must be 16×16 or 26×26 pixels in size and cannot contain more than 256 colors.

Customizing keyboard shortcuts

The *Appendix* to this guide lists the default keyboard shortcuts supplied with Impress. You can change these defaults or add new shortcuts. You can assign shortcuts to standard Impress functions or your own macros and save them for use with Impress only or with the LibreOffice suite.

Caution	Be careful when reassigning predefined shortcut keys used in your operating system or LibreOffice. Many key assignments are universally understood shortcuts, such as *F1* for Help, and are always expected to provide certain results. Although you can easily reset the shortcut key assignments to LibreOffice defaults, changing some common shortcut keys can cause confusion, frustration and possible data loss or corruption, especially if other users share your computer.

Example shortcut key

For example, suppose you wish to assign a shortcut key to easily insert a duplicate slide in your presentation. You could assign the *Insert* key as a logical shortcut for this purpose, as described below.

1) Go to **View > Toolbars > Customize** or **Tools > Customize** on the menu bar, or go to on the menu bar, or right-click in an empty area on the toolbar and select Customize Toolbar from the context menu to open the Customize dialog.

2) Make sure the **Keyboard** page is open (Figure 225).

Figure 225: Customize dialog – Keyboard page

3) As the shortcut key assignment is only relevant with Impress and not LibreOffice, select **Impress** in the upper right corner of the dialog.

4) Select **Insert** in the **Category** list and **Duplicate Slide** in the **Function** list.

5) Select the shortcut key **Insert** in the **Shortcut keys** list and click **Modify**.

6) Click **OK** to accept the change. Now the *Insert* key will insert a duplicate slide immediately after the currently selected slide.

| Note | All existing shortcut keys for the currently selected *Function* are listed in the *Keys* selection box. Since there was no currently assigned shortcut for the **Insert > Duplicate Slide** function the *Keys* list was empty. If it had not been, and you wished to reassign a shortcut key combination that was already in use, you would first have to **Delete** the existing key. |
| | Shortcut keys not available for reassignment are greyed out in the listing on the Customize dialog, for example *F1* and *F10*. |

Saving changes

Changes to the shortcut key assignments (and other configurations) can be saved in a keyboard configuration file for use at a later time. This allows you to create and apply different configurations as the need arises.

1) After making your keyboard shortcut assignments, click **Save** in the Customize dialog.

2) In the Save Keyboard Configuration dialog that opens, select *All files* from the **Save as Type** list.

3) Enter a name for the keyboard configuration file in the **File name** box, or select an existing file from the list. If you need to, browse to find a file from another location.

4) Click **Save**. A confirmation dialog will appear if you are about to overwrite an existing file; otherwise there will be no feedback and the file will be saved.

Loading saved keyboard configurations

To load a saved keyboard configuration file and replace your existing configuration, click **Load** in the Customize dialog and then select the configuration file from the Load Keyboard Configuration dialog.

Resetting shortcut keys

To reset all of the keyboard shortcuts to their default values, click **Reset** in the Customize dialog. Use this feature with care as no confirmation dialog will be displayed and the defaults will be set without any further notice or user input.

Running macros from key combinations

You can also define shortcut key combinations that will run macros. These shortcut keys are strictly user-defined and no macro shortcut keys are supplied with LibreOffice. For information on macros, see the *Getting Started Guide, Chapter 13 Getting started with macros.*

Adding functions with extensions

An extension is a package that can be installed into LibreOffice to add a new function.

Although individual extensions can be found in different places, the official LibreOffice extension repository is at http://extensions.libreoffice.org/. Some extensions are free of charge; others are available for a fee. Check the descriptions to see what licenses and fees apply to the ones that interest you.

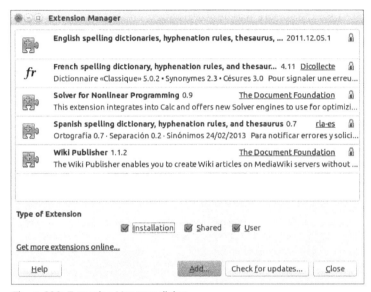

Figure 226: Extension Manager dialog

To install an extension, follow these steps:

1) Download the extension and save it anywhere on your computer.
2) In LibreOffice, go to **Tools > Extension Manager** on the menu bar to open the Extension Manager dialog (Figure 226).
3) Click **Add** and a file browser window opens. Find and select the extension you want to install and click **Open**.
4) If an extension it is already installed, you will be prompted to press **OK** to confirm whether to overwrite the current version by the new one, or press **Cancel** to stop the installation and keep the original extension installation.
5) You are then asked whether to install the extension only for yourself or for all users. If you choose **Only for me** option, the extension is installed only for yourself (the extension will be stored in your user profile and other users will not have access to it). If you choose **For all users**, you must have system administrator rights. In this case, the extension is installed in LibreOffice system folder and will be available for all users.
6) The extension begins installing. You may be asked to accept a license agreement. Click **Accept** after reading the license agreement so that the installation proceeds.
7) When the installation is complete, click **Close** to close the Extension Manager.
8) Close and restart LibreOffice and the newly installed then becomes available for use.
9) If available, check the extension documentation or information on how to use the extension.

Tip	To get extensions that are listed in the repository, you can open the Extension Manager and click the **Get more extensions online** link.

Note	To install a *shared* extension, you need write access to the LibreOffice installation directory.

Note	Normally extensions are OXT file types that are linked to LibreOffice. Double clicking on an OXT file opens the Extension Manager and starts the installation.

Appendix A
Keyboard Shortcuts

Introduction

You can use LibreOffice without requiring a pointing device, such as a mouse or trackball, by using its built-in keyboard shortcuts. Tasks as varied and complex as docking and un-docking toolbars and windows, or changing the size or position of objects can all be accomplished with only a keyboard. Although LibreOffice has its own extensive set of keyboard shortcuts, each component provides others which are specific to its work.

For help with LibreOffice keyboard shortcuts, or using LibreOffice with a keyboard only, search the LibreOffice Help using the "shortcut" or "accessibility" keywords.

In addition to using the built-in keyboard shortcuts (listed in this Appendix), you can also define your own. You can assign shortcuts to standard Impress functions or your own macros and save them for use with Impress only, or with the entire LibreOffice suite.

To adapt shortcut keys to your needs, use the Customize dialog as described in this section and in *Chapter 11 Setting Up and Customizing Impress*.

Tip for Macintosh users

Some keystrokes are different on a Mac from those used in Windows and Linux. The following table gives some common substitutions for the instructions in this book. For a more detailed list, see the application Help.

Windows or Linux	Mac equivalent	Effect
Tools > Options menu selection	**LibreOffice > Preferences**	Access setup options
Right-click	*Control+click* and/or *right-click* depending on computer setup	Open a context menu
Ctrl (Control)	⌘ *(Command)*	Used with other keys
F5	*Shift+⌘+F5*	Open the Navigator
F11	*⌘+T*	Open the Styles and Formatting window

Note	Some of the shortcut keys in this appendix may be assigned to your desktop system. Keys that are assigned to the desktop system are not available to LibreOffice. Try to assign different keys either for LibreOffice in **Tools > Customize > Keyboard**, or in your computer system.

Impress function keys

Shortcut Keys	Effect
F1	Open LibreOffice Impress Help.
F2	Select text tool and edit text.
Ctrl+F2	Starts a slide show.
F3	Enter group and edit group.
Shift+F3	Duplicate object.
Ctrl+F3	Exit group.

Shortcut Keys	Effect
F4	Open Position and Size dialog.
F5	Starts a slide show.
Shift+F5	Restart a slide show at the current slide where the slide show was previously stopped at.
Alt+Shift+F5	Go to the first slide in a presentation when in Normal view.
Ctrl+Shift+F5	Open Navigator.
F6	Forward navigation within the on screen elements without using mouse.
Shift+F6	Backward navigation within the on screen elements without using mouse.
F7	Start spelling checker.
Ctrl+F7	Open thesaurus.
F8	Edit points.
Ctrl+Shift+F8	Fit text to frame.
Shift+F10	Open context menu of a selected object.
F11	Open Styles and Formatting dialog.

Slide show shortcut keys

Shortcut Keys	Effect
Esc or Minus (-)	End presentation.
Down arrow or Right arrow or Page Down	Go to next slide
Up arrow or Left arrow or Page Up	Go to previous slide
Alt+Page Down	Go to next slide without playing effects.
Alt+Page Up	Go to the previous slide without playing effects.
[number] + Enter	Type the number of a slide and press Enter to go to the slide.
Spacebar or Right arrow or Down arrow or Page Down or Enter or Return or N	Play the next effect on the slide. If no previous effect exists on this slide, go to next slide.
Left arrow or Up arrow or Page Up or Backspace or P	Play previous effect again. If no previous effect exists on this slide, show previous slide.
Home	Jump to first slide in the slide show.
End	Jump to the last slide in the slide show.
B or . (period)	Show black screen until next key or mouse wheel event.
W or , (comma)	Show white screen until next key or mouse wheel event.

Normal view shortcut keys

Shortcut Keys	Effect
Plus(+)	Zoom in.
Minus(-)	Zoom out.
Times(×) (number pad)	Fit page in window.
Divide(÷) (number pad)	Zoom in on current selection.
Shift+Ctrl+G	Group selected objects.
Shift+Ctrl+Alt+G	Ungroup selected group.
Ctrl+click	Enter a group, so that you can edit the individual objects of the group. Click outside the group to return to the normal view.
Shift+Ctrl+K	Combine selected objects.
Shift+Ctrl+K	Split selected object. This keyboard combination only works on an object that was created by combining two or more objects.
Ctrl+Plus(+)	Bring to front.
Shift+Ctrl+Plus(+)	Bring forward.
Ctrl+Minus(-)	Send backward.
Shift+Ctrl+Minus(-)	Send to back.

Editing text shortcut keys

Shortcut Keys	Effect
Ctrl+Hyphen(-)	Custom hyphens; hyphenation set by you.
Ctrl+Shift+Minus(-)	Non-breaking dash and is not used for hyphenation.
Ctrl+Shift+Space	Non-breaking spaces. Non-breaking spaces are not used for hyphenation and are not expanded if the text is justified.
Shift+Enter	Line break without paragraph change.
Left arrow	Move cursor to the left.
Shift+Left arrow	Move cursor with selection to the left.
Ctrl+Left arrow	Go to beginning of a word.
Ctrl+Shift+left arrow	Select to the left word by word.
Right arrow	Move cursor to the right.
Shift+Right arrow	Move cursor with selection to the right.
Ctrl+Right arrow	Go to beginning of next word.
Ctrl+Shift+Right arrow	Select to the right word by word.
Up arrow	Move cursor up one line.
Shift+Up arrow	Selecting lines going upwards in the document.
Ctrl+Up arrow	Move cursor to the beginning of the paragraph.

Shortcut Keys	Effect
Ctrl+Shift+Up arrow	Select to beginning of paragraph. Next keystroke extends selection to beginning of previous paragraph.
Down arrow	Move cursor down one line.
Shift+Down arrow	Selecting lines going downwards in the document.
Ctrl+Down arrow	Move cursor to end of paragraph.
Ctrl+Shift+Down arrow	Select to end of paragraph. Next keystroke extends selection to end of next paragraph.
Home	Go to beginning of line.
Shift+Home	Go to and select to the beginning of a line.
Ctrl+Home	Go to start of text block in slide.
Ctrl+Shift+Home	Go to and select to the beginning of text block in slide.
End	Go to end of line.
Shift+End	Go to and select to end of a line.
Ctrl+End	Go to end of text block in a slide.
Ctrl+Shift+End	Go to and select to the end of text block in a slide.
Ctrl+Del	Delete text to end of word.
Ctrl+Shift+Del	Delete text to end of sentence.
Ctrl+Backspace	Delete text to beginning of word. In a list, delete an empty paragraph in front of current paragraph.
Ctrl+Shift+Backspace	Delete text to beginning of sentence.

Impress shortcut keys

Shortcut Keys	Effect
Arrow	Move the selected object or the page view in the direction of the arrow.
Ctrl+Arrow	Move the slide in the normal view.
Shift+drag	Constrain the movement of the selected object horizontally or vertically.
Ctrl+drag	Hold down Ctrl and drag an object to create a copy of the object.
Alt+drag	Hold down Alt to draw or resize objects by dragging from the centre of the object outward.
Alt+click	Select the object behind the currently selected object.
Alt+Shift+click	Select the object in front of the currently selected object.
Shift+click	Select adjacent items or a text passage. Click at the start of a selection, move to the end of the selection, and then hold down Shift while you click.
Shift+drag	Hold down Shift while dragging to resize an object to maintain the proportions of the object.

Shortcut Keys	Effect
Tab	Select objects in the order in which they were created.
Shift+Tab	Select objects in the reverse order in which they were created.
Esc	Exit current mode.
Enter	Activate a place-holder object in a new presentation (only if the frame is selected).
Ctrl+Enter	Move to the next text object on the slide. If there are no text objects on the slide, or if you reached the last text object, a new slide is inserted after the current slide. The new slide uses the same layout as the current slide.
Page Up	Switch to the previous slide. No function on the first slide.
Page Down	Switch to the next slide. No function on the last slide.

Slide Sorter navigation

Shortcut Keys	Effect
Right arrow	Moves the focus to the next slide.
Left arrow	Moves the focus to the previous slide.

Using shortcut keys

Some of the shortcut keys may be assigned to your desktop system. Keys that are assigned to the desktop system are not available to LibreOffice. Try to assign different keys either for LibreOffice, in **Tools > Customize > Keyboard**, or in your computer system.

You can use the keyboard to access Impress commands as well as to navigate through the workspace. LibreOffice Impress uses the same shortcut keys as LibreOffice Draw to create drawing objects.

The following sections give examples of using shortcut keys.

Selecting placeholders

AutoLayouts in Impress use placeholders for slide titles, text, and objects. To select a placeholder, press *Ctrl+Enter*. To move to the next placeholder, press *Ctrl+Enter* again.

If you press *Ctrl+Enter* after you reach the last placeholder in a slide, a new slide is inserted after the current slide. The new slide uses the same layout as the current slide.

Creating and editing drawing objects

1) Press *F6* repeatedly until the Drawing toolbar is active.
2) Press the *Right* or *Left arrow* key until you reach the toolbar icon of a drawing tool.
3) If there is an arrow next to the icon, the drawing tool opens a sub toolbar. Press the *Up* or *Down arrow* key to open the sub toolbar.
4) Press the *Right* or *Left arrow* key to select an icon.

5) Press *Ctrl+Enter* and the object is created at the center of the current slide.

6) To return to the document, press *Ctrl+F6*.

7) Use the *arrow keys* to position the object where you want.

8) To select a command from the context menu for the object, press *Shift+F10* to open the context menu.

9) Use the *Up* or *Down arrow* to select the command.

10) Press *Enter* to execute the command.

11) Press *Esc* key to exit.

Selecting objects

1) Press *Ctrl+F6* to enter the document.

2) Press *Tab* until you reach the object you want to select.

Running a slide show

1) To start a slide show, press *Ctrl+F2* or *F5*.

2) Advance to the next slide or to the next animation effect, press *Spacebar*.

3) Advance to the next slide without playing object animation effects, press *Alt+PageDown*.

4) Return to previous slide, press *Left arrow* or *PageUp*.

5) Go to a specific slide, type the page number of the slide and press *Enter*.

6) Stop slide show, press *Esc* or *−*.

Using Slide Sorter view

When you first switch to Slide Sorter view, press *Enter* to change the keyboard focus to the workspace. Or, press *F6* to navigate to the workspace and then press *Enter*.

Selecting and deselecting slides

1) Use the *arrow keys* to navigate to the slide that you want to select.

2) Use the *Shift+arrow keys* to continuously select more than one slide.

Copying slides

1) Use the *arrow keys* to navigate to the slide that you want to copy and press *Ctrl+C*.

2) Move to the slide where you want to paste the copied slide and press *Ctrl+V*.

Moving slides

1) Use the *arrow keys* to navigate to the slide that you want to move and press *Ctrl+X*.

2) Navigate to the slide where you want to move the slide and press *Ctrl+V*.

3) Select *Before* or *After* the current slide and click **OK**.

Index

N

Navigator 18
Normal view 19
notes
    automatic layout options 204
    fields 204
    formatting 202
Notes Master 202
Notes view 20, 202, 204, 205

O

objects
    converting 130
Open Source Initiative (OSI) 12
outline level 76, 77
Outline view 19, 195, 196

P

Page Setup dialog 197, 203
page style 196
personal key 247
Picture toolbar 97
pictures
    AutoLayout 90
    Color 99
    crop 102
    filters 97
    resizing 96
    rotating 96
    transparency 100
Position and Size dialog 43, 116, 120
position of text 66
PowerPoint format
    save as 248
presentation
    modifying 30
    title slide 27
presentation styles
    AutoLayout text box 64
Presentation Wizard 255
Print dialog 232
printing
    brochure 236

R

Rehearse Timings 218
resizing pictures 96
rotating pictures 96

S

screen settings 197
shapes
    3D 129
    aligning 124
    convert 130
shared extension 269
slide master 29
    apply 36

author information 47
    creat 35
slide show
    Custom 215
    organizing 212
    Rehearse Timings 218
    settings 212
    timing of automatic slide changes 218
Slide Sorter view 21
slides
    animations 219
    hide 30
    master 29
    summary slides 194
    transitions 216
        27
Slides pane 15
snap lines 125
special characters 61
spreadsheet
    cells 173
    moving 172
styles
    Fill Format Mode 167
    image styles 164
Styles and Formatting dialog 164
summary slides 194
support 8
system font 260

T

template
    description 47
templates
    create a template folder 51
    delete a template folder 52
    from other sources 48
    importing 53
    supplied with LibreOffice 48
text
    alignment 71
    animation 162
    character formatting 65
    default formatting 60
    formatting 62, 161
    paragraph formatting 68
    pasting 60
    position 66
    selecting 63
text areas
    handles 42
text box
    AutoLayout 56, 74
    moving 57
Text Formatting toolbar 61, 65
text tool 56
themes 94
three-dimensional objects 129

timing of automatic slide changes 218
title slide 27
toolbar 147
toolbars 17
    curve, 114
transparencies 160
transparency 100

U

User guides 9
user interface, parts of 10

W

Windows Metafile Format (WMF) 131
Workspace 17

www.ingramcontent.com/pod-product-compliance
Lightning Source LLC
LaVergne TN
LVHW042332060326
832902LV00006B/116